HUMAN STRUGGLE

Many of the great thinkers and poets in Christianity and Islam led lives marked by personal and religious struggle. Indeed, suffering and struggle are part of the human condition and constant themes in philosophy, sociology and psychology. In this thought-provoking book, acclaimed scholar Mona Siddiqui ponders how humankind finds meaning in life during an age of uncertainty. Here, she explores the theme of human struggle through the writings of iconic figures such as Dietrich Bonhoeffer, Abu Hamid al-Ghazali, Rainer Maria Rilke and Sayyid Qutb – people who searched for meaning in the face of adversity. Considering a wide range of thinkers and literary figures, her book explores how suffering and struggle force the faithful to stretch their imagination in order to bring about powerful and prophetic movements for change. The moral and aesthetic impulse of their writings will also stimulate intercultural and interdisciplinary conversations on the search for meaning in an age of uncertainty.

MONA SIDDIQUI is Professor of Islamic and Interreligious Studies at the University of Edinburgh. In 2011, she received an OBE for her comparative work and public engagement. As a Muslim scholar in Christian–Muslim relations, she is unique and her book *Christians, Muslims and Jesus* (2013) received international acclaim. She is a fellow of the Royal Society of Edinburgh and a fellow of the American Academy for Arts and Sciences.

Human Struggle

Christian and Muslim Perspectives

MONA SIDDIQUI

University of Edinburgh

 CAMBRIDGE
UNIVERSITY PRESS

CAMBRIDGE
UNIVERSITY PRESS

University Printing House, Cambridge CB2 8BS, United Kingdom

One Liberty Plaza, 20th Floor, New York, NY 10006, USA

477 Williamstown Road, Port Melbourne, VIC 3207, Australia

314–321, 3rd Floor, Plot 3, Splendor Forum, Jasola District Centre,
New Delhi – 110025, India

79 Anson Road, #06–04/06, Singapore 079906

Cambridge University Press is part of the University of Cambridge.

It furthers the University's mission by disseminating knowledge in the pursuit of
education, learning, and research at the highest international levels of excellence.

www.cambridge.org
Information on this title: www.cambridge.org/9781316518540
DOI: 10.1017/9781108609005

© Mona Siddiqui 2021

First published 2021

Printed in the United Kingdom by TJ Books Limited, Padstow Cornwall

A catalogue record for this publication is available from the British Library.

ISBN 978-1-316-51854-0 Hardback

For my parents who always lived with hope

Contents

Acknowledgements		*page* viii
Notes on Text		x
	Introduction	1
1	Human Struggle: Literary, Theological and Philosophical Reflections	8
2	The Search for Salvation in Rainer Maria Rilke and Abu Hamid al-Ghazali	45
3	Community and Divine Calling in Dietrich Bonhoeffer and Sayyid Qutb	83
4	Contemporary Islam and the Struggle for Beauty	139
5	The Struggle for Hope in an Age of Uncertainty	157
	Epilogue	195
Bibliography		198
Index		209

Acknowledgements

Writing this book has been a gift and a task. A gift, because it emerges from my 2016 Gifford lectures at the University of Aberdeen. My sincere thanks to Professor Phil Ziegler for this honour, invitation and hospitality during my time there. But it has also been a task as I quickly realised that speaking about human struggle was far easier than writing about human struggle. This is especially so in a comparative framework where dealing with the lives of thinkers who have attained almost legendary status in their respective religious and philosophical traditions requires a certain level of sensitivity and humility. I am therefore grateful to the reviewers who both encouraged and critiqued my initial ambition and thereby sharpened my approach. I am also very grateful to my editor, Beatrice Rehl, who welcomed the idea from the very beginning and who has guided and supported me with a sharp eye and good humour. In my opinion, the best stage of completing any book is choosing the cover, so a special thanks to Sonya Ahmed from the Glasgow School of Art who designed the striking front cover in her unique style.

Between the delivery of the lectures and the completion of the book, I gave several lectures on human struggle at many universities around the world. I am indebted to all my colleagues who listened and challenged me but a special thanks to Stephen Pickard and Peter Walker at Charles Sturt University. They invited me to present on Bonhoeffer and Qutb and Rilke and Ghazali and I quickly learnt how much more learning was required on my part. I hope to return soon and present them with new and better arguments. My colleagues at the University of Edinburgh provided a very supportive environment, keeping my administrative duties low so that this book could be completed. A particular thanks for the helpful literature given to me by Dr David Robinson, a former PhD student at the Divinity School studying Hegel and Bonhoeffer. The only person who really knew of my own struggle in writing this book is my trusted colleague Dr Joshua Ralston who remains a friend and a joyous conversation partner. I am grateful to him for being an ally, a travel companion on many conference flights, for his sense of humour and his own important work in Christian–Muslim relations. Finally, my gratitude to my husband and children whose unfailing support gives me the emotional space to write and who are always present in my books.

Notes on Text

This book contains translations from Arabic and German. Where I have referred to book titles and words in other languages in the main body of the text, they have been provided in both English and Arabic/German; the Arabic and German titles are in brackets. In the interests of accessibility, however, I have dispensed with diacritical marks except for the ` to indicate the Arabic letter `ayn as in shari'a and ' to indicate the hamza as in Qur'an. For the sake of consistency I have also removed the diacritics from those works which appeared with diacritics in their original transliteration. This style has been applied to the whole book including footnotes and bibliography.

All dates are Common Era. The Qur'anic verses are cited using a variety of translations including my own minor amendments where necessary. This includes replacing Allah with God in many passages.

Introduction

THIS BOOK EMERGES FROM MY GIFFORD LECTURES DELIVERED AT THE University of Aberdeen in September 2016. I'd like to thank the Gifford Committee at Aberdeen for inviting me to give these prestigious lectures; it was an enormous honour. I would also like to thank the School of Divinity at the University of Edinburgh for giving me the space and time to think of how best to write the lectures for subsequent publication. During my academic career I have been privileged to sit on the Gifford committees at the universities of Glasgow and Edinburgh and I know full well the deliberation that goes into thinking, discussing and then finally extending an invitation to someone. When I received the invitation from Professor Philip Ziegler to deliver the lectures in 2016, I knew almost instantly that my chosen theme would be human struggle alongside themes of suffering and hope. Struggle is both a personal and universal reality of human life and always present in theological, philosophical and sociological literature. Yet it has remained somewhat ignored in scholarship as historically greater attention has been given to the phenomenon of human suffering. The terms may often overlap and be used interchangeably and the definition remains a challenge. Struggle seems to be more about hope in the midst of all kinds of moral, societal and personal uncertainties; whereas suffering is often about a certain despair and anguish, a lostness of the human condition. Struggle is part of the learning process and should be expected as essential to life. Human beings can witness each other's struggle and find mutual respect in the process, knowing that at the end of the struggle is a sense of personal achievement.

I also knew from the outset that I wished to explore struggle in a comparative setting, namely Christian and Muslim reflections. There are many approaches to interreligious work and there are potentially many outcomes. Comparative work remains a contested approach, even regarded with confusion and some suspicion at times. Yet the discipline in all its forms, is gaining interest in the academy. Studying religious writings and other forms of reflection outside those of our personal faith or academic discipline, broadens and deepens our scholarly horizon and, in my view, should be encouraged as an intellectual and moral good.

One reason for the rise in intellectual curiosity is because of the fundamental changes in our attitude to conceptualising and defining the word truth. Our understanding of truth has been undergoing a radical shift over the last few decades. More and more of us appreciate the philosophical challenge of speaking of truth in absolutist terms even as we speak of our religious particularities. We also recognise the limits of language when we struggle to speak and write of truth and transcendence. Most importantly, those of us who value dialogical settings also value the spirit of self-reflection, which are necessary ingredients for expanding the parameters of our scholarly life and experience.

My hope was to finish the book by late 2018, but the completion of this book was delayed by a number of research and international scholarly opportunities which came from subsequent grants received from the Henry Luce Foundation, The John Templeton Foundation and the Issachar Fund; I am grateful to all these funders for their generosity in acknowledging my work. The conferences and activities associated with these research grants created an intellectually stimulating and productive intervening period bringing together Christian and Muslim scholars in a number of settings. We met in different parts of the world, debated various theological and philosophical issues and reflected on the importance of doing theology as a scholarly but also as a lived discipline. These encounters over the last few years have hugely enriched my appreciation of both religious traditions. While these conversations and meetings were not on the theme of human struggle, for me, the words 'human struggle' loomed everywhere.

Words such as struggle can be interpreted in multiple ways but in this book, struggle is often allied to theological and anthropological dimensions of human suffering. Despite the differences in meaning, both point to the essence and the paradox of the human condition. We want to avoid struggle and yet it is during times of struggle that we become, we grow and we find deeper purpose and meaning in life. Writers and thinkers from all cultures and civilisations understand that we learn to live as we struggle and that the concept is indispensable to our potential, and central to giving greater weight to our lives.

When I mentioned the word struggle to my colleagues and friends, many immediately said, 'you mean *jihad*?' After all, this word has come into our consciousness in rather dramatic and tragic ways over the last couple of decades. *Jihad* is a central and complex concept in Islamic thought. It has evolved from the early period of Islam and encompasses spiritual and personal struggle as well as the old and new forms of militant struggle that today define the narratives of enmity and hostility towards the West. The central importance of *jihad* in Islam can be illustrated by citing a famous *hadith*, whereby the Prophet is reported to have declared upon returning from battle, 'We have returned from the lesser *jihad* to the greater *jihad*'. When asked what constitutes the greater *jihad*, he replied, 'It is the struggle against oneself'. This lays out the famous distinction in Islam. The greater *jihad* is internalised as a spiritual and moral struggle, a process of honestly and critically engaging the self. The lesser *jihad* involves physical battle often portrayed in the classical world, against enemies and unbelievers. Many Muslim scholars recognised that persistently and patiently trying to improve oneself for the sake of God was a much harder challenge than a simple death on the battlefield. They saw that religious life is ultimately one of constant struggle, perseverance and self-improvement in the presence of God.

The distinction between the greater and lesser *jihad* became particularly influential in Sufi mystical thought. Sufi thinkers understood the greater *jihad* as the daily battle against selfish desires and worldly temptations. These threatened to lead the believer away from the disciplined, religious life. On this note, the eleventh century theologian philosopher Ghazali famously declared, 'Never have I dealt with anything more difficult than my own soul, which sometimes helps me and sometimes opposes me'. Ghazali compared the human body to a city that was governed by the soul and besieged by man's lower, base instincts. He portrayed man's battle against his own selfish desires as the greatest battle facing the believer, yet also as the necessary means of gaining spiritual insight and intimacy with the divine.

Jihad means exertion, striving in the way of God, the internal struggle, the greater struggle, the journey of the self and the soul which has largely now been reduced to offensive and defensive war or erroneously called holy war. Today the words *jihad* and *jihadist* have become part of our English vocabulary and been reduced largely to ideas of terrorism or violent militancy within certain Muslim groups or individuals hostile to the West.

But these lectures are not about *jihad* – there are countless books on *jihad*, martyrdom and the historical, intellectual and mystical dimensions of this concept. When I think of struggle, I think of it as a reality intrinsic to the human condition. Struggle and suffering are fundamental human experiences. The themes of human struggle and suffering are vast but this is not a humanist project or some grand narrative of a universal category. Suffering and struggle arise through all kinds of natural calamities and human injustices – war, famine, exploitation and degradation, the continuing legacies of slavery, colonialism, racism and other inequalities. But this book contends that notwithstanding societal and political injustices, it is our individual struggle, the struggle of our inner lives, which compels us to face our humanity.

The purpose of the book is to explore human struggle expressed by philosophers and cultural theorists but also through the lives of select Christian, Western and Muslim writers. In the two chapters dedicated specifically to this Christian–Muslim comparison, I have taken the writers as a 'pair' and given equal weight and significance to both thinkers. It is the quality of their writing and their individual struggle which has drawn me to them. Not one of these thinkers carries the impossible burden of representing the fullness of their faith, either Christianity or Islam. There is no privileging of one over the other, rather it is their unique place and struggle in their historical settings and their personal lives which distinguishes them. How did these thinkers deal with the personal and social challenges they faced and what did their writings reveal about their understanding of their faith?

One can legitimately ask why these writers and why these pairings? The choice of writers is based largely on my own interest and the ways in which their writings often cross theological and literary boundaries. For different reasons, each of these writers has assumed almost legendary status and each continues to be widely read and debated among the lay and scholarly communities. My humble offering in the following pages does not presume to do justice to their achievements and legacies but I do find the complexity of their personal lives and their writings, an enormously powerful resource for comparative work.

The first chapter provides a range of philosophical and theological perspectives which explore the multiple ways thinkers have reflected on life's meaning, suffering and hope. Beginning with human desire as the basis for all want and restlessness, these reflections show the rich array of perspectives both in Christian and Islamic literature as well as in Western thought more broadly. The chapter attempts to explain how struggle and righteousness are often in contrast to suffering and hope in our understanding of God.

The Christian and Muslim writers explored in Chapters 2 and 3 all responded to personal, political and intellectual challenges. Their writings reflect how their faith and their search for meaning in life inspired them to rethink the universal themes of love, loss, the crisis of faith and personal salvation. They often suffered in their personal lives from their own doubts even as they knew that belief in God was essential to a meaningful life.

I am indebted to the vast resources of primary and secondary literature which are already available to scholars and which I have consulted to present reasonable biographical introductions to each writer, situating them in their historical and political context. The central aim of these chapters is to examine how each writer drew on his religious and philosophical resources to speak of the personal as well as the more universal theme of struggle and suffering. While one particular set of writings is highlighted in each chapter, I have used selections of their other works to explore the theme in its fullness. I hope this approach appeals to scholars of theology, religion, philosophy and literature. There is no one audience and I hope that the appeal of this kind of writing lies in its ability to stretch our imagination, to think in new ways about people and their religious landscapes.

While several centuries divide the Muslim theologian/philosopher Abu Hamid al-Ghazali (1058–1111) and the Austrian poet, Rainer Maria Rilke (1875–1926), both men write of their spiritual struggle and the essence of much of their thinking is to be found in their 'letters'. Throughout history, letters have expressed various intents but they often contain a distilled essence of a writer's deepest anxieties and hopes. In their 'letters' both Ghazali and Rilke try to teach someone younger the wisdom and reverence which emerges from their own restlessness in the search for God and divine beauty. Solitude and the cultivation of the inner life is a persistent theme in their works and brings together two religious thinkers in an unusual symmetry.

Despair and hope are concurrent themes running through most of these writings. In the case of the German theologian and activist Dietrich Bonhoeffer (1906–45) and the Egyptian thinker and activist, Sayyid Qutb (1906–66), the political contexts of Germany and Egypt are crucial to understanding the development of their theological stance. Qutb argued that religion is not a mere theory, but also a programme, a reality and a movement for life. His gradual stance was that any action that is not inspired by faith and divine law has no value in the eyes of God. According to Qutb, that fight is not a temporary phase but rather an eternal state, because 'truth and falsehood cannot co-exist on this earth'. Bonhoeffer's struggle was not just his own conscience in the face of the Nazi regime but his deep concern for the church and what faith in Christ really means for the Christian life. The charge of assassination attempts led to the imprisonment and subsequent execution of both these men. Their deaths immortalised their legacies and for different reasons, they remain two of the most out-standing and controversial religious figures of the twentieth century.

In Chapter 4, I explore the select writings of two contemporary Muslim scholars who have written extensively on what they saw as the crises in Islamic thought and society. Epistemological and philosophical inquiry is essential to articulating Islam in all its intellectual and contemporary diversity. As a faith, Islam is lived, practised, but also contested and challenged from within and by external global events. While both these scholars emerge from Muslim countries, their scholarship has flourished enormously in the Western world making them authoritative and influential voices albeit in different ways. Both the French Algerian academic, Muhammad Arkoun (1928–2010) and the American Egyptian scholar, Khaled Abou El Fadl (1963–) explore particular methodological approaches to the study of Islam. For these scholars, Islamic thought has to free itself from its own epistemological shackles, yet cannot be simply an intellectual enterprise. As Muslim scholars, they have a greater obligation to Islam where their search for the moral and the spiritual is fundamentally tied to the search for the ethical and the beautiful.

The fifth and final chapter focuses on contemporary sociological and political anxieties. Scholars and social and cultural theorists speak of the fragmentation of contemporary Western societies and the fading of religiosity with nothing to replace the human yearning for meaning and the transcendent. Struggle has been manifest in various ways throughout history and the quest for human rights and equality remains acutely relevant in today's world. This chapter also reflects on the issue of racial inequality and Black suffering in the American context. It focuses on the writings of Cornel West., who remains one of America's most celebrated and vocal public intellectuals. He continues to be an important African American voice who speaks of the Black struggle, the indefatigable demand for justice and the force of the prophetic imagination.

A Note on COVID-19

When the manuscript cleared the review process, the world was already suffering the impact of the global pandemic, COVID-19, the highly infectious disease caused by the most recently discovered coronavirus. According to the World Health Organisation, this new virus and disease were unknown before the outbreak began in Wuhan, China, in December 2019. COVID-19 is now a pandemic affecting many countries globally.[1] The outbreak of coronavirus

---

[1] www.who.int/emergencies/diseases/novel-coronavirus-2019/coronavirus-disease-answers

disease has created a global health crisis with a deep impact on the way we perceive our world and our everyday lives. The rate of contagion and patterns of transmission meant that for weeks, the major cities and populations of the world went into lockdown with people staying indoors in their homes and unable to go out or travel except for the most essential needs. The phenomenon of social distancing and not being able to physically meet friends and family became a reality and the emotional and psychological impact of this disease on our lives continues. For the sake of safety, societies had to refrain from the inherently human activity which is to find solace in the company of others. As most businesses and workplaces physically shut for months, the economic and psychological effects of this contagion will be huge. Societies and governments around the world continue to manage public alarm and safety according to scientific advice about the danger from this virus. While the race for a vaccine continues, COVID-19 is still not fully understood as a virus and a disease and all kinds of policies are being put into place to limit the spread and deaths from this contagion. The alarming spread of this virus and the measures to contain it have brought in a particular kind of universal human struggle, in which all the norms and expectations of the world as we experienced it, suddenly changed overnight. For those who have survived, life continues with all its challenges, as the world slowly and gradually comes to terms with the unfolding of 'the new normal'.

1

Human Struggle: Literary, Theological and Philosophical Reflections

'ALL LIFE DEMANDS STRUGGLE', SAID POPE PAUL VI. THERE IS SOME-thing prophetic in the notion of human struggle, in affirming that facing difficulties is essential for human potential and development. We experience struggle in so many aspects of our lives, in broken relationships, in ambition, in accidents and disease, in lost loves, unrequited and forbidden loves, sickness and death, and unfulfilling jobs and failed dreams. We are struggling for or towards something: this gives struggle a hint of hope and potential, the sense that the present pain – physical or emotional – the present injustice will pass, will end by and through human efforts.

The word is used in this book in its broadest philosophical and theological sense where it is often aligned to suffering, although suffering conveys a greater sense of the tragic. For Freud, death and suffering were linked as it is death which takes away all of life's meaning – that not only can we not imagine our own death but that the whole process of civilisation is a self-defence mechanism to substitute for the anxieties of death. Here, culture is a collective means to 'render human mortal life bearable and even mean-ingful'. Yet the paradox for Freud is that it is because of this very civilisation that we suffer. For Freud, modernity may have made our lives easier but not happier and he asks, 'What good is a long life to us if it is hard, joyless and so full of suffering that we can only welcome death as a deliverer?'[1]

Linguistically, suffering can also mean to 'endure' and this is particularly telling, since in Latin *duras* means hard. Hence, to *en-dure* means to harden oneself, so as to be able to take on that which is difficult. Suffering can be seen and interpreted in multiple ways across cultures and throughout history. Suffering is always more than a physical state. As Elisa Aaltola writes, 'Unlike

---

[1] Sigmund Freud, *Civilisation and Its Discontents*, 1941, trans. by David McLintock, London: Imago Publishing, 2002, 24, 26–7.

pain, suffering touches our whole being: our bodies, emotions, and thoughts become governed by it, and thus it is exceedingly difficult to avert attention away from its hold. Suffering stays with us, we cannot escape it, and it becomes the definer of many of our mental contents and even our very existence'.[2] Suffering in its broadest sense, whether mental or physical, 'is always borne by individual human beings, and to recognize suffering is to recognize the suffering of individuals, and not merely of the mass. Suffering, we may say is always *singular*'.[3]

Suffering can also point to anguish and despair, a certain lost-ness of the human condition. As partly owing to its holistic dimension, suffering also often appears hopeless. Thus, it seems there is a difference between struggle and suffering. Struggle contains a sense of hope in the midst of all kinds of moral, societal and personal uncertainties. Struggle is part of the learning process. It's to be expected and honoured. Humans can witness each other's struggle and find mutual respect in the process, knowing that at the end of the struggle is a sense of personal achievement.

Despite the differences in meaning, the words are often used interchangeably. In addition, evil, at least in what is termed the Judaeo-Christian West, also subsumes sin, suffering and death. There are however distinctions in that suffering is often that which happens to us, it affects us whether physically, psychologically or spiritually. As Paul Ricoeur says, 'Suffering sets lamentation against reprimand, for if misdeeds make people guilty, suffering makes them victims'.[4] We will not be able to avoid some struggle or suffering in our lives but our challenge is to find meaning in these conditions. Struggle and suffering are often connected by human hope. Viktor Frankl (1905–97) claimed that man's search for meaning was the primary motivation in his life. He wrote movingly about his own life and experiences in the Nazi concentration camps, including Auschwitz. He argued that suffering is an ineradicable part of life without which life would not be complete and added that 'if there is a meaning in life at all, then there must be meaning in suffering'.[5] While unnecessary suffering should not be seen as heroic, one has to accept one's suffering as a task for we are all unique in the way we accept this burden:

---

[2] Elisa Aaltola, 'Philosophical Narratives of Suffering: Nietzsche, Levinas, Weil and Their Cultural Roots', in *Suomen Antropologi*, 43:3, 2019, 22–40, 23.

[3] Jeff Malpas, 'Suffering, Compassion, and the Possibility of a Humane Politics' in Jeff Malpas and Norelle Lickiss (eds.), *Perspectives on Human Suffering*, Springer: Dordrecht, 2012, 14.

[4] Paul Ricoeur, *Evil: A Challenge to Philosophy and Theology*, trans. by John Bowden, London: Continuum, 2007, 36.

[5] Viktor E. Frankl, *Man's Search for Meaning*, London: Ebury Publishing, 2004, 105 and 76.

The way in which a man accepts his fate and all the suffering it entails, the way in which he takes up his cross, gives him ample opportunity – even under the most difficult circumstances- to add a deeper meaning to his life. It may remain brave, dignified and unselfish. Or in the bitter fight for self-preservation, he may forget his human dignity and become no more than an animal.[6]

For Frankl, when faced with a hopeless situation, 'what then matters is to bear witness to the uniquely human potential at its best, which is to transform a personal tragedy into a triumph, to turn one's predicament into a human achievement'.[7]

It appears that struggle is a particular kind of paradox of the human condition because as much as we think we should avoid struggle, struggle defines the human condition. History throws up countless examples of people who have captured our imagination through their personal struggles and legacies. Dr Martin Luther King Jr (1929–68), Baptist minister and one of the pivotal leaders of the American civil rights movement of the sixties, used the word struggle often when he spoke of the urgency of raising political consciousness to bring about social change and racial justice. In one of his many famous addresses, delivered at the Sheraton hotel in New York City in 1962, he begins by saying, 'Mankind through the ages has been in a ceaseless struggle to give dignity and meaning to human life'.[8] King also saw a positive light in human struggle, the human will to continue despite all obstacles: 'Tragic disappointments and undeserved defeats do not put an end to life, nor do they wipe out the positive, however submerged it may have become beneath floods of negative experience'.[9]

Famous for his oratorical skills, he spoke profoundly and provocatively of freedom for Black Americans and the necessity of ending discrimination, oppression and racial injustice. He wrote and spoke about the challenges for the Black struggle movements which involved other leading players but within which he became one of the most charismatic leaders:

> Human progress is neither automatic nor inevitable. Even a superficial look at history reveals that no social advance rolls in on the wheels of inevitability. Every step toward the goal of justice requires sacrifice, suffering, and struggle; the tireless exertions and passionate concern of dedicated individuals.[10]

---

[6] Frankl, *Man's Search*, 76.   [7] Frankl, *Man's Search*, 116.

[8] https://viewing.nyc/dr-martin-luther-king-jr-1962-civil-rights-speech-in-new-york-city/

[9] https://viewing.nyc/dr-martin-luther-king-jr-1962-civil-rights-speech-in-new-york-city/

[10] Martin Luther King Jr and Coretta Scott King, *Words of Martin Luther King Jr.*, New York: Newmarket Press, 2001, 41.

Often the struggle of one person reflects a societal and civilisational struggle. When King died, the American writer and activist James Baldwin
(1924–87) spoke of his own grief and loss:

> I don't think that any black person can speak of Malcolm and Martin
> without wishing that they were here. It is not possible for me to speak of
> them without a sense of loss and grief and rage; and with the sense,
> furthermore, of having been forced to undergo an unforgivable indignity,
> both personal and vast. Our children need them, which is, indeed, the
> reason that they are not here: and now we, the blacks, must make certain
> that our children never forget them. For the American republic has always
> done everything in its power to destroy our children's heroes, with the clear
> (and sometimes clearly stated) intention of destroying our children's hope.
> This endeavor has doomed the American nation: mark my words.[11]

Baldwin himself was all too aware of the significance of skin colour in
America and the responsibility and struggle of a writer like him. He argued
that American writers do not have a 'fixed society to describe. The only
society they know is one in which nothing is fixed and in which the
individual must fight for his identity'. Baldwin saw this society as one of
tensions and possibilities, one which smashed taboos, and said, 'The time has
come, God knows, for us to examine ourselves, but we can only do this if we
are willing to free ourselves of the myth of America and try to find out what is
really happening here'.[12] Raising social and political consciousness is not
about being consumed with rage alone but a long road towards shaking a
nation out of its indifference or hostility. In her moving tribute to King's
'audacious faith', the Nobel laureate Toni Morrison writes:

> His confidence that we were finer than we thought, that there were moral
> grounds that we would not abandon, lines of civil behaviour we simply
> would not cross. That there were things we would gladly give up for the
> public good, that a comfortable life, resting on the shoulders of others
> people's misery, was an abomination this country, especially, among all
> nations, found offensive. I know the world is better, finer, because he lived
> in it.[13]

Living during what became known as the Jazz Age of the 1920s, the writer
and novelist, F. Scott Fitzgerald (1896–1940) is considered a genius for his
brilliant depictions of that era. Fitzgerald's letters shed light on his life, which
seemed wracked by a strange mix of celebrity, pleasure and failure. Writing

---

[11] www.esquire.com/news-politics/a14443780/james-baldwin-mlk-funeral/
[12] James Baldwin, *Collected Essays*, New York: Literary Classics of the United States, 1998, 142.
[13] Toni Morrison, *The Source of Self-Regard*, New York: Alfred A. Knopf, 2019, 130.

to his daughter Frances, called 'Scottie', he encourages her to move on from her current college, to have new objectives so that she can awaken her mind to developing literary tastes and philosophic concepts. He laments that people become too caught up in the material world to form 'the wise and tragic sense of life'. Fitzgerald writes what lies behind all successful careers in life is that 'life is essentially a cheat and its conditions are those of defeat; the redeeming things are not "happiness and pleasure" but the deeper satisfactions that come out of struggle'.[14]

Thus, all achievement comes through struggle and it is struggle which gives our life meaning. The writer and poet Ralph Waldo Emerson (1803–82), a member of the group, New England transcendentalists, championed the individual in his powerful, philosophical writings. Mary Oliver describes him as one who saw that the whole world is 'taken through the eye, to reach the soul, where it becomes *more*, representative of a realm deeper than appearances: a realm ideal and sublime'.[15] Emerson presents us with a haunting paradox. In his essay 'Compensation', he had presented a theory of spiritual loss and benefit. He wrote: 'As no man had ever a point of pride that was not injurious to him, so no man had ever a defect that was not somewhere made useful to him'. For Emerson, our strength grows out of our weakness and he contends, 'A great man is always willing to be little. While he sits on the cushion of advantages, he goes to sleep. When he is pushed, tormented, defeated, he has a chance to learn something'.[16] But as Emerson realises, suffering can also be banal, leave no mark or be easily forgotten. In his later essay, 'Experience' written two years after losing his five-year-old son to scarlet fever, he wrote that at times we search for grief, we court suffering so that we can find reality and the 'sharp peaks and edges of truth'. Yet he finds:

> The only thing grief has taught me, is to know how shallow it is. That, like all the rest, plays about the surface, and never introduces me into the reality, for contact with which, we would even pay the costly price of sons and lovers . . . Souls never touch their objects. Grief too will make us idealists . . . So is it with this calamity: it does not touch me: something which I fancied was a part of me, which could not be torn away without tearing me, nor enlarged without enriching me, falls off from me, and leaves no scar. I grieve that grief can teach me nothing.[17]

---

[14] Andrew Turnbull (ed.), *The Letters of F. Scott Fitzgerald*, New York: Penguin Books, 1963, 112.
[15] Mary Oliver, 'Introduction' in Brooks Atkinson (ed.), *The Essential Writings of Ralph Waldo Emerson*, New York: The Modern Library, 2000, xiv.
[16] Atkinson, *The Essential*, 166. [17] Atkinson, *The Essential*, 309.

As Dan Chiasson writes, 'This seems nearly callous, but that's the point . . .
Waldo's death was so profound that it went uncompensated, even by grief. It
taught Emerson "nothing"; it was almost as though his son had never existed.
Unluckily, swiftly, even happily, life goes on, only mildly "inconvenienced"
by the most devastating loss imaginable and omnipresence'.[18] But Emerson
sees that every calamity is about human growth. What we humans are unable
to let go because 'we are idolators of the old'. He writes that 'we do not believe
in the riches of the soul, in its proper eternity' because we do not understand
calamity and that misfortune leads to growth:

> A fever, a mutilation, a cruel disappointment, a loss of wealth, a loss of
> friends, seems at the moment, unpaid loss and unpayable. But the sure
> years reveal the deep remedial forces that underlies all facts. The death of a
> dear friend, wife, brother, lover, which seemed nothing but privation,
> somewhat later assumes the aspect of a guide or genius; for it commonly
> operates revolutions in our way of life, terminates an epoch of infancy or of
> youth, which was waiting to be closed.[19]

Yet the connection between the abstraction of thought and the substance of
life comes into sharp focus as we read a letter written by another father who
lost his nine-year-old son and wrote movingly of his bereavement. One of the
greatest Protestant theologian philosophers, Friedrich Schleiermacher
(1768–1834), lost his son Nathanael to scarlet fever in 1829. Albert Blackwell
writes that Schleiermacher's lifelong theological struggle was 'to move
beyond the eighteenth century's mechanistic views of God toward the
Christian doctrine of God's love'. He writes,

> In bringing Schleiermacher to the extremity of life's sorrow in 1829, the
> death of his son brought him to pray for the faith to embrace what his
> theological system had earlier settled upon as the only essential divine
> attribute, God's love . . . His personal struggle at Nathanael's graveside to
> find rest in God's love was the struggle which his theology had formally
> recognized as definitive for Christian faith.

This is reflected in Schleiermacher's Augustinian prayer: 'Let me not only
resign myself to thy omnipotence, not only submit to thy impenetrable
wisdom, but also know thy fatherly love'.[20]

---

[18] Dan Chiasson, 'Ecstasy of Influence' in *The New Yorker*, 91:26, 7 September 2015, 85.

[19] Atkinson, *The Essential*, 170–1.

[20] Albert L. Blackwell, 'Schleiermacher's "Sermon at Nathanael's Grave"', in *Pastoral Theology*,
      26:1, 1977, 23–36, 30–1.

Schleiermacher's 'Sermon at Nathanael's Grave' was written down by Schleiermacher himself after its delivery. The theologian thanks God for the 'undeserved blessings; for a great abundance of joys and sorrows, which, in my calling and as a sympathetic friend, I have lived through with others'. Yet, having been able to live through many of life's trials sustained by both faith and love, he finds this experience has 'shaken my life to its roots'. As he wrestles with his Christian faith, he looks at how others have tried to console him and yet he struggles:

> Still others who grieve generate their consolation in another way, out of an abundance of attractive images in which they represent the everlasting community of those who have gone on before and those who as yet remain behind; and the more these images fill the soul, the more all the pains connected with death are stilled. But for the man who is too greatly accustomed to the rigors and cutting edges of thinking, these images leave behind a thousand unanswered questions and thereby lose much, much of their consoling power.[21]

Schleiermacher still holds onto this faith, for in his theology, the ways of God must still be loving; this is a faith where death does not have the final say:

> Now, thou God who art love, let me not only resign myself to thy omni-potence, not only submit to thy impenetrable wisdom, but also know thy fatherly love! Make even this grievous trial a new blessing for me in my vocation! For me and all of mine let this communal pain become wherever possible a new bond of still more intimate love, and let it issue in a new apprehension of thy Spirit in all my household! Grant that even this grave hour may become a blessing for all who are gathered here. Let us all more and more mature to that wisdom which, looking beyond the void, sees and loves only the eternal in all things earthly and perishable, and in all thy decrees finds thy peace as well, and eternal life, to which through faith we are delivered out of death.[22]

Grief has a poignancy which always needs to be managed. Even when one tries to share it, whether in a sermon or a letter, it never hides the despair one feels over deep loss or misfortune. Oscar Wilde (1854–1900) had requested Emerson's works in his time in prison because they gave him comfort. Imprisoned for two years between 1895–7, on charges of indecency, Wilde's letter, *De Profundis*, was addressed to his lover Alfred Lord Douglas, and written between January and March of 1897, near the end of his internment in Reading prison. Earlier he had served time in Pentonville prison, where he

---

[21] Blackwell, 'Schleiermacher', 33.   [22] Blackwell, 'Schleiermacher', 34.

suffered miserably from dysentery and malnutrition. In Reading prison, he eventually won the right to compose a letter in his cell on the condition that each day's pages were collected at nightfall. *De Profundis* is a long, spiritually rich, seductive and, at times, bitter autobiographical reflection of his life, character and personal failings.[23] Speaking of the dejected Wilde writing in prison, Colm Tóibín says:

> The cell where Wilde wrote 'De Profundis' is filled with a sense of those who recently suffered there, but the view of the sky from the small window and the heaviness of the door as it closes behind you bring back how one of the great spirits of his age was broken in body and soul in this space, and then restored to some dark approximation of life by being given pen and paper so that he too could lighten his sorrow, or make it matter more, by producing something as strange and beautiful as 'De Profundis'.[24]

Wilde writes about the 'paralysing immobility' of such a regulated life which only revolves and does not progress. He wrote about once having everything, in contrast to his now wretched status. Having experienced the 'season of sorrow', he laments that 'suffering is one long moment. We cannot divide it by seasons. We can only record its moods and chronicle their return'.[25] He refers to the sense of loss and personal shame when his mother dies and he has no words in which 'to express my anguish and shame'.

> She and my father had bequeathed me a name they had made noble and honoured, not merely in literature, art, archaeology, and science, but in the public history of my own country, in its evolution as a nation. I had disgraced that name eternally. I had made it a low by-word among low people. I had dragged it through the very mire. I had given it to brutes that they might make it brutal, and to fools that they might turn it into a synonym for folly. What I suffered then, and still suffer, is not for pen to write or paper to record.

For Wilde, 'prosperity, pleasure and success', are the things which occupy us but 'sorrow is the most sensitive of all created things'. Sorrow not only stirs us but carries an 'exquisite pulsation'. But most of all, suffering carries meaning, and for him, the meaning was humility. Having discovered humility, he realises 'it is the last thing left in me, and the best'. And he continues

---

[23] For a useful and quick background, see www.bl.uk/collection-items/manuscript-of-de-profundis-by-oscar-wilde

[24] Colm Tóibín in www.theguardian.com/books/2016/aug/26/oscar-wilde-de-profundis-greatest-love-letter

[25] Rupert Hart-Davis (ed.), *Selected Letters of Oscar Wilde*, New York: Oxford University Press, 1989, 186.

with aligning the tragic to the sacred: 'Where there is sorrow there is holy ground. Some day people will realise what that means. They will know nothing of life till they do'.[26] Wilde had to learn the meaning of survival in prison and through it, the meaning of sorrow.

Literary works often present struggle through the language of human rights. They speak of the denial of rights for those who are oppressed, the silent and the marginalised. When the American writer and monk, Thomas Merton (1915–68) wrote about the black American novelists whose voice was heard even in the days of enslavement, he wrote of their struggle as not only their own liberation but the liberation of the white man. For Merton, the white man cannot even free himself from the only drumbeat he hears – the sound of his own preservation and privilege at all costs.

> In a perfect, unconscious and spontaneous spirit of prayer and prophecy, the Negro spirituals of the last century remain as classic examples of what a living, liturgical hymnody ought to be and how it came into being; not in the study of the research worker or in the monastery library but where mean suffer oppression, where they are deprived of identity, where their lives are robbed of meaning, and where the desire of freedom, and the imperative demand of truth forces them to give it meaning: a religious meaning.[27]

Perhaps one of the most lucid definitions of suffering is to be found in the Apostolic Letter, *On the Christian Meaning of Human Suffering*. Here Pope John Paul II states:

> Even though man knows and is close to the sufferings of the animal world, nevertheless what we express by the word 'suffering' seems to be particu-larly *essential to the nature of man*. It is as deep as man himself, precisely because it manifests in its own way that depth which is proper to man, and in its own way surpasses it. Suffering seems to belong to man's transcen-dence: it is one of those points in which man is in a certain sense 'destined' to go beyond himself, and he is called to this in a mysterious way.[28]

To be human is to suffer, to have life is to suffer. One might claim that it is suffering which is the great constant, the essence of the human condition. One of the most eloquent expressions of humankind's ability to live, seek and

---

[26] All subsequent Wilde quotes taken from www.gutenberg.org/files/921/921-h/921-h.htm
[27] Patrick Hart (ed.), *The Literary Essays of Thomas Merton*, New York: New Directions Paperbook, 1981, 168.
[28] Pope John Paul II, *Salvifici Doloris*, http://w2.vatican.va/content/john-paul-ii/en/apost_letters/1984/documents/hf_jp-ii_apl_11021984_salvifici-doloris.html

be moved by the suffering and indignity of others, is encapsulated in the memorable lines of the philosopher Bertrand Russell who wrote:

> Three passions, simple but overwhelmingly strong, have governed my life: the longing for love, the search for knowledge, and unbearable pity for the suffering of mankind. . . . Love and knowledge, so far as they were possible, led upward toward the heavens. But always pity brought me back to earth. Echoes of cries of pain reverberate in my heart. Children in famine, victims tortured by oppressors, helpless old people a hated burden to their sons, and the whole world of loneliness, poverty and pain make a mockery of what human life should be. I long to alleviate this evil, but I cannot, and I too suffer.[29]

Western philosophical narratives focus more on suffering than struggle. The manner in which they both echo and strengthen culturally common Western meanings of suffering show a variety of approaches to human anguish and sorrow. For the contemporary philosopher, Martha Nussbaum, vulnerability is a fundamental aspect of the human condition and, because we are vulnerable, suffering can enter us. She writes, 'Human beings are vulnerable animals, naked, needy, and weak. They are threatened both by an indifferent nature and by their own hostilities. They need food, drink, shelter, medicine; love, care, protection from violence. But they also aspire, speak, and create'. For Nussbaum, human nature which aspires and chooses, makes us worthy of respect. It is a dignity that 'lifts them above passive objects in nature'. But human beings also need love and 'that is difficult to rank either on the side of dignity or on the side of neediness':

> Love expresses deep needs for connection – whether friendly or erotic – and it becomes a source of further neediness in turn, opening up a great hole of vulnerability in the self. And yet in its splendor it asks to be seen as itself wondrous and divine, a power worthy of respect and awe.[30]

Nussbaum's analysis of love is that 'deep love makes large claims on the self' and involves taking the risk of loss and suffering. Regarding our freedom to exercise our moral agency, she posits: 'If we permit ourselves to love other people deeply, our risk becomes, as well, a risk of wishing and perhaps even of doing evil'.[31]

---

[29] Bertrand Russell, *The Autobiography of Bertrand Russell, Vol. 1, 1872–1914*, London: Allen & Unwin, 1967, 9.
[30] Martha C. Nussbaum, 'Political Animals: Luck, Love, and Dignity', *Metaphilosophy*, 29:4, 1998, 273–288, 274.
[31] Nussbaum, 'Political', 277.

Struggle and suffering often overlap as concepts and realities. In the midst of these realities is that which inspires all human activity and relationships – desire. In the famous words of William Irvine, it is desire that animates life: 'Banish desire from the world and you get a world of frozen beings who have no reason to live and no reason to die'.[32] It is desire which energises us, keeps us moving and creates want and ambition in us, but it is also desire which enslaves us. The German philosopher, Arthur Schopenhauer (1788–1860) was among the first of nineteenth-century philosophers to contend that at its core, the universe is not a rational place. Inspired by Plato and Kant, both of whom saw the world as being more amenable to reason, Schopenhauer developed their philosophies, emphasising that in the face of a world filled with endless strife, we ought to minimise our natural desires for the sake of achieving a more tranquil frame of mind. The pursuit of happiness has become the centre of modern life, but guiding one's life based on pursuing happiness only increases one's misery; our determination to achieve happiness is the root of our malaise. Rather unfortunately labelled the 'philosopher of pessimism', he argued that our will has no purpose, is aimless, because our will's satisfaction is impossible. Schopenhauer's monumental book, *The World of Will and Representation*, (*Die Welt als Wille und Vorstellung*), completed in Dresden and published in 1818, presents the world as having two sides, that of representation (*Vorstellung*), the way things present themselves to us in experience, and that of will (*Wille*), which is, he argues, what the world is in itself, beyond mere appearances. This world is a world of perennial suffering, brought about by the metaphysical drive that moves it and is indifferent to our individual desires, the will. Life is a process of disillusionment:

> If the immediate and direct purpose of our life is not suffering then our existence is the most ill adapted to its purpose in the world.
>
> Work, worry, toil and trouble are indeed the lot of almost all men their whole life long. And yet if every desire were satisfied as soon as it arose how would men occupy their lives, how would they pass the time?[33]

As Christopher Janaway explains:

> Schopenhauer's world is purposeless. His notion of will is probably best captured by the notion of *striving towards* something ... Humanity is poised between the life of an organism driven to survival and reproduction,

---

[32] William Irvine, *On Desire: Why We Want What We Want*, New York: Oxford University Press, 2006, 2.
[33] Arthur Schopenhauer, *On the Suffering of the World*, trans. by R. J. Hollingdale, London: Penguin Books, 2004, 3 & 5.

and that of a pure intellect that can rebel against its nature and aspire to a timeless contemplation of a 'higher' reality.[34]

The essence of existence is insatiable striving, and insatiable striving is suffering, living with the dual miseries of pain and frustration:

> Awakened to life out of the night of her consciousness there will find itself as an individual in an endless and balance world among innumerable individuals, all striving, suffering, and erring and, as if through a trouble dream, it hurries back to the old unconsciousness. Yet still then, its desires are unlimited, its claims inexhaustible, and every satisfied desire gives birth to a new one. No possible satisfaction in the world could suffice to still its craving, set a final goal to its demands, and fill the bottomless pit of its heart ... Everything in life proclaims that earthly happiness is destined to be frustrated, or recognized as an illusion. The grounds for this lie in the very nature of being. (W2, 573)[35]

Schopenhauer argued that tragedy, and tragedy alone, is able to reveal the world that lies beyond the level of representation, beyond ideology. Tragedy is not only a supreme art form, like many philosophers contend, rather it is tragedy which is 'uniquely able to portray human life in what he regards as its true colours, containing the right degree of unfulfilled desire, conflict and unmitigated suffering'.[36] No satisfaction achievable in human existence can compensate for the suffering that it must also contain. To alleviate ourselves of this kind of suffering, to achieve a certain kind of salvation, he presents a Buddhistic minimisation of desire. It is this gradual denial of the will which will eventually lead to a disconnection from this temporal world and precipitate a more ascetic lifestyle, one that achieves inner tranquility and meaning. This is a more mystical transcendent state, where suffering or pain is virtually dissolved. 'Far from condoning suicide in response to the world's violence, Schopenhauer advocates living in a state as close to will-less-ness as possible'. While non-existence would be preferable and the world is the worst possible world, Schopenhauer also states that the world does not owe us happiness nor are we meant not to suffer. As the cultural theorist Terry Eagleton writes:

---

[34] I have relied primarily on Christopher Janaway's analysis in Christopher Janaway, *Schopenhauer: A Very Short Introduction*, Oxford: Oxford University Press, 2002, 7–8. This section serves to highlight Schopenhauer's view on will and suffering only.

[35] Janaway, *Schopenhauer*, 103. Janaway's reference is to *The World as Will and Representation*, vols. 1 & 2 (1819, 1844), Dover, 1969.

[36] Janaway, *Schopenhauer*, 83.

We bear a dead weight of meaninglessness at the very core of our being, as though permanently pregnant with monsters. It is as though Schopenhauer's macabre world view derides the idea of God at the same time as it mocks the post metaphysical progressivists who imagine they can get on without it. The futility which Schopenhauer finds in human existence manifests itself in exactly the places which the Romantics and the sentimentalists thought most precious – in our instincts and affections, in the stirrings of desire and the motions of the spirit. Desire is no longer a positive capacity.[37]

The Russian novelist, Leo Tolstoy (1828–1910) mentions Schopenhauer when writing of his own search for the meaning of life. In depicting his personal journey of struggle, depression and estrangement from the world, Tolstoy, speaks of his desire to find the answer to that fundamental question in human life:

Expressed another way the question can be put like this: why do I live? Why do I wish for anything, or do anything? Or expressed another way: is there any meaning in my life that will not be annihilated by the inevitability of death which awaits me?[38]

For Tolstoy, reason, rationality and human knowledge had failed to give an answer to the meaning of life. In trying to find an explanation, he writes,

Life is a senseless evil, that is certain, I said to myself. Yet I have lived and still live, and so too humanity has lived and still lives. How can this be? Why do men live when it is possible not to live? Can it be that only Schopenhauer and I have been intelligent enough to understand the senselessness and evil of life?[39]

What Tolstoy discovers is that to understand the meaning of life, he must not look at those who 'have lost it and wish to kill themselves' but rather among the millions of those living and dead who 'have created life, and who carry the weight of our lives together with their own'. It is this humanity, the masses who see meaning in irrational knowledge, who seemed to have a comprehension of life. Tolstoy was to realise this was faith, 'this irrational knowledge is faith, the very thing that I could not help rejecting, This God, one in three, the creation in six days, the devils and angels and all the rest which I could not accept without going mad'.[40]

---

[37] Terry Eagleton, *Culture and the Death of God*, New Haven: Yale University Press, 2015, 153.
[38] Leo Tolstoy, *A Confession and Other Religious Writings*, London: Penguin, 1987, 35.
[39] Tolstoy, *A Confession*, 47.　　[40] Tolstoy, *A Confession*, 50.

Both Schopenhauer and the German philosopher Friedrich Nietzsche (1844–1900) agreed that there is something wrong with scientific attempts to uncover the truth about the human predicament. If anything, such attempts prevent us from reaching the truth, only allowing us to pursue a truncated form of existence. Schopenhauer advocated the slow destruction of human desire by encouraging a more ascetic world view, as desiring is the source of suffering. As far as Nietzsche is concerned, the deaths of his father, Carl Ludwig, in 1849 when Nietzsche was just five, and his brother, Joseph, the following year had a profound effect on his adolescence and adulthood. The cognate issues of suffering and nihilism throughout much of his works, may also owe their presence to his own physical afflictions 'including paralysing headaches, digestive problems, and a painful eye condition that meant that most of his books needed to be at least partly dictated'.[41] For Nietzsche, who once considered himself a student of Schopenhauer, suffering should be seen as a critique of western culture. Modern man has forgotten that suffering is necessary and must be included in the human world view. The modern attitude towards suffering is predominantly negative where human suffering is perceived as an unnecessary evil, as burdensome, something which we don't wish to include in our world view. But for Nietzsche, suffering is not an argument against the value of life, rather it is meaningless suffering which causes distress.

> To those human beings who are of any concern to me I wish them suffering, desolation, sickness, ill treatment, indignities – I wish that they should not remain unfamiliar with profound self-contempt, the torture of self – mistrust, the wretchedness of the vanquished: I have no pity for them, because I wish them the only thing that can prove today whether one is worth anything or not – that one endures'[42]

Amena Coronado writes,

> While the death of God brings the joy and new sense of freedom that overflow from *The Gay Science*, the loss of desire and meaning that accompanies this event demands a response. At stake for Nietzsche, just as it had been for Schopenhauer, is the value of life – how we might live in the absence of our cherished idols and how we might come to live joyfully despite our suffering.[43]

---

[41] Stewart Smith, *Nietzsche and Modernism*, London: Palgrave Macmillan, 2018, 23.

[42] Friedrich Nietzsche, *The Will to Power*, London: Penguin, 2017, 481.

[43] Amena Coronado, *Suffering and the Value of Life*, a PhD dissertation submitted to the University of California, Santa Cruz, 2016, 14.

Nietzsche's anger was that humankind continues making only minor adjustments to their existence after the death of God, failing to recognise that this is a momentous event of human history. Expanding this point, Eagleton writes that we are the assassins: we humans have committed deicide but have 'repressed all memory of the traumatic event'. Secular societies have disposed of God but pretend otherwise. He writes that belief is a pretence but 'God is too vital a piece of ideology to be written off, even if it is one that their own profane activities render less and less plausible'.[44] However, for Christian faith, the death of God is not a question of his disappearance. On the contrary, it is one of the places where he is most fully present. Jesus is not man standing in for God. He is a sign that God is incarnate in human frailty and futility.[45]

It is worth mentioning in relation to desire, albeit briefly, the mimetic theory thesis of René Girard (1923–2015). In the religious aspects of desire, a distinction emerges between the desire for God, as the *summum bonum*, and disordered desire, which is the desire for things other than God: false gods or idols. It is 'disordered desire which leads to rivalry and violence; religious violence is the idolatry of disordered desire'. It is claimed that all desire is mimetic, albeit not all desire is conflictual or negative:

> My years of research and clinical observation have convinced me that it is indeed desire that humanises us, that impels us to unite with each other, to associate with each other, to assemble in groups, and also, as we will see, to resemble each other. It forms us in proportion as it animates us and arouses our thoughts and feelings. Desire leads us to seek out the company of others, their approval, their friendship, their support, and their recognition. But this can also be accompanied by rivalry and hatred; it can arouse both love and violence.[46]

Mimetic Theory, Christianity, and Islam all offer narratives of origin, locating the beginnings of violence and estrangement between God and humanity in the trauma of misguided desire.[47]

Discussions on human suffering in the West have assumed a more complex nature also because of the different kinds of evil and suffering which many see as the product of the modern age. But Peter Dews rightly questions

---

[44] Eagleton, *Culture*, 157.   [45] Eagleton, *Culture*, 160.

[46] Jean-Michel Oughourlian, *The Genesis of Desire*, East Lansing, MI: Michigan State University Press, 2010, 11.

[47] Michael Kirwan, 'Vox victima, vox moderna? Modernity and Its Discontents' in M. Kirwan A. Achtar (eds.), *Mimetic Theory and Islam*, Cham: Palgrave Macmillan, 2019, 173.

why, in a post-theological intellectual universe, should there be philosophical difficulty in coming to terms with the concept and phenomenon of evil:

> It would seem that the problem of theodicy, of justifying the ways of God to a suffering world, should have disappeared for us who live after Nietzsche's proclamation of the death of God. And yet as the recent burgeoning of philosophical literature on the topic of evil suggests, the problem of theodicy seems in some sense to have outlived the explicit belief in a divine creator that first gave rise to it.[48]

As can be seen, much of western literature's focus on suffering and struggle, comes from a number of different sources, but principally religion, psychology, arts and philosophy. These are thinkers who construct myths in which they embody their own struggle for coping with the questions of life and are generally considered 'prophetic' in the sense that they anticipate in their solitude the struggles and the general consciousness of later generations. But it is religion which has the longest and most persistent history of interest. Theological discussions have ranged from the contradiction posed by the existence of suffering (thought by to some be an evil) in a world which was created and governed by a benevolent God to the question of whether or not God suffers (*Patripassianism*) in his essential nature. Christianity in particular has been preoccupied with the redemptive possibilities of suffering and the entry of pain and struggle in human life. Christianity speaks of a God who knows suffering but also hope from the inside namely in Jesus on the cross. In his second letter to the Corinthians, St Paul established the link between the redemptive suffering of Jesus and the redemptive character of suffering among all humans:

> We are hard pressed on every side, but not crushed; perplexed, but not in despair; persecuted, but not abandoned; struck down, but not destroyed. We always carry around in our body the death of Jesus, so that the life of Jesus may also be revealed in our body. For we who are alive are always being given over to death for Jesus' sake, so that his life may also be revealed in our mortal body.[49]

In Romans 5:3–4, St Paul writes, 'Not only that, but we rejoice in our sufferings, knowing that suffering produces endurance, and endurance produces character, and character produces hope'. So much of human struggle is linked to scriptural stories which have been subject to a variety of theological

---

[48] Peter Dews, '"Radical Finitude" and the Problem of Evil' in María Pía Lara (ed.), *Rethinking Evil*, London: University of California Press Ltd, 2001, 46–7.

[49] 2 Corinthians 4:8–12, *NIV*.

and philosophical interpretations over the centuries. This includes the Christian doctrine of 'original sin' as resulting from the Fall. Robert Saler argues that while this Fall is not made explicit in Genesis 2–3, where it is the suffering rather than the sinfulness of man which is derived from the Fall, Paul's reading of Genesis 2–3 casts the story in uniquely Christocentric terms; this has crucial implications for the tradition that would come to regard Adam's transgression as the advent of knowledge's corruption. Saler provides a neat summary:

> In Paul's theology, Adam the transgressor becomes the rhetorical and theological counterpoint to Christ the redeemer. 'Therefore, just as sin came into the world through one man, and death came through sin, and so death spread to all because all have sinned . . . death exercised dominion from Adam to Moses, even over those whose sins were not like the transgression of Adam, who is a type of the one who was to come' (Romans 5:12, 14). Moreover, just as the individual character 'Adam' serves as the prototype for all of humanity (adam), the individual redeemed by Christ signals a new mode of being human, a 'new man' to replace the old: 'Therefore, just as one man's trespass led to condemnation for all, so one man's act of righteousness leads to justification and life for all. For just as by the one man's disobedience the many were made sinners, so by one man's obedience the many will be made righteous' (Romans 5:18–19).[50]

Not until the end of the second century did the Fall come to be discussed by the Church Fathers and it was only with St Augustine (354–430) that the doctrine of original sin and the Fall take on its particular severity.[51] St Augustine's most famous contribution to this topic is his idea that the 'ontological deficiency in humanity brought about by Adam and Eve's sin is biologically transmitted through the act of reproduction'. As Saler explains, Augustine understood this effect as an 'epistemological deficiency as well: while in Eden the primeval couple was *posse non peccare* (able not to sin) after the Fall, all of humanity becomes *non posse non peccare* (not able not to sin)'. While the Fall is interpreted in various ways in Christian thought and doctrine, Saler notes that one of the difficulties Christians face is that the Jesus of the canonical Gospels nowhere explicitly references the idea that Adam's transgression 'is the decisive locus through which sin and mortality enter the human experience'.[52] St. Paul advances this

---

[50] Robert Saler, 'The Transformation of Reason in Genesis 2–3: Two Options for Theological Interpretation', *Currents in Theology and Mission*, 36:4, 2009, 275–86, 276–7.
[51] For an incisive overview of Christianity and perfectibility, see John Passmore, *The Perfectibility of Man*, London: Gerald Duckworth and Company, 1970, 86–7.
[52] Saler, 'The Transformation', 277.

story into the starting point for humanity's subsequent rebellion and disobedience against God.

This duality of before and after, the breaking apart (*entzweiung*), innocence and sin, good and evil has been a major theological focus in Christian thought. For the German pastor and theologian, Dietrich Bonhoeffer, 'the fall *really* makes the creature – humankind in the imago dei – into a creator sicut deus' [emphasis original].[53] The serpent promises Adam that he will be 'like God' but mortality undercuts human likeness to God. Bonhoeffer writes:

> Nothing in the nature of humankind or of creation or of the serpent can be uncovered as a basis on which to explain this event. No theory of *posse peccare* or of *non posse peccare* is able to comprehend the fact that the deed was done. Every attempt to make it understandable merely takes the form of an accusation that the creature hurls against the Creator. *Second*, however, from a human point of view this deed is final; it cannot be abrogated. Otherwise Adam would be able to absolve himself from his guilt. Then his guilt would not be guilt, and Christ would have died in vain.[54]

Man is now his own centre and alone in his creatureliness. For Bonhoeffer, being a creature means being in relation to God. Freedom is not autonomy, as freedom from something, but as freedom for someone. For Bonhoeffer, 'We are creatures in relation; our freedom is not autonomy but a relational freedom that is free for God, and in this free for the other and creation'. He adds that 'we can lose our creatureliness when this relation to God (and with this to the other and the creation) is destroyed'. As he writes, humankind's transgression is not the eating of the fruit but 'the calling into question God's words'. Instead of obedience, human beings call into judgement God's words from the standpoint of their own rationality.[55] This is the first and the deepest split between God and humankind.

The Genesis story has explicit resonances in the Qur'an but, as with so many Qur'anic and biblical versions of the same event, the moral consequences are different. Max Weber is right to say that Islam lacks the sense of tragedy which comes from the feeling of sin. This is true in terms of a strict comparison with the historical weight of the Christian doctrine of the Fall

---

[53] Dietrich Bonhoeffer, *Creation and Fall: A Theological Exposition of Genesis 1–3*, John W. De Gruchy (ed.), trans. by Douglas Bax, Minneapolis: Fortress Press, 2004, 116.

[54] Bonhoeffer works, *Creation*, 119. I am grateful to David Robinson for sending me his article which explores this in greater depth. David Robinson, 'A Cleaving Mind: Hegel and Bonhoeffer on the Fall and Creation', *Modern Theology*, 32:4, 2016, 544–68.

[55] Nadine Hamilton, 'Dietrich Bonhoeffer and the Necessity of Kenosis for ScHiptural hermeneutics', *Scottish Journal of Theology*, 71:4, 2018, 441–59, 448. Cf. DBWE 3.

with all its shades. Furthermore, the centrality of sin and redemption can be compared with the whole Muslim theological framework which instead focuses on human transgression and divine forgiveness. If Adam's story is a story of disobedience, it is also a story of repentance. Repentance is the path to God and patience and trust the foundation of the pious life. The whole context of our earthly existence is based on human transgression, struggle, forgetfulness and divine forgiveness. The Qur'anic equivalent of the Genesis story is a paradigm of human disobedience and the acquiring of a certain kind of knowledge. Adam falls at the very first step, having given in to Iblis's seduction and temptation, thereby making his first act of freedom an act of disobedience and human vulnerability. But this disobedience goes deeper – it is a turning away, a repudiation of God and divine attention and care. Iblis begins by destroying the sexual innocence in Adam and Eve's relationship by luring them away from the divine and arousing in them both an awareness of the profane. It is this contested knowledge that defines human moral consciousness. Feeling ashamed at his actions and the consequences, Adam desperately tries to hide from God in shame and remorse. He asks for one parting glance at paradise as he tries to run away beseeching God to restore him to dust. Yet this dramatic entry of sin/disobedience entering the world is a story of human struggle; it is a struggle from the fear of the unseen. Adam wants forgiveness and his suffering to end. But he also wants that God re-establish the former relationship of love and care that they had prior to his own disobedience. He wants to be close to God, he wants to be cleansed so that he and God are in dialogue again. This cleansing is a cleansing of the spirit, a purification and an overcoming of the rupture between the sacred and the profane. Adam is unaware that God has already forgiven him and restored the divine–human relationship. The Qur'anic verse, 'I am placing on the earth a vicegerent', (Q2:30) alludes to Adam's destiny in that Adam was always created for the earth and not for the heavens. Human beings remain God's creatures, but they are now creatures with a different purpose. God's response is solace, 'O Adam how can I restore you to dust when I have known for all eternity that I would fill the earth and hell from your loins'.[56] The Qur'anic story is about human struggle in the light of that first 'slip' and the quest for divine forgiveness and or divine mercy. There is a life of hope here even if it is set against the tragic realisation that the heavens could not contain human desire, human freedom or human knowledge.

---

[56] Muhammad ibn 'Abd Allah al-Kisa'i. *Tales of the Prophets, Qisas al-anbiya'*, trans. by Wheeler M. Thackston Jr, Chicago: Great Books of the Islamic World, 1997, 44.

The Hanbali jurist Ibn Qayyim al-Jawziyya (1292–1350) sees the Iblis/human relationship as defining the human condition. While there is no particular understanding of Adam's goodness prior to his temptation, the assumption is always that this state of being can no longer be restored and human beings now act and respond within a different kind of existence. Human goodness and progress is a response to Iblis. He writes that 'although many evils and sins have occurred due to the existence of Iblis, the enemy of God, many pious deeds have also resulted [indirectly]. These pious deeds include waging battle in his path, denying oneself of desires and temptations, and enduring hardships and adversities in order to attain his love'.[57] Suffering (ibtala) is both a trial from God and a source of hope in God. Prophets are at the forefront of this. Ibn Qayyim continues, 'Even though God was displeased with Adam eating from the tree, he was pleased with his repentance, return back to him, submission, brokenness and humility in front of him. Even if God was angered by the expulsion of his Messenger [from Mecca] by his enemies, he was more pleased with Muhammad's return to it [victorious]'.[58] For Ibn Qayyim, these trials occur so humankind can witness the vastness of divine forgiveness and generosity.

In his explanation of how we 'witness' God's wisdom, Ibn Qayyim focuses on tawba or repentance. For Ibn Qayyim, patience and repentance are the dual roads to regaining God's love. He writes that there is 'no greater or more complete joy than this:' Quoting the gnostics he writes:

> If it had not been for the fact that repentance is one of the most beloved things to him, God would never have allowed the lapse of the most noble of humanity to him [i.e. Adam] to occur. Thus, repentance is the perfect and ultimate objective of all humanity; and the perfection of their father [Adam] occurred through it.

For Ibn Qayyim, 'since Adam's perfection was only achieved through repentance, the perfection of his offspring can only occur likewise'. But in Islamic thought, the necessity of human repentance is associated with the magnanimity of divine forgiveness. So powerful is this emphasis that the Qur'anic message contains an almost desperate sense of divine forgiveness.

> Say, 'O my servants who have transgressed against themselves, despair not of the mercy of God, for God forgives all sins: for He is oft-forgiving, most merciful. (Q39:53)
> My mercy engulfs everything. (Q7:156)

---

[57] Ibn Qayyim, On Divine, 136.   [58] Ibn Qayyim, On Divine, 138.

He has at heart that which you suffer, He has care for you, for the believers, compassionate and merciful. (Q9:128)

And perhaps the most poetic and moving Prophetic *hadith*:

O son of Adam, so long as you call upon me and ask of me, I shall forgive you for what you have done, and I shall not mind. O son of Adam, were your sins to reach the clouds of the sky and were you then to ask forgiveness of me, I would forgive you. O son of Adam, were you to come to me with sins nearly as great as the earth and were you then to face me, ascribing no partner to me, I would bring you forgiveness nearly as great as it [i.e., the earth].[59]

In his analysis of the influential Shafi'i jurist and Sufi Abu Talib al-Makki, Atif Khalil` writes that for al-Makki, 'there is nothing more obligatory on creation than repentance'. Khalil explains that there is nothing optional about *tawba* because '*tawba* is an essential and inescapable requirement for anyone who surrenders to God. Nor is repentance meant only for individual sins, but must, instead, be an all-embracing process of self-purification'.[60] *Tawba* is therefore a turning to God which neither relies on wrong doing nor petition – it is simply a state of being.

However one understands this narrative, at one level the Qur'anic story is essentially a story of struggle but not alienation from a transcendent God. Adam must now experience distance from God to understand what nearness was and while this might lie at the root of human struggle and yearning, it is also a route to human development. This view finds resonance in Christian theology namely emanating from St Augustine's view that God judged it better to bring goodness out of evil than not to permit any evil to exist – the concept of *felix culpa* or 'happy fault'.[61] In Christianity, human salvation lies in the atoning sacrifice of Christ but there is still a new inner battle being waged. St Paul describes this in Galatians 5:17: 'For the flesh lusts against the Spirit, and the Spirit against the flesh; and these are contrary to one another, so that you do not do the things that you wish'. The doctrine of sanctification or sanctifying grace, while understood in various ways, is the process of making holy and defines the continual human struggle with sin and

---

[59] *Hadith* 25 related by Bukhari and 34 related by al-Tirmidhi respectively, cited in Ezzeddin Ibrahim and Denys Johnson Davies, *Forty Hadith Qudsi*, Cambridge: Islamic Texts Society, 1997, 126.

[60] Atif Khalil, 'Tawba in the Sufi Psychology of Abu Ṭalib al-Makki', *Journal of Islamic Studies*, 23:3 2012, 294–324, 301.

[61] 'O Felix Culpa' is sung within the *Exultet*, the Church's prayer during the Easter Vigil service. 'O Happy Fault that merited such and so great a Redeemer!'

obedience to God. It is an inward spiritual process whereby God brings about holiness and change in the life of a Christian by means of the Holy Spirit. It is a process of transformation within the effects of living in a fallen world where all struggle. But sanctification means that humankind can be raised to something greater and better after sin and struggle.

For their part, most Muslim thinkers did not see this descent to earth as a loss or a fallen state nor did they interpret Adam's actions as a betrayal of divine trust. While disobedience may have led to an expulsion from paradise, many saw a positive ray in the first human act of disobedience. The Indian philosopher poet Muhammad Iqbal saw the creation of Adam as the creation of a being who, driven by desire and passion, would tear away all veils:

> Desire, resting in the lap of life
> And forgetful of itself,
> Opened its eyes, and a new world was born.
> Life said, 'Through all my years
> I lay in the dust and convulsed
> Until at last a door appeared
> In this ancient dome'.[62]

In Iqbal's view, human freedom is a risk which God has taken in his wisdom. Adam was guided but gave in to Iblis. There is an inevitability to this disobedience. Iqbal writes that Iblis persuaded him that, 'A life of passion and longing is better than eternal quiet' and that 'good' and 'bad' are "figments of the imagination of your Lord'.[63] He writes, 'That God has taken this risk shows his immense faith in man; it is for man now to justify this faith'. It is not that God desires to keep humankind from becoming more aware as Adam's inherent human impulse is to reach out for autonomous experience and knowledge; his sin is that of disobedience but it is also one of impatience. For Iqbal, good and evil fall within the same whole of creation because both are predicated on God's risk taking, faith in humanity and human freedom to use reason and to choose. In Iqbal's poetry it is Iblis who 'sets the soul astir'.[64] Iblis then becomes a symbolic but necessary player in the human quest for good since without him there is nothing for intelligence to master. In Iqbal's poetry, Gabriel is a mere spectator of the struggle between good and evil whereas Iblis is part of it; he is a rival of God. At one point, he taunts Gabriel, 'I rankle in God's heart like a thorn. But what about you? All you do is chant "He is God" over and over'. Yet, later, it is Iblis

---

[62] Muhammad Iqbal, *Tulip in the Desert: A Selection of Poetry*, trans. and ed. by Mustansir Mir, London: Hurst & Company Publishers, 2000, 26.
[63] Iqbal, *Tulip*, 28.   [64] Iqbal, *Tulip*, 27.

who is bored of man and exclaims 'The son of man is only a handful of straw and for that one spark of mine is enough. If straw is all that this world had, why was I given so much fire?'[65] For Iblis, causing human suffering and evil is no great challenge because humankind falls at every step; Iblis wants to be resisted, to be denied. But for Iqbal, human struggle on earth is not a damnation, it is precisely what gives meaning to life and is the route for our return to God. Unlike Adam, ordinary mortals have not experienced creation without suffering, but nor have humans experienced creation without love, beauty, joy, reason and the quest for success (*falah*).

While the ordinary believer struggles to stay away from wrongdoing, from temptation, for many Sufis, this struggle (*mujahada*) is a form of ascetic self-discipline which is part of the various stages (*maqamat*) on the Sufi's journey. However for some Sufis, the struggle is not even real for the world itself is not real:

> Though he is fallen asleep, God will not leave him
> In this forgetfulness. Awakened, he
> Will laugh to think what troubled dreams he had.
> And wonder how his happy state of being
> He could forget, and not perceive that all
> Those pains and sorrows were the effect of sleep
> And guile and vain illusion. So this world
> Seems lasting, though 'tis but the sleepers' dream.[66]

The journey in both Christianity and Islam is from sacral injunction to a form of moral reasoning. The Edenic state is one of blissful ignorance whereas the post-Edenic knowledge is one of freedom and rationality as well as struggle and dissent. In his analysis of Christian approaches to original sin, Saler sees Immanuel Kant (1724–1804) as describing Adam's humanity as 'substantially incomplete prior to its own appropriation of human reason – a process epitomized by the rebellion against God's prohibition'. For Kant, the exercise of human reason was 'rooted in sadness as well as joy, as humanity moves beyond the simplicity of the garden/nature into the 'conflict-ridden world of rational choice'.

> So long as inexperienced man obeyed this call of nature all was well with him. But soon reason began to stir ... The original occasion for deserting natural instinct may have been trifling. But this was man's first attempt to be conscious of his reason as a power which can extend itself beyond the

---

[65] Iqbal, *Tulip*, 40.
[66] Jalaluddin Rumi, 'The Progress of Man' in R. A. Nicholson, *Persian Poems*, ed. by A. J. Arberry, Everyman, 1972. https://www.rumi.org.uk/poems/#TheProgressofMan

limits to which all animals are confined. As such its effect was very important and indeed decisive for his future way of life. . . . He discovered in himself a power for choosing for himself a way of life, of not being bound without alternative to a single way, like the animals. Perhaps the discovery of this advantage created a moment of delight. But of necessity, anxiety and alarm as to how he was to deal with this newly discovered power quickly followed.[67]

Christian theology and philosophy focuses more deeply on evil and suffering in relation to divine and human freedom and subsumes human struggle within suffering. It also tends to collapse human affliction, suffering, natural calamities and wrongdoing within the larger framework of evil. In an article written in 1938 John Bennet wrote:

Evil is the source of the most acute theoretical problem which Christians must face. Also, it is for many sensitive souls the most formidable practical obstacle to the religious life. But it must also be recognised that evil is the stimulus without which among men as they are there would be little religious faith at all. If there were no evil in the world the intellectual life of the Christian would run smooth but he would be so self-sufficient and would fit so comfortably in his environment that there would be little room for faith in anything but himself.[68]

Bennett argued that many human qualities which we value most could hardly be possible without evil or the strong possibility of evil.[69] While he does not advocate that evil must be alive for us to develop the deeper levels of all virtues, he argues in relation to suffering that

The greatest mystery of all is why some souls are able to transmute evil into good in their own lives and others are shattered by it. But when we have said all this, it still remains true that without suffering life is lived on a superficial level; we become self-sufficient, complacent and proud. Suffering deepens and strengthens every quality we have. It can purify us from preoccupation with trivial things. It raises love and friendship to the highest level. It forces us out of ruts and often gives life a new beginning.[70]

The German philosopher and polymath, Gottfried Wilhelm von Leibniz (1646–1716) defended the justness of God and argued for the doctrine that this world is the best of all possible worlds, coining the word theodicy. He

---

[67] Saler, 'The Transformation', 282. See Immanuel Kant, 'Conjectural Beginnings of Human History', trans. by Emil Fackenheim, from Lewis White Beck (ed.), *Kant on History*, Indianapolis: Bobbs-Merrill, 1963, 55–6.

[68] John C. Bennett, 'The Problem of Evil', *The Journal of Religion*, 18:4, 1938, 401–21, 401.

[69] Bennett, 'Problem', 416.   [70] Bennett, 'Problem', 417.

presented this concept in its fullest form in his essay *Théodicée* (1710). Leibniz used the word in its original sense to demonstrate that divine justice remains uncompromised by the manifold evils of existence. He writes at the beginning of the essay 'Concerning the origin of evil, in its relation to God, I shall offer a vindication of his perfections that shall extol not less his holiness, his justice and his goodness than his greatness, his power and his independence. I show how it is possible for everything to depend upon God'. He adds,

> I explain how evil has a source other than the will of God, and that one is right therefore to say of moral evil that God wills it not but simply permits it. Most important of all however, I show that it has been possible for God to permit sin and misery, and even to cooperate therein and promote it, without detriment to his holiness and his supreme goodness; although generally speaking, he could have avoided all these evils.[71]

While recognising that God could have 'avoided' evils, for Leibniz, theodicy was a problem of an imperfect ontology. Resolve the fundamental structure of the world, discover the essential harmony and freedom in all things, and the justice of God would be vindicated. More specifically, theodicy is the common term for the vindication of God's goodness in the face of the existence of evil, or the apparent contradiction between the assumption that God is omniscient and omnibenevolent and the evidence of evil which includes sin and suffering. In agreement with Leibniz, Hegel (1770–1831) too is committed to the principle of sufficient reason and the view that there is an exhaustive explanation for innocent suffering that is accessible to human reason; nothing exists beyond the scope of human reason. As Matthew Eggemeier writes,

> Hegel interprets suffering as a necessary moment in the dialectical movement of history that is overcome (*aufheben*) by being transformed into the positivity of progress in history. Hegel's philosophy confers meaning on innocent suffering in history by viewing it within a broader field of vision that sees the telos of history and interprets even the most brutal experiences of suffering as necessary byproducts of the progressive realization of Spirit in history.[72]

In this concept of theoretical theodicy, God functions as the final cause of reality that makes sense of and finally serves to justify the catastrophes of history. But as many philosophers have also noted, there comes a point when

---

[71] Gottfried Wilhelm Leibniz, *Theodicy*, Dumfries and Galloway: Anodos Books, 2019, 6.
[72] Matthew T. Eggemeier, 'Lévinas and Ricoeur on the Possibility of God after the End of Theodicy', *Philosophy and Theology*, 24:1, 2012, 23–48, 25.

physical suffering is so extreme or on such a massive scale that 'any attempt to justify it in terms of God's plan or the march of progress is morally repugnant, and the worst exercise of (philosophical) bad faith'.[73] Within this context, Eggemeier explores how both Lévinas (1906–95) and the French philosopher Paul Ricoeur (1913–2005) criticise Hegel's theodicy as 'representative of a more widespread criticism of the manner in which the Western tradition has used God as a means of justifying the suffering of the innocent'.[74] For Lévinas, the distinctive feature of the twentieth century is the collapse of all forms of theodicy before the scandal of innocent suffering:

> Perhaps the most revolutionary fact of our twentieth-century consciousness – but it is also an event in Sacred History – is that of the destruction of all balance between Western thought's explicit and implicit theodicy and the forms that suffering and its evil are taking on in the very unfolding of this century. This is the century that in thirty years has known two world wars, the totalitarianisms of right and left, Hitlerism and Stalinism, Hiroshima, the Gulag, and the genocides of Auschwitz and Cambodia. ... [A]mong these events the Holocaust of the Jewish people under the reign of Hitler seems to me the paradigm of gratuitous human suffering, in which evil appears in its diabolical horror.[75]

To rationally comprehend this level of suffering of the innocent in the twentieth century is 'intellectually untenable, but also as ethically suspect insofar as theodicy imposes meaning and order on suffering and thereby justifies it'. Lévinas's God is not 'the God of the promise who will redeem the victims of history at the end of time'. After Auschwitz, Lévinas rejects hope as an example of the consolation provided by theodicy and instead points to an 'ethics without hope as the only legitimate meaning of God after the end of theodicy'.[76] For Lévinas, it is the ethical relationships between human beings which bring one closer to God.

Similar to Lévinas, Paul Ricoeur argues that the 'death of God should be understood in a very precise sense as the death of the omnipotent, providential God'. But Ricoeur claims that the focus of the Judeo-Christian tradition is not merely on what is, but more profoundly what is to come and that that the living God is not 'the God who is but the God who is coming' or 'the God of promise'. Jesus's preaching

[73] Richard White, 'Lévinas, The Philosophy of Suffering, and the Ethics of Compassion', *The Heythrop Journal*, 53, 2012, 111–23, 111.

[74] Eggemeier, 'Lévinas', 26.

[75] Eggemeier, 'Lévinas', 29. Emmanuel Lévinas, *Entre Nous: Thinking-of-the-Other*, trans. by Michael Smith and Barbara Harshav, New York: Columbia University Press, 1998.

[76] Eggemeier, 'Lévinas', 34.

was centered around the eschatological event, then the whole of theology must be reinterpreted according to the norm of eschatology; theology can no longer take as its leading thread a notion of logos or of manifestation that would be independent from, and prior to, the hope concerning things to come. The task of a theology of hope would be to revise all the theological concepts on the basis of an exegesis ruled by the preaching of the kingdom to come.[77]

In contrast to Lévinas, Ricoeur points to both a narrative and eschatological theology as consistent with the basic commitments of his own hermeneutics of hope. Ricoeur claims that the believer is able to maintain faith in the midst of suffering and absence of answers, through the affirmation that God is both the creator and eschatological end of history. Because there is originary goodness at the beginning of time it follows that one is permitted to hope that evil will not have the last word at the end of time.

As Eggemeier writes, Ricoeur's mature response to the problem of theodicy is that the reasons for believing in God have nothing to do with the capacity to articulate a definitive explanation that makes sense of the suffering of the innocent. Ricoeur observes that 'it is in spite of evil that we believe in God, rather than that we believe in God in order to explain evil. Evil – and by evil I mean exactly unjust, undeserved suffering – remains what is and ought not to be'.[78] For Ricoeur, the belief in God in spite of evil is the act of a mature faith that leaves behind the idolatrous conception of God tied to retribution and theodicy. Lévinas describes the God 'that survives the end of theodicy as a trace that passes in the ethical relation with the human other and refuses what he views to be the pseudo-consolation of hope in any future redemption'. By way of contrast, Ricoeur defends hope as the privileged post-metaphysical path to God. Hope, as a passion for the possible, amidst all the suffering we face, stands at the centre of Ricoeur's philosophical project,

Much of twentieth-century philosophical literature on suffering focuses on the belief in a transcendent God as a manifest deceit where God mediates relations between people, turns man into an object and then man becomes not a value in himself but only in relation to God and because of God. Christianity more than Islam is said to involve a radical calumny, the rejection of man. An example of this hermeneutic of suspicion lies in the writings of the German philosopher Ludwig Feuerbach (1804–72). In his most famous work, *Das Wesen des Christentums*, translated by George Eliot

---

[77] Eggemeier, 'Levinas', 43. Emmanuel Levinas, *Figuring the Sacred: Religion, Narrative, Imagination*, trans. by David Pellauer and ed. by Mark I. Wallace, Minneapolis: Fortress Press, 1995, 204.

[78] Eggemeier, 'Levinas', 39. Emmanuel Lévinas, 'Figuring', 292.

as *The Essence of Christianity* (1841), Feuerbach held that theologians are correct when they say we can discern the divine attributes. They are right to believe in such things as divine love, justice, mercy, sagacity – even in eternal life and omniscience. Theologians are merely wrong in ascribing these to some divine person beyond humanity:

> The essential standpoint of religion is the practical or subjective. The end of religion is the welfare, the salvation, the ultimate felicity of man; the relation of man to God is nothing else than his relation to his own spiritual good; God is the realized salvation of the soul, or the unlimited power of effecting the salvation, the bliss of man.[79]

Feuerbach's thesis claims that since language about God is drawn from nature or human self-consciousness it does not succeed in speaking about God, but only about the world or humanity. Any speech about a god distinct from humanity is an illusory project. For Feuerbach, religion is the relation of man to his own nature. He writes, 'The personality of God is thus the means by which man converts the qualities of his own nature into the qualities of another being – of a being external to himself. The personality of God is nothing else than the projected personality of man'.[80] On this argument, the grandeur of human nature, of the human race collectively, truly *is* divine. It is also a terrific burden to bear. Our problem is that we shirk the burden of our own divine greatness. We create the devil as the scapegoat for the evil that we do, both trivial and titanic; and we create God as a paradoxical scapegoat to take the burden of our righteousness. Feuerbach insisted that he was the genuine believer, because he revered true divinity where it was really to be found – in the human breast, or in humanity as a whole. As regards suffering, in Feuerbach's view, 'To suffer is the highest command of Christianity – the history of Christianity is the history of the Passion of Humanity'. He contends that the Christian should make Christ's suffering his own because Christ has purchased man's salvation. He questions, 'shall I share only the gain and not the cost also? Do I know merely that he has redeemed me? Do I not also know the history of his suffering?'[81]

While the problem of theodicy features in Islamic thought in conceptions of God's unqualified omnipotence, human suffering is very often conceptualised as a necessary component of humanity's spiritual journey. In Sunni Islam, the focus on theodicy was a major theological debate during the ninth and tenth centuries. One of the earliest problems in Muslim theological

---

[79] Ludwig Feuerbach, *The Essence of Christianity*, trans. by George Eliot, United Kingdom: Create Space Independent Publishing Platform, 2018, xcv.
[80] Feuerbach, *The Essence*, cxv.   [81] Feuerbach, *The Essence*, xxxi and xxxii.

scholasticism (*kalam*[82]) was how to reconcile the divine attribute of omnipotence with the notion of human free will. The reconciliation of certain divine attributes, predominantly the aspect of an all-powerful God, with the idea of human free will – the broader frame within which human suffering was enclosed – was the first attempt to initiate a theodicy within the context of Islam. While the debate began among several groups, it crystallised between the Mu'tazilite and Ash'arite, the two main schools of thought, with a divergence of opinion. Broadly speaking, the Mu'tazilite school advocated for human free will and opposed the idea that God creates human acts that include suffering and bad deeds. They argued that human beings are the creators of their own acts, good or bad, and emphasised an Islamic free will theodicy. By emphasising the importance of the divine attribute of justice ('*adl*), they 'obligated God to do what is beneficial and most advantageous (*al-salah wa'l-aslah*)'.[83] Evil which included suffering was the result of human freedom and human choice and that what may appear as suffering serves a purpose in the creational cosmic plan. The Ash'arites got round the problem of preserving complete justice and complete omnipotence by developing the theory of acquisition (*kasb*) where God creates man's actions and humankind appropriates them thereby becoming responsible for individual actions.[84] God creates appropriation in man and is its real agent but the act is performed in man, not in God. In one of his most famous works, the *Kitab al-Luma'*, Al-Ash'ari is asked if God is free to inflict pain on infants in the next life?

> God [is free] can do that and if he does that he is just. In the same way whenever he inflicts a never ending punishment for a finite wrong and some living things to others and blesses and not others and creates some with the knowledge that they will not believe, that is all just on his part. It would not be morally bad (*aqbah*) on God's part to create them in perpetual, painful punishment. It would not be shameful on God's part to inflict pain on the believers and to allow the unbelievers to enter the gardens. We only say that he will not do this because he has told us that he will punish the unbelievers and lying in his knowledge [information] is not permitted.

[82] The word *kalam* has several interpretations of Muslim intellectual thought including both theology and scholasticism.

[83] Tallal M. Zeni trans. by *Ibn Qayyim al-Jawziyya on Divine Wisdom and the Problem of Evil*, Cambridge: The Islamic Texts Society, 2017, xiv.

[84] For an examination of Al-Ash'ari's theory of *kasb*, see Binyamin Abrahamov, 'A Re-examination of Al-Ash'ari's Theory of 'Kasb' According to "Kitab al-Luma'"' in *Journal of the Royal Asiatic Society of Great Britain and Ireland*, 2, 1989, 210–221. In his analysis, Abrahamov also draws on Frank's much earlier article on created causality in Al-Ash'ari in R. M. Frank, 'The Structure of Created Causality According to Al-Ash'ari: An Analysis of the *Kitab al-Luma'*, pars 82–164', *Studia Islamica* 25, 1966, 13–75.

The proof that whatever he does it is for him to do is that he is the king, not subject to anyone. There is no one above him who can permit, or command or be an obstacle or prohibit or decree for him or fix boundaries for him. If this is so nothing can ever be morally bad from him. If a thing is so, it is only morally bad from our part because we transgress the limits and decrees set and bring about what we have no right to bring about. Since the Creator (al-bari') is subject to no-one and not under the command of anyone, nothing can be morally bad on his part.[85]

Al-Ash`ari's God is the creator of everything, including evil, but cannot be defined by that which is bad or unjust in the world. The focus of his theology was not so concerned with the consequences of human moral choices associated with any kind of freedom to act, as with attributing complete freedom and omnipotence to God. From the arguments in the Luma`, the presence of evil and suffering in the world does not reflect negatively on a good God. Lying is bad only because God has declared it so and for Al-Ash`ari God can create lying for others but not lie himself, as this would mean a divine imperfection. Ayman Shihadeh writes that Al-Ash`ari advances a theological voluntarism, the view that 'God's will and acts are free and never subject to ethical considerations'. But he adds that 'classical Ash`arism ... did not subscribe to a simple divine command theory of ethics, but in fact grounded this theory in a fairly developed anti-realism'.[86] Frithjof Schuon attributes a 'mental weakness' to the intellectual argument of Al-Ash`ari in that Al-Ash`ari tries to humanise the Absolute. Schuon states that 'What, in God is an overflowing of infinity, becomes for the Ash`arites and their like an unfathomable tyranny, at least in certain sectors of their thought'.[87] But Jon Hoover contends

> The voluntarism of Ash`ari Kalam theology rejects the notion of theodicy as meaningless. God's unfettered will, sufficiency apart from the world and exclusive power preclude asking why God does this or that. God is not limited by any reason, and His acts require no deliberation, rational motive or external cause. Thus, God's creation of injustice, unbelief and other evils is not susceptible to any explanation except that God wills it.[88]

[85] For a fuller analysis on this, see Mona Siddiqui, The Good Muslim, Cambridge: Cambridge University Press, 2012, 106–36. Al-Ash`ari, Kitab al-Luma" fi al-radd `ala ahl al-zaygh wa'l-bida`: The Theology of Al-Ash`ari, ed. and trans. into English by R. J. McCarthy, Beirut, 1953.

[86] Ayman Shihadeh, 'Theories of Ethical Value in Kalam: A New Interpretation' in Sabine Schmidtke (ed.), The Oxford Handbook of Islamic Theology, Oxford: Oxford University Press, 2016, 402 and 384.

[87] Frithjof Schuon, Islam and the Perennial Philosophy, United Kingdom: World of Islam Publishing Company, 1976, 129.

[88] Jon Hoover, Ibn Taymiyya's Theodicy of Perpetual Optimism, Leiden: Brill, 2007, 1–2.

While much of Islamic thought tried to absolve God of actively creating human suffering and evil, it recognised that goodness and wrong reflect on God's essence. Despite debates around theodicy, Muslim theologians touched on human vulnerability and suffering largely through the philosophical analysis of divine omniscience and the human need to understand how God is involved or distant from all kinds of human suffering. While the concept of 'best of all possible worlds' is a phrase attributed to Leibniz in the West, the Sunni theologian and jurist, Abu Hamid al-Ghazali had made a similar statement in the late tenth century. For Ghazali, the issue is one of trust and reliance (*tawakkul*) in God. There is neither 'rift nor discrepancy' in what God creates:

> Everything which God apportions to man, such as sustenance, life –span, pleasure and pain, capacity and incapacity, belief and disbelief, obedience and sin, is all of it sheer justice, with no injustice in it; and pure right with no wrong in it.

Ghazali then continues:

> There is not in possibility anything whatever more excellent, more perfect, and more complete than it. For if there were and He had withheld it, having power to create it but not deigning to do so, this would be miserliness contrary to the divine generosity and contrary to the divine justice. But if he were not able, it would be incapability contrary to divinity.[89]

Eric Ormsby investigates this comment in great detail saying that this statement 'engendered a controversy that lasted from [Ghazali's] own lifetime until well into the 19th century'.[90] For Ghazali, the world as it is, is superior to any hypothetical alternative.

Sunni Islam however lacks a motif of human suffering, when speaking of this life or the afterlife. Despite philosophical disputes around theodicy, human suffering was debated but largely dissolved within debates about divine goodness. Shi'ism however had a markedly different approach to the place of suffering in human life. In writing about redemptive suffering, Mahmoud Ayoub states, 'Human life has been marked by a great mystery, the mystery of suffering and death'. For Mahmoud, human consciousness has always been a consciousness of suffering. These attempts could be characterised as the search for identity and permanence, and for meaning and value in an otherwise ephemeral and desperate existence. For Mahmoud,

---

[89] Eric Ormsby, *Theodicy in Islamic Thought: The Dispute over al-Ghazali's 'Best of All Possible Worlds'*, Princeton: Princeton University Press, 1984, 39.
[90] Ormsby, *Theodicy*, 39.

meaning and fulfilment in human life can be attained 'not in spite of, but through, suffering and even death'. He writes that the 'quest for the redemption of man, and, indeed, of the totality of phenomenal existence, is the essence of faith':

> Faith, to be sure, is a divine gift of grace to man; yet man's acceptance of it, working out in his life its implications and demands, is what we mean by the quest of faith. This search for meaning in the most meaningless aspects of life has dominated myth and ritual, spiritual quests and cultural achievements since the dawn of recorded history. Considered from the point of view of the history of religion, this process becomes the history of revelation, or of divine providence at work in human history, shaping and guiding its course toward final fulfillment in God.[91]

Ayoub's study is mainly focused on the suffering and martyrdom of Imam Husayn, grandson of the Prophet and spiritual head of the Shi`i community. Husayn is seen as the seal of the martyrs after his assassination at the battle of Karbala in 680. For Ayoub 'All suffering and martyrdom after him are only modes of participation in his martyrdom'.[92] There is a strong and passionate narrative and theology of suffering in Shi'ism centring on the Prophet's family and on the martyrdom of the imams. Shi`ite theology and hagiography allow for a number of perspectives on human suffering that lend it a sacred purpose of spiritual and moral examples of selflessness. Exoteric interpretation of various Qur'anic stories mean that different types of suffering are often intertwined.

While images and references to paradise (*janna*) encapsulate salvation, the central story of Sunni Islam is not suffering or redemption but rather *falah* or success. *Falah* refers to human prosperity and success after human striving and struggle. Righteousness and hopeful perseverance rather than suffering give form and weight to our earthly existence. The Qur'an sees human patience as a virtue bringing one closer to God, a virtue essential to human piety:

> Piety is not to turn your faces to the east or the west; rather, piety is [personified by] those who have faith in Allah and the Last Day, the angels, the Book, and the prophets, and who give their wealth, for the love of Him, to relatives, orphans, the needy, the traveller and the beggar, and for [the freeing of] the slaves, and maintain the prayer and give the zakat, and those who fulfil their covenants, when they pledge themselves, and those who are patient in stress and distress, and in the heat of battle. They are the ones who are true [to their covenant], and it is they who are the Godwary. (Q2:177)

---

[91] Ayoub, *Redemptive*, 23   [92] Ayoub, *Redemptive*, 27.

Seek God's help with patience and prayer. It is indeed hard except for
those who are humble. (Q2:45)

O you who believe! Seek help with patience and prayer, for God is with
those who are patient. (Q2:153)

Be sure we shall test you with something of fear and hunger, some loss in
goods, lives, and the fruits of your toil. But give glad tidings to the patient.
Those who, disaster strikes them, say 'To God do we belong, and to him do
we return'. They are those on whom descend blessings from their Lord, and
mercy. They are the ones who receive guidance. (Q2:155–157)

As for those who fear God and are patient, God does not allow to waste
the wage of a people who do good. (Q12:90)

The dominant ethos at the core of the Qur'an is *sabr*, patience or endurance
(*sabr*) in the face of adversity. Patience as endurance seems to be a defining
characteristic of the believer. *Sabr* is not a virtue like other virtues, it lies at
the core of belief in God; *sabr* is in reality another word for faith/*iman* itself.
In ibn Qayyim we find that patience is the outward manifestation of an inner
struggle;

It is said that 'patience is that intellect and religion stand firm when faced
with lusts and desires'. The meaning of this is that human nature runs after
that which it loves, but intellect and religion prevent it. As such the two are
at continuous war with each other, and this war has its ups and downs. The
battle field is the heart, patience, courage and firmness.[93]

The Qur'an speaks consistently of *sabr* as a virtue which will be the true test
of humankind, adding frequently that God is with those who are patient.
Notwithstanding all of life's blessings, life is struggle and God is with us as we
struggle. We cannot exercise patience and fortitude without struggle. But
patience is not only about being able to 'bear' trial and tribulations. While
Islamic thought sees affliction as that which reminds us of God, reminds us
to turn to God, exercising patience is also exercising wisdom and gratitude.
While many exhort that to be patient is to abandon any form of complaint,
there is a distinction between complaining about affliction in itself and
turning to God to complain about the affliction; the latter is itself is a form
of piety.

A question that was sometimes very poetically discussed by the Sufis was
which was superior of the two stations on the mystic path – patience or
gratitude – with many praying for struggle as a way of being certain that God
had not forgotten them. To be afflicted with adversity meant that God had

---

[93] Ibn Qayyim, *On Divine*, 93.

not forgotten you. If remembering God is an act of piety, being remembered by God is the ultimate destination.

Patience (*sabr*) and trust (*tawakkul*) are bound to a certain kind of steadfastness and righteousness (*taqwa*). The words 'God loves the patient' underpin the entire ethos of the Qur'an, namely, that the believer will face affliction, for that is what it means to have faith and to recognise the deep and desperate human trust in God. The issue is not why struggle and suffering is not a question raised in despair or lament but rather that human struggle is recognised as bringing benefit to humankind. So much of Islamic thought centred on struggle as the human experience through which one turns to God: all faith is a journey of a return to God. There is no faith and thus no success without patience and perseverance because patience and righteousness are the route to success/*falah*.

> You who have faith! Be patient, be supreme in patience, be firm on the battlefield, and have *taqwa* of God so that hopefully you will be successful. (Q3:200)
> Truly man is in loss- except for those who have faith and do right actions and urge each other to the truth and urge each other to patience. (Q103:2–3)
> When harm touches a man, he calls on us, lying on his side or sitting down or standing up. Then when we remove the harm from him he carries on as if he had never called on us when the harm first touched him. (Q10:12)

Despite understanding God as the transcendent other, Islamic thought has from the earliest times wrestled with how divine presence manifests itself in this world and how humans can understand themselves as God's agents of the 'divine breath'. Though Adam's descent on earth is regarded as a new paradigm for human existence, something between the human and the divine has been ruptured in this exile and thus our longing for return, the restlessness and the yearning we endure remains; this separation is conceived of as a supernatural defect which can be remedied only by divine grace. Sunni Islam has for the most part focused on the divine exhortation to turn to God and human need for divine mercy. To desire God in this existence is to be rewarded by God, to share intimacy with God. The distinguishing signs of such people is that when darkness spreads and everyone is alone with their loved ones, these people direct their step towards God and whisper confidences to him:

> So amid calling out and weeping and moaning and lament, between standing and sitting, between bowing down and prostration, with My own eye, I see what they endure for My sake, with my ear I hear what complaint they make about my love. And I shall give them three things:

First, I will cast my light into their hearts so that they bear witness to me, as I to them. Second, if the heavens and the earth and all that is within them were placed in the balance with them, I would account it of little worth compared to them. Third, I shall draw my face close unto them; and to whom I draw near, who will be privy to what I shall give him?[94]

Prayer is about the desire for God. It is desire (*irada*) that calls out to God. The Sufi scholar Al-Qushayri (986–1072) wrote that 'Desire is the beginning of the path of the wayfarers and the name of the first station of those who aspire to God Most High. This feature is called "desire" because desire precedes every matter'. True desire is the absence of all desires other than God. For Qushayri, one who desires God (*murid*) is also the one desired by God (*murad*). Nothing happens unless God desires it, and thus, one who desires is 'not other than he who is desired'. This again shows a God in waiting for the *murid*, that is, the disciple on the path to God, while the *murad* is the one who is assisted and protected by God. According to al-Junayd, the difference between them is that 'the *murid* walks, while the *murad* flies'.[95]

Obedience and righteousness are in themselves a struggle including the experience of the prophets. The Qur'anic verses on struggle and affliction are at times addressed to individual believers, to a particular context and sometimes to the prophets themselves. Their struggle humanises them but it also illustrates how God's chosen always face conflict:

Do you suppose that you would enter paradise without facing the same as those who came before you? Poverty and illness afflicted them and they were shaken to the point that the Prophet and the believers with him said, 'When is God's help coming? Be assured that God's help is very near. (Q2:214)

Many of the Qur'anic and biblical prophetic lives have become central to literary explorations of belief struggle and hope. The prophet par excellence who represents all these moral complexities is Job. The book of Job begins with an introduction to Job's character – he is described as a blessed man who lived righteously and it was his praise of God which prompts Satan to challenge Job's integrity, suggesting that Job served God simply because God protected him. God removed Job's protection, allowing Satan to take his

---

[94] Al-Ghazali, *Love, Longing, Intimacy and Contentment, Kitab al-mahabba wa'l-shawq wa'l-uns wa'l-rida*. Book xxxvi of *The Revival of the Religious Sciences, Iḥya' `Ulum al-din*, trans. Eric Ormsby, Cambridge: The Islamic Texts Society, 2011, 92–3.

[95] *Al-Qushayri's Epistle on Sufism*, trans. Alexander D. Knysh, Reading: Garnet Publishing, 2007, 216–17.

wealth, his children and his physical health (but not his life) in order to test Job's character. Job's sufferings and the direction of the questioning it inspires would seem to lead to a position of pessimism, but the dramatic conclusion of his 'dialogue' with God allows for a more optimistic outlook. Inflicted with painful boils from head to foot, he comes to regret the day he was born. In the midst of his afflictions, he is visited by his friends who argue that suffering is always a punishment for wrongdoing and that good fortune is always a reward for righteousness. Job responds by saying that God is omnipotent and that man is sinful, while denying that he has done anything to deserve punishment. His innocent suffering thus challenges the notion that there exists a direct relationship between human actions and human fortunes. In other words, righteousness is not necessarily rewarded; nor is sinfulness necessarily punished. Job endures his suffering and does not accuse God of injustice, rather feels vindicated that God has spoken to him. God does not answer questions on demand.

There have been several interpretations of the book of Job in modern biblical scholarship. God makes no attempt to justify why the innocent suffer as Job is a victim of undeserved suffering; others have argued that Job realises that God is neither just or unjust, that God is God and Job comes closer to God through his struggle and integrity in faith. In her literary analysis of the Russian novelist Fyodor Dostoevskii (1821–81), Vanessa Rampton writes that Dostoevskii used the book of Job as a convincing model of an attempt to demonstrate the goodness of God in the face of human struggle and suffering. The book of Job is a text 'which de-emphasizes the apparent contradictions between faith and doubt by reminding us of the fact that the world exists in all its incomprehensible forms, and that we can do no more than try to grapple with the implications of this'. This biblical book arrives at a paradoxical conclusion whereby Job is comforted by the knowledge that suffering is inexplicable and that all reasoned attempts to comprehend suffering only take us so far. This then makes the resolution of these matters less urgent. Rampton elaborates:

> Dostoevskii's great insight was to turn this potential weakness into an advantage, both as a novelist and as a religious thinker. According to this reading, Job does not provide Dostoevskii with a cognitive answer to the question of why the innocent suffer or explain the existence of evil in the world, but rather acts as a confirmation that faith is a process in which doubts play a crucial and ongoing role.[96]

---

[96] Vanessa Rampton, 'Dostoevskii and the Book of Job: The Struggle to Find Faith', *Studies in Religion*, 39:2, 2010, 203–17, 204.

In Dostoevskii's view, western civilisation had largely fallen way from God and many readers see in his writing attempts to vindicate the Christian worldview. For some, the book of Job is the ultimate vindication of faith over reason exemplifying the ultimate struggle between reason and revelation. Creation is a mystery, human existence is defined by both beauty and tragedy. There can never be a concrete understanding of either human nature or of where human reason ends and faith begins. Exploring the multiple ways of approaching the issue of theodicy in this story, some critics have interpreted God's response to Job as a study, not of how to understand undeserved suffering, but rather how to react to it. Dostoevskii believed that anguish impels individuals to find spiritual satisfaction and that certain types of suffering can be morally valuable. But Rampton writes that 'By drawing on the book of Job, Dostoevskii is able to develop his insight that suffering impels one to make peace with God. At the same time, his sense of the complexity of the task made him aware that the redemptive value of suffering could not be the whole solution to his character's problems'.[97]

The Qur'anic story of Job (Ayyub) is similar in content and style. Job is one of many prophets who faces trials, albeit he is subjected to extreme hardship. All prophetic stories in the Qur'an contain an element of prophetic struggle, the elect caught between divine favour and earthly trials. Within the prophetic paradigm, we see that blessings such as children and wealth are means by which humankind is tried. Whatever the struggle, the implication is that humankind must continue to cultivate patience. Ayyub's patience in the face of adversity becomes exemplary: 'Truly, we found him patient. How excellent a slave! Verily, he was always returning in repentance' (Q38:44). The focus of the Qur'anic story is belief based on trust, patience and gratitude in all circumstances. It is not gratitude for suffering but gratitude for God's purpose. It is the combination of these three virtues which means that, unlike Job, the story of Ayyub is not plagued by the question of theodicy. The distinction between human wrongdoing and human affliction is blurred – both are in themselves reflections of the human condition. Human life is struggle and success in this life requires living with our individual struggle and suffering holding onto faith. Our existence is not whole without struggle but nor is our existence complete without our need for hope.

---

[97] Rampton, 'Dostoevskii', 214.

2

The Search for Salvation in Rainer Maria Rilke and Abu Hamid al-Ghazali

> What is wanted, in art, is to harness the power of the unfinished. All earthly experience is partial. Not simply because it is subjective, but because that which we do not know, of the universe, of mortality, is so much more vast than that which we do know. What is unfinished, participates in these mysteries. (Louise Glück)[1]

The contemporary decline in letter writing constitutes a huge cultural shift in the way society had communicated for centuries. Letters are among the earliest examples of writing in the history of humankind. Although the writing of letters was common during the classical period, it was not till the Middle Ages that the written letter became a central concern of rhetorical theory. Different things were achieved through the medium of letters. Besides being the main medium as administrative and clerical documents, letters are a very rich source ranging from church and state correspondence to social hierarchies and fiction. Furthermore, while medieval society, in general, was largely illiterate and rural, historians depend on the letters of ordinary people to create a picture of the past. Letter writing reached a peak between the fifteenth and twentieth centuries because of the availability of paper and also ease of travel and distribution by courier and the development of post. The letters people left behind are invaluable evidence of how past societies lived and worked and reflect their most sublime and their most mundane concerns. Yet it's important to bear in mind that written words, unlike spoken words, have time on their side, meaning they can be subject to human mediation:

> Of course letter writers don't always tell the truth in their letters and there can be an editing process in the choice of which letters they destroy and

---

[1] Louise Glück, 'Disruption, Hesitation, Silence', *Proofs & Theories: Essays on Poetry*, New York: Ecco, 1994, 74–5.

which they preserve. But either way, a letter reflects a single moment in time and experience – what Goethe called the 'immediate breath of life'. Many bonfires of letters were lit to hide secret deals and scandals. But to destroy a letter, Goethe thought, out of discretion, was destroying life itself.[2]

The literary genre of letter writing carries its own aesthetic value. During the Middle Ages, writing was a way of ordering one's thoughts and preserving the past. Letters formed an intrinsic aspect of how knowledge and thought were communicated. In pre-modern Islamic societies, as well as in most societies in Antiquity, the letter was first and foremost an essential mode of communication, one that often transmitted meaning across countries and even continents.[3] Consciously or unconsciously, the letters of most authors are intended for a wider circle than for the individual recipients alone. Richard and Mary Rouse open their introduction to their collection of articles, *Bound Fast with Letters*, with a quote from Isodore of Seville: 'use of letters was devised to remember things: things are bound fast with letters lest they escape into oblivion'.[4] Letters retained their literary popularity and distinction as they are also witnesses to change, in human thinking, morality, society and politics. They are about communicating ideas as well as personal stories of love, loss and anguish. In addition to being a comment on social and political history, some letters are epic tales of correspondence between two friends or two people who are romantically inclined. Others – like the example of *De Profundis* by Oscar Wilde written from prison – are a dramatic monologue of self-reflection. They resonate profoundly with their audience, being rich in both self – revelation and self-indulgence. Their form is the letter-monologue in which the writer speaks of all that matters to him; his thoughts on his life, his downfall, his decadence his wrongful passions, art and spirituality and religion. Letter writing can be seen as the writer's gift to posterity.

Letter writing was a form of slow communication in a period of limited literacy. Today, greater literacy and diverse forms of technology allow us to connect with an unprecedented immediacy. The speed and convenience of modern technology has replaced many traditional forms of correspondence where letter writing may not be a dying art but has become precious and rarefied. In the efforts to revive this art form is a lament that we have lost the

[2] Simon Sebag Montefiore, *Written in History: Letters that Changed the World*, London: Weidenfeld and Nicolson, xvii.

[3] Adrian Gully, *The Culture of Letter Writing in Pre-Modern Islamic Society*, Edinburgh: Edinburgh University Press, 2008, 2.

[4] Richard H. Rouse and Mary A. Rouse, *Bound Fast with Letters*, Notre Dame, IN: University of Notre Dame Press, 2013, 1.

shared intimacy experienced in the physical process of letter writing, that this gradual decline has robbed us of a certain romance in the way we communicate.

Letters have always had various forms, styles and purposes. In the following chapter, we can see a glimpse of the education-philosophical dimension of a letter form as we compare a scholar and a poet whose works continue to inspire through their religious and philosophical wisdom. Their letters are a collection of religious, wisdom narratives and personal reflections on life, faith and God. Despite their very different historical, civilizational and cultural backgrounds, and the distance of time and space, their works explore one of the fundamental human struggles, namely how to reconcile ourselves to impermanence and yet look for meaning and salvation in life. The two writers have been chosen not as representatives of East and West or Islam and Christianity, but for the literary and philosophical merit of their respective works. Their works are expansive, covering a range of philosophical, autobiographical and literary themes. They are separated by several centuries and came from very different religious, cultural and political backgrounds. While Abu Hamid Muhammad al-Ghazali was a famous Sunni philosopher-theologian and mystic, Rainer Maria Rilke is not even considered a believing Christian by many and in fact he writes against Christianity at times. Yet he is considered a profoundly religious man and, for that reason, his reflections on life and death, good and evil, human desire and searching, as well as his copious references to God and religion, supremely qualify him for this comparison. Rilke's reflections on God and religiosity scattered throughout his works are a compelling testament to his own faith and speak of a man consumed with how to understand the transcendent. Frederick Vanson compares him to Dylan Thomas; not a self-professed Christian but it was undeniable that he was a religious poet dealing with the eternal themes of birth, death and destiny. He writes that 'if ever a man was obsessed by God with God as the immanent power informing all natural and human life, that man was Rilke'.[5] Rilke's embrace of death is an embrace of God: a God who did not promise immortality in the next life but who is the metaphor for the most intensely conscious part of mankind. As Joanna Macy and Anita Barrows state, 'Rilke's God is an intimate partner, beyond all dualism of matter and spirit'.[6] Both writers compose their work in different didactic tones but they share that elusive quality of the author's personal quest for meaning, truth and salvation.

---

[5] Frederic Vanson, 'Rilke's "Stories of God"', *Renascence*, 14:2, 1962, 90.

[6] Joanna Macy and Anita Barrows (eds.), *A Year with Rilke*, London: Harper Collins, 1996, xiii.

The Islamic intellectual tradition can boast many names but maybe none
stands out as much as the supremely eminent Abu Hamid Muhammad al-
Ghazali (1058–1111), deemed by some to be the greatest ethical thinker in
Islamic intellectual history. In fact his contemporaries were in such
admiration of his work that they gave him the honorific, Proof Islam
(Hujjat al-Islam). Ghazali was a polymath, a jurist of the Shafi`i school of
law, but also a philosopher, a theologian and a Sufi of Sunni Islam. He is
described as figurehead of a revived Sunnism of the Seljuk period which
managed to reverse the political dominance of various forms of Shi'ism
during the tenth century. Born around 1058 in Tabaran in the district of Tus
in Iran, he studied with the influential Ash'arite theologian al-
Juwayni (1028–85) at the Nizamiyya Madrasa in nearby Nishapur.
Ash`arism had become the dominant school of theological scholasticism
by the eleventh century. In 1091, at the invitation of Nizam al-Mulk
(d.1092), he was appointed to the prestigious Nizamiyya Madrasa in
Baghdad where he became closely connected to the royal court.[7] He
wrote many of his most significant works here and soon came to be
regarded the most influential and acclaimed thinker of his time.
Although Ghazali is considered to be one of the greatest Muslim scholars
by Muslims, he has also earned huge accolades from certain Christian
theologians and writers impressed with his deep learning and piety. As
far back as 1910, Claud Field's quote attributed to the renowned Protestant
theologian, August Tholuck, is worth citing in full: Field wrote:

> Theologians are the best judges of theologians, and in conclusion we may
> quote Dr. August Tholuck's opinion of Ghazzali: 'This man, if ever any
> have deserved the name, was truly a "divine", and he may be justly placed
> on a level with Origen, so remarkable was he for learning and ingenuity,
> and gifted with such a rare faculty for the skilful and worthy exposition of
> doctrine. All that is good, noble, and sublime that his great soul had
> compassed he bestowed upon Muhammadanism, and he adorned the
> doctrines of the Koran with so much piety and learning that, in the form
> given them by him, they seem, in my opinion, worthy the assent of
> Christians. Whatsoever was most excellent in the philosophy of Aristotle
> or in the Sufi mysticism, he discreetly adapted to the Muhammadan
> theology; from every school he sought the means of shedding light and
> honour upon religion; while his sincere piety and lofty conscientiousness

---

[7] Abu `Ali Hasan al-Tusi known as Nizam al-Mulk (d.1092) was the vizier to three of the greatest
Seljuk sultans and is generally credited for reviving Sunni learning and intellectual life through
founding the system of colleges known after him as *al-madaris al-nizamiyya*. Ghazali's life is
linked with what was considered the 'mother' college in Baghdad itself.

imparted to all his writings a sacred majesty. He was the first of Muhammadan divines'.[8]

While his intellectual breadth and brilliance are widely recognised, there are various tensions in much of the work attributed to him. Thus, scholars are often divided over aligning the changing circumstances of his personal life with his intellectual position on many of his theological and philosophical works. The sheer range of his work and his personal reflections on philosophy, *kalam* and Sufism reveal both a life and a thinker in gradual reflection and transition, rather than sudden epistemological ruptures. A life of introspection and refinement of character through prayer and piety, he came to represent an equilibrium between letter and spirit in religious faith. This may be a more accurate way of assessing his life, despite Ghazali vocalising his crises and his search for transcendence in his often-dramatic manner.

In one of his letters, Ghazali mentions that he had written 70 books but today there are some 400 works attributed to him. Authenticity is always an issue in the reading of pre-modern writings and sometimes the same work is found in different manuscripts with different titles. As far back as the 1950s, in his discussion of the genuine works of Ghazali, W. Montgomery Watt wrote, partly on the findings of earlier scholars, 'Indeed nothing short of a radical examination of the whole Ghazalian corpus is a prerequisite of any advance in our understanding of that great Muslim thinker. Of each work as a whole we must ask: Are we certain that this is a genuine work of Ghazali?'[9] Nevertheless, the works which are attributed to him are some of the most engaging works of devotion and reflection in Islamic intellectual history.

His works both present the essentials of Islamic belief and reveal his slightly ambivalent preoccupation with philosophy. Ghazali is celebrated for far more than his philosophical critiques, for it seems that ultimately he wanted to preach and live the life of a practical and moral mystic. His aim was to lead the faithful away from merely notional acquiescence of Islamic creeds to a deeper knowledge and experience of God. In his quasi-autobiographical work, written shortly before his death, *Deliverance/The Deliverer from Error, (Al-Munqidh min al-Dalal)*, he confesses that he had from an early age, searched for the true reality of things. While the tone is often sensational and open to interpretation, Ghazali writes:

> The thirst for grasping the real meaning of things was indeed my habit and wont from my early years and in the prime of my life. It was instinctive,

---

[8] Claud Field, 6, http://data.nur.nu/Kutub/English/Ghazali_Alchemy-of-Happiness.pdf

[9] W. Montgomery Watt, 'The Authenticity of the Works Attributed to al-Ghazali', *The Journal of the Royal Asiatic Society of Great Britain and Ireland*, 1:2, April, 1952, 24–45, 25.

natural disposition placed in my makeup by God Most High, not something due to my own choosing and contriving. As a result, the fetters of
servile conformism fell away from me, and inherited beliefs lost their hold
on me, when I was still quite young:

So I began by saying to myself: 'What I seek is knowledge of the true
meaning of things (*haqa'iq al-umur*). Of necessity therefore, I must inquire
into just what the true meaning of knowledge is'. Then it became clear to
me that sure and certain knowledge is that in which the thing known is
made so manifest that no doubt clings to it, nor is it accompanied by the
possibilities of error or deception, nor can the mind even suppose such
a possibility.[10]

The quest for certainty dominated Ghazali's struggle with his faith even
during his early years. It led him to what has been called an epistemological
Odyssey in search of the essence of knowledge. The desire for the essence of
knowledge drove him to physical and mental paralysis. According to
Ghazali, this malady lasted almost two months, during which time he was
a 'skeptic in fact, but not in utterance and doctrine'. He writes that it was
God who 'cured me of that sickness'. Ghazali was cured not by putting
together proofs or arguments, but by a beatific answer, a divine light,
'which God Most High cast into my chest'.[11] It is this light which is the
key to knowledge.

Ghazali studied all different approaches in his struggle with reason's
reliability. Theological scholasticism or *kalam* was important for the defence
and elaboration of creedal belief but it was not an end in itself, and could not
be a substitute for the experiential. He writes that he found *kalam* 'a science
adequate for its own aim, but inadequate for mine. For its aim is simply to
conserve the creed (*aqida*) of the orthodox for the orthodox and to guard it
from the confusion introduced by the innovators'. The creed had to be
guarded as, over time, Satan, through the 'whispering of the innovators',
had brought about distortions to the Prophetic message.[12] Thus, while
theological scholasticism had status and showed 'an earnest desire for
attempting to defend orthodoxy,' in the end it could not reach primary
truths and thus for Ghazali, 'it was not sufficient in my case, nor was it

---

[10] Richard Joseph McCarthy (trans.), *Al-Ghazali, Deliverance from Error, Al-Munqidh min al-Dalal*, Originally Twayne Publishers and this edition Louisville, KY: Fons vitae, 1980, 54–5. *Al-Munqidh min al-Dalal* was written in the very late stages of al-Ghazali's life and as Montgomery Watt proposes, it's 'an account of the development of his religious opinions, but not exactly an autobiography, since it is arranged schematically not chronologically'. See https://reference works-brillonline-om.ezproxy.is.ed.ac.uk/entries/encyclopaedia-of-islam-2/*-COM_0233.

[11] McCarthy, *Al-Ghazali*, 57.

[12] McCarthy, *Al-Ghazali*, 59. I prefer 'whispering' rather than the translation 'sinister suggestions'.

a remedy for the malady of which I was complaining'.[13] This malady or
sickness could be his scepticism, his scholarly dissatisfaction or his inner
desire for certainty and truth. The book discusses the various epistemologies
he encounters and subsequently rejects. However, Ghazali does recognise
that his malady and search is specific to him and that his aim is 'not to
express disappointment of anyone who sought a cure in *kalam*. For healing
remedies differ as sickness differs, and many a remedy helps one sick man
and harms another'.[14]

It was during his time as head of the Nizamiyya College from around
1091 AD, that he wrote some of his most prominent philosophical critiques,
works including his denunciation of the Batiniyya, a pejorative label for the
Ismailis. Ghazali's term translates as the 'esotericists' and is used as a polemical
construct. His books are part of a longer history of critiques by Muslim
scholars against Ismaili Shi'ism. Since the beginning of the eleventh century,
Muslim theologians who were close to the 'Abbasid court had written refuta-
tions of Ismaili teachings. The famous Sunni Ash'arite theologian, Al-Baqillani
(d.1013) had composed such a work in the years preceding the official condemnation of the Fatimid caliphs as unbelievers by the 'Abbasid court in 1012.

Ghazali has acquired the status of being the greatest proponent of Sunni
orthodoxy through his celebrated philosophical critiques. The refutation of
certain philosophical concepts became a turning point in the religious
history of medieval Islam. This was not because it proved to be the end of
philosophy but rather that it brought to the fore a particular critique of
philosophy which was also present in the writings of Ghazali's teacher al-
Juwayni. Juwayni argued that it was the philosophers who had failed the
standard of rationality, not the theologians:

> One of their strange declarations is for them to reject the convincing proofs
> given by the theologians by insisting that they are sophism, that the best of
> them are merely dialectical, and that none of them consist of demonstrative
> syllogisms. Yet, . . . they accept, without argumentation, what conforms to
> nature, despite admitting that it is a matter as obscure as can be.[15]

On the one hand, Ghazali wrote extensively on Aristotelian logic and the
philosophies of Al-Farabi (d.950) and Ibn Sina or Avicenna (d.1037) informed
his own learning even though ultimately they were also the objects of his

---

[13] McCarthy, *Al-Ghazali*, 60. See also Michael E. Marmura, 'Ghazali and Ash'arism Revisited',
Arabic Sciences and Philosophy, 12, 2002, 91–110.

[14] McCarthy, *Al-Ghazali*, 60.

[15] Imam al-Haramyan al-Juwayni, *A Guide to Conclusive Proofs for the Principles of Belief*, trans. by
Paul E. Walker, Doha: Garnet Publishing, 2000, xxxii.

attack.[16] In order to reject certain philosophers and their thinking, he had to first of all explain their philosophies and, in doing so, he made philosophy very accessible to those who were not philosophers. In his most famous philosophical work, *The Incoherence of the Philosophers*, (*Tahafut al-Falasifa*), Ghazali lays out the reasons why he rejects many of the claims of the ancient philosophers who thought that their way of knowing by 'demonstrative proof' was superior to theological knowledge drawn from revelation and its rational interpretation. He accuses them of being foolish and ignorant (*al-aghbiya'*) but also rebukes the particular Muslim transmitters and exponents of ancient philosophy who have embarked on this road. Ghazali is scathing at times and accuses them of having abandoned Islam. He writes that they have done this 'thinking that the show of cleverness in abandoning the imitation of what is true (*taqlid al-haqq*) by embarking on the imitation of the false (*taqlid al-batil*) is a beautiful thing, unaware that moving from one kind of imitation to another is stupidity and confusion'.[17] Some of Ghazali's philosophical points are that God's creation of the world was decided in the eternal past, and therefore it does not mean any change in God; indeed, time itself is God's creation, an argument based on the Aristotelian concept of time as a function of change. Furthermore, if God has complete knowledge of a person from birth to death, there will be no change in God's eternal knowledge, even though the person's life changes from moment to moment. Human beings consist of soul and body, but their essence is the soul. The human soul is a spiritual substance totally different from the body. It is something divine which makes possible human knowledge of God. The body is simply a vehicle for the soul in the journey to the hereafter.

Despite outlining twenty critiques of the teachings of the *philosophers*, it is erroneous to claim that Ghazali's *Incoherence of the Philosophers* began the decline of philosophy as a distinct, intellectual discipline in the Islamic world. His legacy, wherein we find the interweaving of philosophy and theology, points to the fact that the discipline of, Muslim scholastic theology, as it had

---

[16] Tim Winter's introductory biographical notes claim, 'There is little firm evidence to suggest that Ghazali ever studied Aristotle directly, as he preferred to read the Arab philosophers, whose ideas presented the more immediate challenge to the Ash`ari position'. See an informative introduction to Ghazali in *Al-Ghazali on Disciplining the Soul, Kitab Riyadat al-nafs & On Breaking the Two Desires (Kitab kasr al-shahwatayn)*, Books XXII and XXIII of *The Revival of the Religious Sciences, Ihya' `ulum al-din*, trans. T. J. Winter, Cambridge: The Islamic Texts Society, 1995, xlix.

[17] Michael E. Marmura, *Al-Ghazali, The Incoherence of the Philosophers*, Provo UT: Brigham Young University Press, 2000, 2. This is an excellent source with a brief but very useful Introduction to Ghazali and the *Tahafut al-falasifa*. I have inserted minor changes in translation where appropriate.

been developed by the Mu'tazilites onwards, was the new homeland for philosophy. In his introduction to Ghazali's life, Frank Griffel writes that 'the situation was in this respect similar to that in the Latin Middle Ages, during which the study of philosophy could not be distinguished from Christian theology'. He writes against the claims by some of the most famous twentieth century historiographers of Islamic Studies in the West such as Ignaz Goldziher and W. Montgomery Watt, for whom Ghazali's critiques had caused the decline of Islamic philosophy. For Griffel, Ghazali 'is indeed the first Muslim theologian who actively promotes the naturalization of the philosophical tradition into Islamic theology. His works document an attempt to integrate Aristotelian logic into the tradition of *kalam*, of rationalist Islamic theology'.[18] Michael Marmura also states that after Ghazali, *kalam* or speculative theology 'became, as it had never been before, thoroughly involved with the theories of the *falasifa*'.[19] Ghazali succeeded in bringing philosophy and philosophical theology within the range of ordinary people. A century later, the famous Andalusian jurist, philosopher and polymath, Ibn Rushd or Averroes (1126–98) tried to defend Aristotelian philosophy and its decline in his own landmark work *The Incoherence of the Incoherence*, refuting many of Ghazali's claims. However, it is argued that, by then, much of Muslim philosophy had been absorbed into mysticism.

We learn from *al-Munqidh*, that, by 1095, Ghazali had grown frustrated with scholasticism and was once again restless by his inability to devote himself purely to God. This is often described as his spiritual crisis which the physicians 'lost hope of treating' as it was a matter of the heart. Ghazali realized that he had to shun fame, fortune and all worldly attachments as his teaching and speaking activities were instigated and motivated by 'the quest for fame and widespread prestige' and not directed to God. But even as he resolved to go, he was torn between his 'mundane desires' to stay, with Satan whispering that he would regret giving up his wealth and position. Conversely he was also pulled by the call of his faith, that 'If you do not prepare now for the afterlife, when will you do so? And if you do not sever these attachments now, then when will you sever them?'[20] Ghazali sought help in prayer and states that God made it easy for him to turn away from his present life.

Under the influence of Sufi writings and practice, Ghazali saw his life in a different way; the virtuous life demanded higher standards of ethical living

---

[18] Frank Griffel, *Al-Ghazali's Philosophical Theology*, New York: Oxford University Press, 2009, 5–7.
[19] Marmura, *Al-Ghazali*, xvi.   [20] McCarthy, *Al-Ghazali*, 79.

which for him weren't compatible with being in the service of sultans, viziers and caliphs. For Ghazali, virtuous acts predispose the soul to receive God's grace, a thinking located in the Qur'anic verse, 'The mercy of God is near to those who do good' (Q7:56). He was convinced that the primary evidence for God was not *per se* rational; there was no way to certain knowledge except through the practice of asceticism; through prayer and the development of the inner life, a virtuous life. He acknowledged that he already had faith in God, in 'the prophetic mediation of revelation' and in the Last Day. These three fundamentals of faith were rooted in his soul 'not because of any specific, precisely formulated proofs, but because of reason and circumstances and experiences'.[21] In devoting oneself to Sufism, one devoted oneself to rituals of the faith, to prayer and mystical practice. Again he writes in *al-Munqidh*, 'I knew with certainty that the Sufis were masters of states, not purveyors of words, and that I had learned all I could by way of theory. There remained, then, only what was attainable, not by hearing and study, but by fruitional experience and actually engaging in the way'.[22]

Ghazali wanted to restrain 'his soul from passion' and sever his attachment to the world 'by withdrawing from this bode of delusion' in order to devote himself completely to God. He had mastered theory and now wanted experience. The Sufi way of life was the best and the most pure as everything they do is 'learned from the light of the niche of prophecy. And beyond the light of prophecy there is no light on earth from which illumination can be obtained'. Ghazali makes the bold claim that it is only the purity of the Sufi way which makes it possible for them to really understand prophecy.[23]

In his search for solitude and seclusion, Ghazali gave up his teaching and left the city for almost ten years. He abandoned most of his material possessions but was thankful that his family would be well supported through various religious endowments for scholars which had been set up in Iraq. He travelled to Damascus as a wandering Muslim *religieux*. He gave himself up, as he says, to 'seclusion and retreat, spiritual exertion and struggle' in his attempts to purify his soul. This included a trip to Jerusalem and to Mecca and Medina to perform the Hajj pilgrimage. One of the many criticisms Ghazali levels at some of the philosophers during this time (he specifically names Ibn Sina), is that while they pay lip service to the *shari'a*, they do not give up 'winebibbing and various kinds of depravity and debauchery'.[24] He questions himself, that even though he had studied the ways of a variety of scholars and practitioners, nevertheless, 'what will solitude and seclusion avail you when the disease has become endemic, the

---

[21] McCarthy, *Al-Ghazali*, 78.   [22] McCarthy, *Al-Ghazali*, 78.   [23] McCarthy, *Al-Ghazali*, 81.
[24] McCarthy, *AL-Ghazali*, 90.

physicians are sick, and men are on the brink of perdition?' Thus, Ghazali sought a compromise to emerge from his religious retirement and on the basis of other people's testimonies saw himself as one who would revivify Islam at the beginning of the century.

Thus, despite his vow never again to serve the political authorities, he did towards the end of his life return to such teaching, being lured back to the Nizamiyya College in Nishapur in 1106 AD; he states that his seclusion lasted eleven years. A year later, he returned to Tus where he founded a small private school and a Sufi convent (khânqâh). For about four years, he surrounded himself here with Sufi disciples living an almost monastic communal life. He died in 1111 AD in Tus, the place of his birth.

While most of his writings are in Arabic, there are a few in Persian, of which his most famous work is *The Alchemy of Happiness*, (*Kimiya Sa`dat*), his own shorter version of his magnum opus, the celebrated *The Revival of the Religious Sciences*, (*Ihya' 'Ulum al-din*). The first four chapters of *The Alchemy of Happiness*, are a commentary on the famous *hadith* 'he who knows himself knows God'. For Ghazali, self-knowledge is the key:

> Knowledge of self is the key to the knowledge of God, according to the saying: 'He who knows himself knows God,' and, as it is written in the Koran, 'We will show them our signs in the world and in themselves, that the truth may be manifest to them'. Now nothing is nearer to you than yourself, and if you do not know yourself, how can you anything else?[25]

Knowing oneself is a path to happiness and it consists in realizing that we have a heart or spirit which is perfect but which has been covered with dust by the accumulation of passions derived from the body and its animal nature. The essence of oneself is likened to a perfect mirror which, if polished, would reveal one's true divine nature. The key to this polishing is the elimination of selfish desires. As he writes, 'the aim of moral discipline is to purify the heart from the rust of passion and resentment till, like a clear mirror, it reflects the light of God'.[26] It is the heart that is the seat of all knowledge:

> It is the heart which knows God, which draws near to God, which strives for God and which discloses what is in and with God. The other members are simply subordinates and servants and instruments which the heart employs and uses as a master uses a slave and a shepherd uses his flock and a craftsman uses a tool.[27]

---

[25] Claud Field, 8, http://data.nur.nu/Kutub/English/Ghazali_Alchemy-of-Happiness.pdf. I have modified this translation by replacing some of the more archaic pronouns for ease of reading.

[26] Field, *Alchemy*, 9.

[27] McCarthy, *Al-Ghazali*, contained in *The Book of the Marvels of the Heart*, 309.

Ghazali's greatest work however remains the monumental *The Revival of the Religious Sciences*. Spanning some forty books, it is divided into four 'quarters' covering various aspects of faith and life, and has inspired scholarship and popular piety throughout the generations for successfully combining orthodox Sunni theology with Sufi practice as a guide to the pious, reflective Muslim life. His purpose is to show how the doctrines and practices of Islam can serve as the basis of a profound devotional life. For Ghazali, observance of the *shari'a* was essential to the moral path and religious knowledge should not be seen as a means of worldly advancement, but rather essential for the attainment of salvation in the hereafter. The work is rich in scope and poetic in style yet it is also extremely accessible. Ghazali quotes the Qur'an, *hadiths*, traditions attributed to the early Muslims (*salaf*), and stories of the Qur'anic and biblical prophets including repeated references to Jesus. His overriding pastoral concern was to encourage the societies around him to participate in the religious life, to recognize the personal benefits and salvific force of faith in God.

The Revival brings together Ghazali's fundamental conviction that neither scholastics nor conventional knowledge could lead you to God consciousness, to the encounter and direct knowledge of God. Ultimately, gnosis of God is experienced, tasted (*dhawq*), directly. He is one of the few writers to give a systematic account of love between God and man. He describes the mystical states and stations towards God by concluding that the love of God is the highest in rank and the last stage in drawing towards God before repentance and patience. Love is not a means to God; love is the end station, for the acquisition of the love of God is the end and what is important is the human endeavour to nourish that love:

> The ultimate rule of perfection of the servant of God is that the love of God
> Most High triumph in his heart, so that his totality is engulfed (by that). If it
> is not this, well, it should be more dominant than the love for other things.
> Coming to understand the true nature of love is so difficult that some of the
> scholastic theologians have denied it and have said: 'It is not possible to love
> a person who is not of your kind. The meaning of love is obedience and
> nothing else'. Whoever thinks this way has no inkling of the basis of
> religion.[28]

This state of genuine happiness is not something most people attain and Ghazali claims that it is only the prophets who are truly happy because they

---

[28] *Al-Ghazali on Love, Longing and Contentment*, trans. by Muhammad Nur Abdus Salam, Chicago: Great Books of the Islamic World, 2002, 15.

have achieved this ultimate goal of human existence. For us ordinary mortals, we are so distracted by our desire for physical and earthly pleasures to remedy the pain of our souls that we've lost the ability to see the unseen. It is our enslavement to desire which causes our unhappiness. And yet Ghazali is keen to stress that it would be absurd to imagine that the purpose of spiritual struggle is to completely efface all traits such as anger, desire and worldliness from ourselves; what is important is that we work to restore balance and moderation in our lives.[29]

While one can read most of the Qur'an as an exhortation and a reminder to the believer of death and the Day of Judgement, one can also read Ghazali's *The Revival* in a similar manner. The final book, book forty, titled *Remembrance of Death and the Afterlife* (or what follows death) combines the themes of repentance, the virtues of remembering death and our fate in the next world. Ghazali is keen to explain that it is by purifying the heart from worldly preoccupations that we remember death and repent, and repentance is central to human salvation. For Ghazali, 'The penitent man recalls death frequently, so that fear and apprehension might thereby proceed from his heart, making his repentance complete'. Furthermore this world is a prison for the believer from which death is a release (*itlaq*) and this release is a gift (*tuhfa*).[30]

It is his intellectual and emotional preoccupation with salvation and the hereafter which dominates much of the moral discourse in Ghazali's *Letter to a Disciple*, literally 'O boy/disciple' (*Ayyuha'l-Walad*). Considered to be one of his last works, written during his time in the *khânqâh* in Tus, the short book is full of clear advice on what is important for the believer to know and practice for his salvation. Salvation is dependent on our remembering death, which underpins all of devotional life. Ghazali takes salvation to be the most serious concern for the believer, where salvation belongs to the victorious (*al-fa'izun*), the ones who will be in heaven. It is said that around a third of the Qur'an is eschatological whereby belief in the Day of Judgement and the afterlife became articles of faith. The Qur'an mentions, in different and overlapping ways, concepts of life immediately after death, the period between death and the day of resurrection, signs of the end times here on earth for all and images of the various abodes of the afterlife. The two ideas of damnation and forgiveness in God's final judgement dominate this eschatological narrative. At the heart of Qur'anic eschatology is the

---

[29] Winter, *Al-Ghazali, Disciplining*, 27–8.

[30] Al-Ghazali, *The Remembrance of Death and the Afterlife, Kitab dhikr al-mawt wa-ma ba'dahu*. Book XL of *The Revival of Religious Sciences*, trans. by Tim Winter, Cambridge: The Islamic Texts Society, 1989, 9.

conviction that human beings are called to account by God. This is a warning repeated in the Qur'an; that all prophets cautioned their communities about this day but they were mocked with people refusing to live in the light of this eschatological dawning. According to the Qur'an, death is the one event affecting all life – 'Every soul will taste death,' (Q29:57) – but it is also the event through which human life enters into another stage of its destiny. In Islamic thought, this transformation of earthy life is real and God ordained. We do not comprehend fully what a future life after death means but the depiction and events of an afterworld form one of the central motifs of the Qur'an. Righteousness and wrongdoing are to be understood in the light of the reality of the Day of Judgement for the whole of human history is a movement from creation to the eschaton. Although the Qur'an repeatedly mentions a life beyond this earthly existence and events of the eschaton, the relationship between humankind, resurrection and death is a rich didactic theme in Islamic thought, capturing the imagination of scholars throughout history.

In her intriguing and detailed analysis of the distinction between a Christian afterlife and a Muslim afterworld, Nerina Rustomji writes:

> Islamic eschatology provides an *afterworld*, while Christian eschatology focuses on an *afterlife*. While some Eastern Christian texts incorporate metaphors of a physical world, Christian texts in general present the quality of future lives through relationships with humans, angels and the divine. By contrast Muslims enjoy an afterlife within the parameters of a physically described afterworld. The connotation of 'The Garden' and 'The Fire' involves spaces and objects more than states of being.[31]

Like much of Islamic orthodoxy, Ghazali also imagines salvation as the physical abode of paradise, the destination for those who believed and were righteous.

The epistolary framework is a common feature in this kind of didactic writing and does not relate to a letter as we would think of a letter today. The preamble is an addition to the main body of the letter and may well have been added later. *Ayyuha'l-Walad* reads as a reply to the request of a former student or disciple who is clearly precious and beloved to Ghazali. The student wants advice from his master as guidance for the rest of his life. It is difficult to ascertain the age and situation of the student and despite the title of the work implying boy, youth or jeunesse, it is most probable that he

---

[31] Nerina Rustomji, *The Garden and the Fire*, New York: Columbia University Press, 2009, xvi–xvii.

was an older man.[32] Whatever his age, he knows that the answers to his questions are already contained in works such as the *Ihya' 'Ulum al-din*, but he wants the 'master to write down what I need in a few pages to be with me for the rest of my life'. But more specifically, the student really wants that learning 'which will be of use to me on the morrow, to keep me company in my grave'.[33] This clear request reflects so much of Ghazali's own concerns about the afterlife. Tobias Mayer describes the work as having the pathos of a 'spiritual last testament'.[34] It is contended by Mayer that the disciple didn't exist and that Ghazali was in fact writing to himself – a mirror image of a young man whom Mayer says was a preacher 'steeped in learning, prone to vanity and possibly on course for spiritual disaster'.[35]

The very first question however is why seek advice from Ghazali when the student should be seeking it from the words of Prophet. And if a person has not learnt from the Prophet, then what have they achieved in the years gone by? But this short question is immediately followed by the main theme running throughout the book which is that the true purpose of life is worship of God. And yet alongside this truth is the human truth, the human struggle which is how one stays true and faithful to this worship. Ghazali is too aware from his own experience that humankind is easily tempted, too quick to give into desires and longings which take one away from the worship of God. He writes, 'O disciple, advice is easy, what is difficult is accepting it, for it is bitter in taste to those who pursue vain pleasures, for forbidden things are dear to their hearts'.[36] But it is not only our desires but also the vanity of the learned like the philosophers who think that we can attain salvation through traditional learning and knowledge alone. As Ghazali was to discover in his own life, not only could knowledge alone not save you from yourself, knowledge had to be accompanied by action and so he writes, 'O disciple, knowledge without action is madness and action without knowledge is void. Know that the knowledge which does not remove you from sins today and does not convert you to obedience, will not remove you tomorrow from hellfire'.[37] Our whole life is a provision for the next life: 'Even if you had studied for

---

[32] Manuscript np. 4932 at the Bibliothèque Nationale, Paris (dated 1090/1679), gives the name of the man or disciple as 'Abd Allah ibn al-Hajj Khalil'. See Tobias Mayer, *Al-Ghazali, Letter to a Disciple, Ayyuha'l-Walad*, Cambridge: The Islamic Texts Society, 2005, xxiii. This is an excellent book in bilingual English/Arabic edition. It contains very useful but concise biographical material on Ghazali and notes on the text. An earlier translation by George Scherer was published in 1951 by the Catholic Press in Beirut. This was a reissue of Scherer's doctoral dissertation but has been dismissed as 'an unacceptable translation' in William Thompson's review in *Speculum*, 29:3, 1954, 561–4.

[33] Mayer, *Letter*, 2.   [34] Mayer, *Letter*, xxii.   [35] Mayer, *Letter*, xxiv.   [36] Mayer, *Letter*, 6.

[37] Mayer, *Letter*, 16–17.

a hundred years and collected a thousand books, you would not be eligible for the mercy of God except through action'.[38]

To support his stance, Ghazali refers to the eminent tenth-century Sufi, al-Junayd, whom Ghazali saw in his sleep after he had died and who confessed that 'Nothing was of benefit to me except some prayers I made in the middle of the night'.[39] These few prayers may have been voluntary or ritual but what is important is genuine intention and the practical faith in worshipping God in the middle of the night. God does not need our religious observance but God responds to that which the believer does from the heart. Citing a range of Qur'anic verses and *hadiths*, Ghazali's repeated advice for the disciple and all believers is to observe righteous practice and follow the Prophetic *shari'a*. However, worship of God must be accompanied by conformity to divine law so that if you pray 'in a garment unlawfully acquired, though there is the appearance of worship, you sin'.[40]

Moreover, the message for the learned and the scholars is that if all the learning they do is for worldly glory then it is of no use, it must be for the cultivation of a righteous character and spiritual ethics. The reality of impermanence is everywhere in this work: 'Live as long as you want, but you must die, love whatever you want but you will become separated from it'.[41] Death is the fate awaiting us all after which the truth of our faith would become clear. There was no room for complacency; indeed faith was strengthened not just by deeds but supererogatory acts of worship such as prayer during the night: 'a large quantity of sleep at night will leave its owner a poor man on resurrection day'. For most Muslim thinkers and devotees, prayer was what eased human struggle and suffering, and it was prayer which brought you nearer to God. Prayer is the remembrance of God at all times. A most poignant image of prayer is given by the famous poet Rumi for whom prayer was the centre of his life in his search for the divine: 'I have prayed so much that I myself turned into prayer, everyone who sees me begs a prayer from me'.[42] Prayer is the supplication of the created to the creator. An early Sufi, Abu Hazim al-Makki said, 'To be deprived of prayer (*du'a'*) would be for me a much greater loss than to be deprived of being heard and granted'. Annemarie Schimmel writes, 'This is the keynote for an understanding of the moderate Sufic point of view concerning prayer. Prayer is an intimate conversation between man and God which consoles the afflicted heart even if it is not immediately answered'.[43]

---

[38] Mayer, *Letter*, 8–9.   [39] Mayer, *Letter*, 6   [40] Mayer, *Letter*, 22.   [41] Mayer, *Letter*, 14.

[42] Annemarie Schimmel, *Rumi's World: The Life and Work of the Great Sufi Poet*, Boston and London: Shambala Publications, 2001, 5.

[43] Annemarie Schimmel, 'Some Aspects of Mystical Prayer in Islam', *Die Welt des Islams*, 2:5, 1952, 112–25, 112.

Much of Ghazali's attitude to the need for increased worship and prayer is predicated on his views of disciplining the soul. These ideas are found predominantly in his other works such as *Kitab Riyadat al-nafs, Ghazali on Disciplining the Soul* and *Kitab kasr al-shahwatayn, On Breaking the Two Desires*.[44] In *Breaking the Two Desires*, Ghazālī writes that 'the greatest of the mortal vices which man may harbour is the desire of the stomach'.[45] While fasting (*sawm*) and eating frugally were established as pious practices early on in Islamic history and regarded as beneficial to humankind, it would seem that very soon, hunger itself was seen as sort of virtue. This was not because hunger and fasting were ends in themselves, rather they were a means to a higher ideal, purification of the heart and God consciousness. In these books, Ghazali extols the virtue of frugality, recounting the stories of saints and prophets who ate little or fasted most of the time in order to purify their hearts and minds and thereby draw nearer to worship and prayer. In Ghazali's view, the merits of hunger or the renunciation of certain kind of food, were multiple, including the purity of one's heart and sharpening of the mind; over indulgence or even just a satiated stomach made one lazy causing the intellect to sleep. It was important to master one's soul by emptying it from desire through hunger as hunger breaks ones desire for sin. He writes 'all sins originate in one's desires and strengths, the stuff of which is food in every case: when one eats less, every one of one's desires and strengths will be enfeebled'.[46] Muslim and Christian ascetics both extolled the virtues of fasting and by 200 AD, Tertullian was one of the first to link flesh with lust and carnal desire. In the fourth century, St Jerome stated that a stomach filled with too much food and wine leads to lechery; indulging in food incited lust and, for this reason, 'fasting was seen as a way of both cleansing the body and controlling sexuality'.[47] There is a strong theme running in both Christian and Islamic thought that the believer should not be too greatly concerned about the food which fills the body but leaves the soul to die.

Ghazali's concern is that man must discipline his soul for the sake of the righteous life, for a gradual detachment from worldly temptations which

---

[44] *Al-Ghazali on Disciplining the Soul, Kitab Riyadat al-nafs* and *On Breaking the Two Desires* (*Kitab Kasr al-Shahwatayn*), Books XXII and XXIII of *The Revival of the Religious Sciences, Iḥyā' 'Ulum al-Din*, trans. T. J. Winter, Cambridge: The Islamic Texts Society, 1995.

[45] Al-Ghazali, *On Breaking the Two Desires*, 106.

[46] Al-Ghazali, *On Breaking the Two Desires*, 122.

[47] Melitta W. Adamson, *Food in Medieval Times*, Westport, CT: Greenwood Press, 2004, 185.

allows us to become nearer to God. This *jihad* against the soul is mentioned in multiple ways:

> The believer is beset with five afflictions: a believer who envies him, a hypocrite who hates him, an unbeliever who makes war on him, a devil who misguides him and a soul which struggles against him.
>
> Man has three enemies: the world, the devil and the soul. Be on your guard against the world through renunciation, against the devil by disobeying him, and against the soul by abandoning desire.

We are all *mujahids*, engaged in the greater *jihad*, warriors struggling against our soul for 'Ghazali; our very being is to be in a state of desperation. He quotes al-Mawsili who used to say to his soul, 'O soul! Neither do you revel in the world with the sons of kings, not so you struggle for the Afterlife with the ascetics. It is as though you had imprisoned me between Heaven and Hell. O soul! Are you not ashamed?'[48]

For Ghazali, humankind remains suspended between the two worlds, caught in his desires for this world and his hopes of the afterlife. But the purpose of self-discipline, this long inward strife, is to find oneself constantly in the presence of God.

While Ghazali recognizes the value of moderation in life, the important thing is to kill the ego, otherwise the heart will not be illumined by gnosis (*anwar al-ma'rifa*). His advice to his disciple is 'work for this world in proportion to your stay in it, work for your afterlife in proportion to your eternity in it, work for God in proportion to your need of him and work for the fire in proportion to what you can bear of it'.[49]

For Ghazali, knowledge and learning must improve the heart and purge the ego. The most eloquent expression of this is the question, 'if mere knowledge were enough for you and you did not need deeds besides it, God's call 'is there any suppliant? Is there anyone seeking forgiveness? Is there anyone repentant?'[50] This is based on the tradition which says that during the last third of the night, God descends into the lowest heaven and asks these questions of anyone who is awake and praying.

In Ghazali's view, human struggle is linked to the conviction that we need to work on our character so that our life is a life of God consciousness, a life devoted to God in prayer and observance. Alongside this imperative is the painful recognition that this devotion is difficult, requiring extreme self-discipline, and that so much of our lives is occupied with worldly desires and not in preparation for the Day of Judgment. We can only immerse ourselves

---

[48] Winter, *Al-Ghazali on Disciplining*, 56–8.   [49] Mayer, *Letter*, 14–15.
[50] Mayer, *Letter*, 18–19.

in this love for God through banishing our desires for the earthly life. In fact, the other moment of illumination is when we fully realise that all we carry in life as in death are our good deeds. This was a theme expressed poignantly in his reference to Hatim al-Assam who spoke of the many lessons he had learned from his own master, the first of which was:

> I observed mankind and saw that everyone had an object of love and infatuation which he loved and with which he was infatuated. Some of what was loved accompanied him up to the sickness of death and some to the graveside. Then all went back and left him solitary and alone and not one of them entered his grave with him. So I thought and said, the best of what one loves is what will enter one's grave and be a friend to one in it. And I found it to be nothing but good deeds. So I took them as the object of my love, to be a light for me in my grave, to be a friend to me in it and not leave me alone.[51]

These words of advice are as much a salutary reminder for Ghazali as they are for his student:

> I saw mankind being guided by their pleasures and hurrying to what their egos desired, so I meditated on his saying (the Exalted), 'But as for him who feared the station of his Lord, and kept the soul back from pleasure, the Garden is his abode'. I was certain that the Qur'an is genuine truth, so I hurried to what my ego was opposed to, and I set to work, combatting it and restraining it from its pleasures, until it was satisfied with obedience to God the Glorified and Exalted, and it gave up.[52]

Self-discipline relies on trust in God and this, in Ghazali's view, requires belief in predestination. The student must sincerely believe that 'what has been predestined for you (*qaddara laka*), will inevitably reach you, even if all that is in the world tried to divert it from you. And what is not written will not come to you, even if the whole world helped you'.[53] The theme of God working in and through humankind is reflected towards the end of Ghazali's *Al-Munqidh* when he writes that on returning to teaching after his spiritual crisis:

> I believe with a faith as certain as direct vision that there is no might for me and no power save in God, the Sublime, the Mighty; and that it was not I who moved, but He who moved me; and that I did not act, but He acted through

---

[51] Mayer, *Letter*, 28.

[52] McCarthy, *Al-Ghazali*, 30. The verse is Q70:40–1. Mayer has the adjective 'vain' linked to 'pleasures' on the first mention. However, it would seem from a close reading of Ghazali that all worldly pleasures are vain and that this is implied in the word 'pleasures' on its own.

[53] McCarthy, *Al-Ghazali*, 38.

me. I ask him then to reform me first, then to see me as an instrument of reform; to guide me then to use me as an instrument of guidance; to show me the true as true, and to grant me the grace to follow it.[54]

His emphasis on doing good deeds notwithstanding, running through this short work is the sub-doctrinal issue of whether doing good deeds is itself enough to attain paradise or salvation. Ghazali presents the Ash'ari position whereby no one is actually saved by their own actions but only through divine mercy (*rahma*). Prayer and good works should form the life of the believer but they cannot in themselves determine our individual salvation. Quoting Hasan al-Basri, he writes, 'God the Exalted will say to his worshippers on the day of Resurrection, "O worshippers of Mine, enter the Garden by my mercy and divide it between you according to your works"'.[55]

Throughout much of the book, Ghazali speaks as if humankind has control over life, the ability to discern spiritual ethics from a life of worldly temptation. There is a growing sense that the order of life, from revelation to the eschaton, defines being and purpose. There is an urgency here and no room for complacency; faith demands everything from us. This realisation is painful for Ghazali who has himself struggled to find the essence of what it means to believe in God and the hereafter. Ghazali ends his short treatise saying that he has given his disciple the necessary advice but also requests that the disciple remember him in his prayers. Ghazali is always aware of his own weaknesses and the work ends with an emotional prayer which he advises the disciple to recite as part of supererogatory prayers. The master-disciple relationship may have been hierarchical but there was no hierarchy in the eyes of God; it was always a sign of humility to ask someone to remember you in their prayers. He devoted himself to writing and thinking about God the only way he knew through prayer and reflection which for him were the essence of belief. In this short but absorbing work, his words of exhortation and encouragement to a former student reflect fully Ghazali's own spiritual struggle. There is a sense of immediacy and self-reflection, the acute sensitivity of a man wishing to emphasise and prioritize what our faith demands from us. This is a man who is drawn to the intellectual and scholarly life even as he speaks of its limitations. This is also a man who finds himself humbled as he reflects on God, truth and salvation. Throughout his work, despite the constant affirmation of prayer and good deeds, it would seem that the very remedy he advocated could not give him the certainty and solace for which he struggled his whole life.

Even against the stunning array of writers and poets of the nineteenth century, Rainer Maria Rilke (1875–1926) is often described as the most

---

[54] McCarthy, *Al-Ghazali*, 93.   [55] Mayer, *Letter*, 10. Mayer translates this as grace.

cosmopolitan and arguably the most important modern German-language poet. Born in Prague to middle-class German-speaking parents, he became famous for combining philosophical, literary and poetical genres in his diverse and eclectic range of writings. He read literature from an early age and was writing poetry from the 1890s. However, his literary legacy has been important for philosophy, religion and the visual arts.

> The fact is that Rilke developed tropes of style and attitude that have proved essential for the cultural life of the twentieth century and beyond. To speak of Rilke is to speak of world literature. It is almost impossible to grasp the key elements in the development of modern culture without reference to him.[56]

His description of his early years in Prague as 'an anxious, heavy childhood' reflect the family life of one whose parents, Josef and Sophie Rilke, suffered from unfulfilled ambitions for themselves. Rilke's father had hoped for a major military career but had to confine his hopes to advancing within the offices of the North Bohemia railway. His mother Sophie, or Phia as she was known, always dressed in black as if in perpetual mourning. Her dreams for living a life of high society came to nothing and it seems that the parents' frustrated aspirations were projected on the young Rene; they eventually separated in 1885.[57]

Rilke's father pushed him into the military partly because he despaired of him ever having a proper job and the young poet served for five rather miserable years at a military academy. He then left for Prague University where he studied art history, literature and philosophy.[58] He returned to Prague where he found in his uncle, Jaroslav Rilke, a relative who was most sympathetic to his intellectual needs and provided the means for Rilke to complete his school-leaving certificate. But Rilke left for Munich where he continued his studies for another year. While Rilke was to attend several universities, he never graduated from any of them, yet he always considered himself a scholar. According to Baer, Rilke travelled to Italy and Russia in his resolve to become a poet. Russia inspired him deeply, allowing him to

---

[56] Karen Leeder and Robert Vilain, 'Introduction' in K. Leeder and R. Vilain (eds.), *The Cambridge Companion to Rilke*, Cambridge Companions to Literature, Cambridge: Cambridge University Press, 2010, 1–5.

[57] Donald Prater, *A Ringing Glass: The Life of Rainer Maria Rilke*, Oxford: Clarendon Press, 1986, 5–11; and see, Rudiger Görner, 'Rilke: A Biographical Exploration', in Karen Leeder and Robert Vilain (eds.), *The Cambridge Companion to Rilke*, Cambridge: Cambridge University Press, 2010, 9–26.

[58] Ulrich Baer, *The Poet's Guide to Life: The Wisdom of Rilke*, New York: The Modern Library, 2005, xvii. Baer provides an accessible biographical introduction.

reconnect with the Slavic side of his Prague childhood, and he came to see Russia as his spiritual homeland in both the people and the landscape. He travelled with his lover Lou Andreas Salome, the older woman to whom Friedrich Nietzsche once proposed marriage and who would be amongst the first female psychoanalysts trained by Sigmund Freud. It was she who encouraged him to change his name René to the more masculine Rainer 'and to practice a signature and penmanship with the verve and flourish befitting a poet'.[59] Rilke had been impressed with her books, *Female Figures in Ibsen's Plays* (1892) and *Friedrich Nietzsche* (1894). She taught him the essence of Nietzscheanism and, in his *Florentine Diary*, which he kept for Lou, Rilke attempted to see art from the perspective of Nietzsche's *Zarathustra* and engage in reflections on the meaning of art and the existential condition of the artist: 'Every artist is born abroad as it were; and his home is nowhere but within himself'.[60] Salome's s husband, the Orientalist Friedrich Carl Andreas had a special interest in Muslim minorities within Russia, and it is most likely he played a part in Rilke's exposure to Islam. This draw to Islam is reflected in various works and while Islam or the Qur'an is often painted in a favourable light, it is not because he is anti-Christianity, rather it is because he is frustrated with what Christianity has become in his view. It was also under Andreas's tutelage that Rilke became acquainted with the Qur'an and an influential popular account of the Prophet's life that had been circulating in Europe since the eighteenth century, Boulainvillier's *La vie de Mohamed*, published in 1730.[61] Russia's archaic world was a decisive experience for Rilke and his encounters with Leo Tolstoy, the painter Leonid Pasternak and the peasant poet Spiridon Dimitrievich Drozhzhin, left a huge impression on him.

While Lou remained his lifelong friend, Rilke married a young German sculptor, Clara Westhoff with whom he had a daughter, Ruth, in December 1901. In 1911 Rilke undertook a trip to Tunisia and Egypt, following the example of Clara, who had been to North Africa some years before. Even though Rilke's actual knowledge of the world was mainly confined to continental Europe, except for this journey to North Africa in 1910–11, the poet's outlook was international and he remained open-minded towards other cultures until the end of his life.

---

[59] Baer, *The Wisdom*, xvii.
[60] Ruth Sieber-Rilke and Carl Sieber (eds.), *Rainer Maria Rilke, Das Florenzer Tagebuch, 1942,* Frankfurt and Leipzig: Insel, 1994, 38. See Görner, *Cambridge Companion*, 12.
[61] I have taken this account from Karen J. Campbell's brief comments on Rilke and Islam from her detailed analysis, 'Rilke's Duino Angels and the Angels of Islam', *Alif : Journal of Comparative Poetics*, 23, 2003, 191–211.

While Rilke had been lonely as a child and often struggled during adulthood, he was to turn the negativity of loneliness into a positive search for solitude which he thought indispensable to the life of the artist. He eventually left his family for Paris where he worked briefly for the sculptor Auguste Rodin.[62] It was during his time working as Rodin's secretary that Rilke realised the importance of self-discipline in the life of the artist and how this life is connected to the sacred. Rilke's *The Book of Hours* (*Das Stunden-Buch*), written in three bursts between 1899 and 1903, appears at the end of 1905, is his most formative work and covers this period of his life and his rapid ascent as a poet with a distinctive urban modern voice.[63] The book is a kind of unfinished dialogue between Rilke and God, his search for the divine in the material existence around him. In 1910, he completes his only novel, a unique prose work, *The Notebooks of Malte Laurids* (*Die Aufzeichnungen des Malte Laurids Brigge*), often described as the first truly post-realist novel of international stature. The book tells the story of Malte, a twenty-eight-year-old aristocratic Dane whose artistic aspirations bring him to Paris. Here he begins to record his life crises, experiences and memories in a series of diary-like notations. But this fictional plot soon gives way to a 'series of literary and historical reflections that push the work toward allegory and essayism rather than providing narrative and plot'. The book becomes fragmented readings focusing on Malte's traumatic reactions to city life, delving into the deepest layers of Malte's unconscious memory. The reader wonders how much of this is autobiographical, Rilke's own struggle as a young poet, looking for purity of language and expression and the crisis of subjectivity in modern life. Rilke speaks of the sheer labour of writing poetry – 'For the sake of one line of poetry, one must see many cities, people and things' – and that poetry demands time:

> Poems don't come to much when they are written too soon. One should wait and gather the feelings and flavours of a whole life, and a long life if possible, and then just at the end, one might perhaps be able to write ten good lines. For poems are not, as people suppose, emotions – these come easily and quickly enough. They are experiences.[64]

This work marks a crisis in Rilke's ideal of God. Having failed to accurately depict God in his poetry, his attention was even more focused on how one

---

[62] It appears from his biographical accounts that he always seemed to be returning to Paris.

[63] The name refers to the liturgical booklet or office-book of the Orthodox Church, corresponding to the Latin breviary and containing prayers for every hour of day and night.

[64] Macy and Barrows, *A Year*, 357.

turns life into art. But he was sceptical of his own abilities as an artist. In a key passage, Malte conjures up an image of apocalypse in writing and language:

> For the time being, I can still write all this down, can still say it. But the day will come when my hand will be distant, and if I tell it to write, it will write words that are not mine. The time of that other interpretation will dawn, when there shall not be left one word upon another, and every meaning will dissolve like a cloud and fall down like rain.[65]

Rilke's life in Paris often made him feel alone and he wrote that while there, before going to bed at night, he used to read the Book of Job for solace, 'It was all true of me, word for word'.[66] Time and time, Rilke comes across as honest and self-indulgent about his own insecurities and vulnerabilities.

Yet according to Baer, Rilke was irresistible to women and had affairs with several women only to end them when he wanted to return to his writing. He acknowledges late in life that while he had paid for his wife and daughter's living expenses throughout his life, he had been neither a good husband nor a good father.[67] Rilke lived in Paris and after a short stint on the front during World War I, he left and sought army release. He left Germany in 1919 with a great ambivalence towards the country he held responsible for the war and its aftermath. In 1922, thanks to the patronage of Werner Reinhart, who bought and renovated the castle/tower Muzot in the Valais in Switzerland, Rilke was able to live there in relative seclusion until his death from leukaemia in 1926. Many of the poems in French evoked the beauty of his beloved Valais, the Swiss canton where he now lived. His time in Muzot was intensely productive. It was here that, in 1922, he completed both his *Duino Elegies* (*Duineser Elegien*) which he had begun writing a decade earlier in 1912 in the old castle of Duino near Trieste. The castle at Duino was the property of Rilke's patron Princess Marie von Thurn and Taxis-Hohenlohe. It had been damaged by bombardment from the Italian navy when Italy entered the Great War in 1915 and, while it proved to be a unique setting, Rilke wrote that he soon felt like a prisoner within its immense walls.[68] He did complete two

---

[65] Andreas Huyssen, 'The Notebooks of Malte Laurids Brigge' in *Cambridge Companion*, 78.

[66] Rainer Maria Rilke, *Letters to a Young Poet*, trans. by Charlie Louth, London: Penguin Books Ltd, 2011, xxv.

[67] Baer, *The Wisdom*, xviii.

[68] The 'Elegies' are ten long philosophical poems and are called elegies because of their form and content. According to Graham Good, it is the 'perceptible dactylic base', a loose variant of the elegy which reinforces the exploratory nature of the content. 'The tentative, unsettled quality of the verse produces a sequence of possible approximations, and provisional insights rather than established uncertainties'. See Graham Good, *Rilke's Late Poetry*, Vancouver: Ronsdale Press, 2015, 13.

of the *Elegies* and other fragments during his stay here. But the war seemed to have hurt Rilke's poetic inspiration and it was not until his time in Muzot that he both completed the *Duino Elegies* and produced *The Sonnets to Orpheus* (*Die Sonnette an Orpheus*) in bursts of frenzied inspiration. Both these works are considered to be Rilke's poetic masterpieces and two of the finest achievements of twentieth century European literature. He wrote to Princess Marie that his writing had taken over him with such a force that 'all that was fibre, fabric in me, cracked and bent'.[69] This unique period of inspired literary productivity is mentioned by W. H. Auden who referred to Rilke's experience in 1938 in his Sonnets from China:

Tonight in China let me think of one

Who for ten years of drought and silence waited,
Until in Muzot all his being spoke.
And everything was given once for all.

According to Leeder and Vilain, Rilke's 'long creative crisis and effective silence between 1910 and 1922' was born out of death in the terrible reality of the First World War. But 'when this was broken with the publication of the *Duino Elegies* and *Sonnets to Orpheus* in 1923, it was in the context of a changed world'.[70] However, Baer contends that Rilke was not silent during these years, rather that, during this time, he wrote countless letters which reflect on 'grace', which Rilke found in his perseverance against great adversity and wartime silence was only partial.[71] 'The *Elegies*, in particular, chime with T. S. Eliot or Wallace Stevens to speak of a world after God, after catastrophe, and after any sense of coherent wholeness has been lost. The only place it can be regained is in the work of art itself'.[72]

The opening lines of the *Duino Elegies* are dramatic and it is worth recounting the full circumstances surrounding their inception. Rilke was staying at Duino Castle, the residence of Princess Marie.[73] He had received a troubling business letter and wanted to deal with it so he went out to the cliffs where a violent bora was blowing:

Rilke went down to the bastions that jut out to east and west. . . . From there the rocks drop down steeply to the sea, which lies two hundred feet below. He was walking up and down immersed in thought, for the answer he had

---

[69] Good, *Rilke's Late*, 12.   [70] Leeder and Vilain, *Cambridge Companion*, 3.
[71] Baer, *The Wisdom*, xx.   [72] Leeder and Vilain, *Cambridge Companion*, 3.
[73] Rilke 'was fortunate in finding Princesses and Countesses with castles and mansions who gave him hospitality', in Stephen Spender, 'Rilke and the Angels; Eliot and the Shrines', *The Sewanee Review*, 61:4, 1953, 557–81.

to write to the business-letter preoccupied him. All of a sudden, in the middle of his cogitations, he stopped still, for it seemed to him that he heard a voice call through the roaring of the wind: 'Wer, wenn ich shrie, hörte mich den aus der Engel Ordnungen?' (If I cried out aloud, would anyone hear me among the ranks of the angels?)

It is said that Rilke wondered who or what it was that he heard, but he wrote down these words as well as a few more lines. He knew who was coming – It was 'the god'. The opening lines continue, 'And if one of them suddenly took me to heart, I'd be overwhelmed by his more powerful being. For beauty is simply the onset of terror'.[74] He calmly climbed back up to his room, set his notebook aside, and replied to the difficult letter. But by that same evening the entire first elegy had been written.[75]

For Kathleen Komar, 'Rilke's ten elegies form a response not so much to this question as to the impulse to ask it'. They record the isolation of individual human consciousness seeking some escape from the trauma so strongly felt by writers and artists between the two world wars. Rilke ponders how self-conscious man could gain access to the transcendent realm represented by the angels.[76] Humankind is separated from the divine and for Rilke, angels reconciled the inner and outer worlds of our existence as he writes, 'the angel is the creature in whom the transformation of the visible into the invisible we are performing is already complete'. It is said that Rilke told his Polish translator that the angel in the *Elegies* had nothing to do with Christian heavenly angels. Rather in Rilke's angelology, the angels he is referring were the angelic figures of Islam. Alluding to the Islamic belief in the angel Gabriel's mission to Muhammad to recite the heavenly Qur'an, the angels represent the transcendent realm to which Rilke wants access.[77] On this point, Stephen Spender writes, 'There is something terrifying about the concept of the isolated poet, acting as substitute-spiritual-institution, projecting in to the world the idea of the angels, in whom the individual is made impersonal, isolated vision made objective. Rilke himself is terrified'.[78]

---

[74] This is from the first elegy from Good, *Rilke's Late*, 25. A variation on this translation is 'Who, if I cried out, would hear me among the angelic/orders? And even if one of them pressed me/ suddenly to his heart: I'd be consumed/in his stronger existence'. See Campbell, 'Rilke's Duino Angels', 191+.

[75] This description is taken from Princess Marie Von Thurn und Taxis, *The Poet and the Princess: Memories of Rainer Maria Rilke*, Amazon printed, UK, 2017, 34–5.

[76] Kathleen L. Komar 'The Duino Elegies' in *Cambridge Companion*, 82.

[77] Komar 'The Duino Elegies' in *Cambridge Companion*, 82.

[78] Spender, 'Rilke and the Angels', 571.

The theme of impermanence and transience is central in our search for meaning:

> It seems,
> Our own impermanence is concealed from us.
> The trees stand firm, the houses we live in
> Are still there. We alone
> Flow past it all, an exchange of air
>
> Everything conspires to silence us,
> Partly with shame,
> Partly with unspeakable hope.[79]

On the one hand, Rilke is all too conscious of the violence of death and yet the knowledge and experience of mortality contains a delicacy (*leise*).[80] In other words, the divine conveys itself delicately and is a far more intimate presence. As Komar rightly says, by the end of the *Elegies*, there is a new realization:

> The poet instead must immerse himself in the physical and the earthly in order to create fruitful transformation. The reader too comes to understand that this limited human world is indeed enough; human consciousness and larger existence are reunified; self-conscious man finds a way to expand his consciousness without abandoning the human realm by death.'

It takes courage to love the world in the face of death. Our griefs are part of us, death is part of this life and in his journey Rilke ultimately realises that 'intensely experienced immanence replaces the desire for transcendence'.[81]

> We waste our sorrow,
> We look beyond them into the sadness of time
> To see if they end. But they are really our winter foliage, our
>   dark evergreen
> One of our secret seasons – no, more than that –
> They are place, plot, hearth, earth, home.[82]

Similarly, in the *Sonnets to Orpheus*, Rilke sees the realm of death as not something after this life but an aspect of this life. As Martinec explains:

> Rilke's attempt to reintegrate death into life is part of a more comprehensive endeavour to free human existence from the limits of the visible world. The prime target of this endeavour is not so much to enhance death by supporting our recollection of those passed away, but rather to enhance life

---

[79] From Rilke's Second Duino Elegy in Macy and Barrows, *A Year*, 5.
[80] See Antonella Castelveder, 'Neither Religion nor Philosophy', *German Life and Letters*, 63:2, 2010, 133–45.
[81] Komar, 'The Duino', *Cambridge Companion*, 94.   [82] Good, *Rilke's Late*, 52.

by extending its boundaries far beyond the area of what is commonly regarded as life.'[83]

The visible world was only one dimension of our existence. For Rilke, ancient myths and stories could continue to give meaning to this life: mythology had been replaced by the Enlightenment and rationality but the latter had failed to answer the deeper existential questions on the meaning of life. As a result, life was not better, it was more impoverished. The work is based on the tenth and eleventh book of Ovid's *Metamorphoses*, in which Orpheus journeys to the underworld to bring back his beloved Eurydice who has died from a snakebite. While Orpheus does not succeed in Ovid's poem and is killed at the end, his severed head continues to sing and his lyre continues to play. Thus, for Rilke, Orpheus not only confronts death but comes back singing:

> Always be dead in Eurydice – singing
> And praising more, rise to that purer state.
> Here in the this realm of decay, be a ringing
> Glass that shattered as it rang.
> Be – at the same time know non-existence,
> The infinite ground of your inner vibration,
> So that you fully perfect it just this once.[84]

Rilke felt that with regard to the invisible world, humankind was confronted with a twofold challenge: on the one hand, we are asked to achieve the spiritual act of metamorphosis on which the universe relies in order to reach a deeper level of reality; on the other hand, we have to appreciate our present nature, because it, too, is a crucial dimension of our existence.[85]

Even during his seclusion, Rilke maintained his correspondence with hundreds of people, from his patrons and benefactors to aristocrats and businessmen. There are approximately 17,000 letters, although not all published. In many of the letters, we gain insight into Rilke's daily concerns and his struggles in outlining various artistic projects. Rilke's letters all originate in an urgent inquiry into himself, into the world, into the things around him and into other people. Rilke's poetry might be said to encapsulate many of the dilemmas of the twentieth century and beyond: the loss of belief in a divinely sponsored universe, the struggle with industrialisation, a preoccupation with war and death and the atomisation of society. Love, suffering and fragility as well as the human struggle with impermanence lie at the heart of his work. But this earthly existence is also joyful and, while transient, it must be lived with integrity, courage and gratitude. Artists and thinkers had to portray the beauty of the physical and natural world.

---

[83] Thomas Martinec, 'Sonnets to Orpheus' in *Cambridge Companion*, 98.
[84] Good, *Rilke's Late*, 97.   [85] Martinec, 'Sonnets' in *Cambridge Companion*, 100.

Despite his deteriorating health during 1923–5, he continued to be prolific in his poetic and epistolary productivity. In addition, he continued to receive huge numbers of visitors, especially in Paris in January 1925. Görner writes that 'the cream of the French literati came to see him, from André Gide to Paul Valéry (whose reputation in the German-speaking world rested on Rilke's translations), Edmond Jaloux, Jules Supervielle, Jean Cassou, Jean Giraudoux and Charles Du Bos'.[86] He was admired by all quarters of society and his biography paints the portrait of a man who could not afford the expensive lifestyle he lived and mostly relied on others for the luxuries to which he had become accustomed. Yet people lavished praise and money on him and despite his erratic publishing record, his correspondents knew that with each letter 'they were given something that would far outlast anything bought with their money'.[87] Indeed Princess Marie von Thurn writes of her meeting with Rilke with huge admiration and gratitude:

> Never have I seen a human countenance more radiant, or listened to more ecstatic words. The poet seemed to have solved the riddle of existence, accepting pleasure and pain, joy and sorrow, life and death ... I ought to have understood: he had attained the summit, scaled the highest peak and looked upon the face of God.
>
> The days we spent together will always remain in my memory. The more I saw of the poet, whom I had met so fleetingly in Paris, the more I was fascinated by his unique charm. I was deeply touched at the pleasure he expressed at being with us, and his gratitude – for which I know no explanation. It was we who had to be grateful – for the mere fact of his existence.[88]

In his biographical introduction, Baer writes that on 4 December 1926, his fifty-first birthday, Rilke asked from his hospital bed for cards to be printed in German and French and mailed to over a hundred correspondents. The card read:

> Monsieur Rainer Maria Rilke, seriously ill, asks to be excused; he finds himself incapable of taking care of his correspondence. December 1926.

Rilke died on 19 December 1926. For Rilke, writing had become a moral responsibility and he did not wish to disappoint those waiting for his correspondence. As Baer writes, 'to ask his correspondents to forgive him for not writing means, in this poignant card, effectively to be excused for being taken 'seriously ill' and thus, ultimately, to be excused for dying'.[89]

---

[86] Görner, 'A Biographical' in *Cambridge Companion*, 24.   [87] Baer, *The Wisdom*, xxi.
[88] Princess Marie von Thurn und Taxis, *The Poet*, 3 & 8.   [89] Baer, *The Wisdom*, 1i.

In 1902 Franz Xaver Kappus was a nineteen-year-old military cadet who wrote to Rilke seeking critical guidance on his own poetic efforts. He writes that he sent his 'verses accompanied by a letter in which I revealed myself more unreservedly than to anyone ever before, or to anyone since'. Rilke's response in the ten letters between 1903–8, became one of his most famous and widely quoted works, (*Letters to a Young Poet, Briefe an einen jungen Dichter*). The book is regarded as a modern classic. Rilke never met Kappus who pursued his military studies and served for fifteen years as an officer in the Austro-Hungarian Army. During the course of his life, he worked as a newspaper editor and journalist, writing poems, humorous sketches, short stories and novels, and adapted several works (including his own) into screenplays for films in the 1930s. However, Kappus did not achieve lasting fame. He died in Berlin in 1966, and while immortalised in Rilke's *Letters*, he has been largely forgotten by history. In his short note to the *Letters*, clearly grateful to Rilke, he writes 'and where a great and unique person speaks, the rest of us should be silent'.[90]

Letter writing was Rilke's literary mode of exploration during his creative bursts of poetry. During his life, Rilke had corresponded with several other 'young poets' who had sought his guidance and these ten letters contain universal themes whether in his advice to the young poet or his own sentiments on life. One should remember that Rilke was himself a young poet at that stage and like Ghazali, he may have been writing these letters to himself; Kappus' struggles are Rilke's struggles. Rilke's style is reflective, full of philosophical sermonizing for this young poet. The young Kappus is only eight years younger than Rilke and wanted to open himself to Rilke both as a man and a poet. He writes that he wanted Rilke's advice and insights as he too wished to write poetry. But it seems that other than a few pieces of advice on how to approach the art of writing poetry, Rilke was more interested in Kappus the man than Kappus the poet. One could argue that the *Letters*, while deeply moving in places, are also hyperbolic, reaching in and out of the extremes of the human condition. Yet he seems pleased to be given yet another opportunity to correspond, to liaise with another human being on what is important to hold onto for one's art. He thus often asks forgiveness for being late in his replies. At the beginning, his question is to ask the poet why he is seeking advice because he should not be looking for help from the outside as 'there is only one way. Go into yourself'. Rilke encourages the young Kappus to reflect: 'Examine the reason that bids you to write; check whether it reaches its roots into the deepest region of your heart, admit to

---

[90] Rainer Maria Rilke, *Letters to a Young Poet*, trans. by Charlie Louth, London: Penguin Books Ltd, 2011, 5.

yourself whether you would die if it should be denied you to write'.[91] It is as if only when you know you can't live without writing, then that's when you write or when you write the very best that is within you. In fact if your everyday life lacks material its because 'you are not poet enough to summon up its riches, for there is no lack for him who creates and no poor, trivial place'.[92] Interiority and seeking depth are constant reminders in these *Letters*.

Throughout this work, the theme of solitude as a gift is the most poetically resonant. Rilke had suffered from loneliness as a child and concluded in his *Letters* that 'we are lonely'. However, rather than suffer from loneliness, he takes isolation to be a given, something to be embraced and this is what he urges Kappus to do as well. Solitariness is a spiritual state; it is about going into oneself embracing the struggle – the suffering that life presents – but then turning that into some kind of artistic creation. Suffering and solitude were modes of being for Rilke. 'Love your solitude and bear the pain it causes you with melody wrought with lament. For the people who are close to you, you tell me, are far away, and that shows that you are beginning to create a wider space around you'.[93] For Rilke this was a sign of internal growth. On suffering he wrote, 'Long must you suffer, not knowing what, until suddenly, from a piece of fruit hatefully bitter, the taste of the suffering enters you. And then you already almost love what you've savoured. No one will talk it out of you again'.[94]

For Rilke, 'Every artist is born abroad, as it were; and his home is nowhere but within himself'.[95] Solitude is not a state, it is something we should seek and enter into for our art. Solitude is not a curse, it is a blessing. There are resonances here of Oscar Wilde's reflection on suffering in *De Profundis*-that sorrow might be the only truth, pain unlike pleasure wears no mask:

> I now see that sorrow, being the supreme emotion of which man is capable, is at once the type and test of all great Art. What the artist is always looking for is that mode of existence in which soul and body are one and indivisible: in which the outward is expressive of the inward: in which Form reveals.[96]

Living with patience is part of being an artist, and it doesn't happen in the way we understand time: true artistic creativity may take years to manifest itself and in that time while we wait we should know that art is a way of living. Words do not always come easily, 'for even the best of us gets the words

[91] Rilke, *Letters*, 7.   [92] Rilke, *Letters*, 8.   [93] Rilke, *Letters*, 28.

[94] Galway Kinnell and Hannah Liebmann, *The Essential Rilke*, New York: HarperCollins Publishers, 2000, 67.

[95] Rainer Maria Rilke, Ruth Sieber-Rilke and Carl Sieber (eds.), *Das Florenzer Tagebuch*, Frankfurt and Leipzig: Insel, 1994, 38.

[96] Rupert Hart-Davis (ed.), *Selected Letters of Oscar Wilde*, New York: Oxford University Press, 1989, 201.

wrong when we want them to express such intangible and almost unsayable things'.[97] Patience and holding 'close to nature' is required. It is here that we come across, Rilke's famous lines in which he advises Kappus

> Be patient towards all that is unresolved in your heart and to try to love the questions themselves liked locked rooms, like books written in a foreign language. What matters is to live everything. Live the questions now, for gradually without noticing it, live your way into the answer, one distant day into the future.[98]

The positive affirmation of life, of wonder, is to be cherished. Rilke urges the young poet to live and grow with uncertainty, to embrace all the unknowns for that represents beauty, faith and trust in this life. This includes our fears because all that we experience comes from within us. We have to let life happen to us rather than be anxious quite simply because we misunderstand the world and our own impulses:

> We have no reason to be mistrustful of our world, for it is not against us, if it holds terrors they are our terrors, if it has its abysses these abysses belong to us, if there are dangers then we must try to love them.
>   The myths about the dragons who at the last minute turn into princesses? Perhaps all the dragons in our lives are princesses, only waiting for the day when they will see us handsome and brave? Perhaps everything terrifying is deep down a helpless thing that needs our help?[99]

He advises that everything serious is difficult and everything is serious. In all this seriousness, love is the most serious thing we do: 'Love between one person and another; that is perhaps the hardest thing it is laid on us to do, the utmost, the ultimate trial and test, the work for which all other work is just preparation'.[100] The love to which Rilke seems to be referring often contains the element of sexual desire but is not a youthful abandon or 'trivial and frivolous games behind which people have hidden'. Physical desire is a sensual experience, 'no different from pure sensation' and not to be held lightly but in awe. Questions of love, he writes cannot be solved publicly; they are questions that touch the quick of what it is to be human. For Rilke, love was the experience that had the potential to lift us out of our self-involved selves. Love is work and requires patience and maturity. When we are in love, as he describes so beautifully, we are capable of being slightly more alive than we normally are. This is so despite the fact that life is both beauty and unspeakable suffering.[101] Rilke had observed the vanishing of all kinds of

[97] Rilke, *Letters*, 23.   [98] Rilke, *Letters*, 23–4.   [99] Rilke, *Letters*, 57.
[100] Rilke, *Letters*, 42–3   [101] Rilke, *Letters*, 44–5.

master narratives of redemption. He believed in love, even when, and maybe because, he understood how love can be the deception we need and want in life, to make life liveable.

While the themes of solitude, love, death, art and suffering suffuse his writing in concrete and abstract ways, underlying all of these is his complex relationship to God and religion. The search for God was the search for life's greater meaning. God is a great conviction in Rilke for he was brought up in a Christian environment and refers to God and leading biblical figures in a fairly orthodox way. But he is often described as a post-Christian poet who rejected Christianity. This seems to be more a disillusionment with the way Christianity has developed rather than a rejection of its essential message. Both suffering and joy are not mere interruptions to the Christian life, but give it form and meaning. Rilke may not have written as an orthodox Christian – in fact he writes against Christianity at times – but he constantly explored the artist's relationship to God's presence in and through creation. Frederick Vanson writes that 'if ever a man was obsessed by God with God as the immanent power informing all natural and human life, that man was Rilke'.[102] His gospel is the gospel of God immanent. God is the Invisible and the Unsayable. The restlessness, uneasiness and dreaminess of his early poetry gave way to his grappling with God, an obsession with God's presence in the world and our struggle with what divine presence means. His God is not the God of angels and heavens but is imagined in nature and as nature everywhere:

> Often when I imagine you
> Your wholeness cascades into many shapes
> You run like a herd of luminous deer
> And I am dark, I am forest
> You are a wheel at which I stand,
> Whose dark spokes sometimes catch me up
> Resolve me nearer to the center.[103]

God is 'the dream you are dreaming' and, if he is waiting for us, we are also yearning for him. Rilke asks the young poet why he feels he has lost God when in reality he never yet possessed him at all. He writes,

Do you think a child can hold him, him whom grown men only bear with difficulty and whose weight bows down the old? Do you believe that anyone who really has him could lose him like a little pebble, or don't you think that whoever had him could only be lost by him alone?

[102] Frederic Vanson, 'Rilke's "Stories of God"', *Renascence*, 14:2, 1962, 90.
[103] Taken from *The Book of Hours* in Macy and Barrows (eds.), *A Year*, xiii.

Rilke advises the young poet to think of God 'as a coming god, who since eternity has lain ahead of us, the future one'.[104] In another poem, it is God himself who wishes to be desired;

> God speaks to each of us as he makes us,
> Then walks with us silently out of the night.
> These are the words we dimly hear:
> You, sent out beyond your recall
> Go to the limits of your longing.
> Embody me.[105]

Rilke wrote that the same things belong to God and the artist, be it riches or poverty. There are parallels here with Oscar Wilde's reflection on Christ and the artist. Wilde writes that for Christ, the spirit alone was of value and that to Christ, imagination was simply a form of love. Wilde saw 'a far more intimate and immediate connection between the true life of Christ and the true life of the artist' and he wrote,

> I remember saying once to André Gide, as we sat together in some Paris cafe, that while meta-physics had but little real interest for me, and morality absolutely none, there was nothing that either Plato or Christ had said that could not be transferred immediately into the sphere of Art and there find its complete fulfilment.[106]

In *Letters from a Young Worker*, (*Der Brief des jungen Arbeiters*), Rilke complains that, when speaking of God, 'the whole of creation says this word without deliberation'.[107] He critiques Christianity for ignoring the gesture Christ makes on the cross which was to point to a different way of being in their search for God; Christ's way on the cross was a signpost, not the destination itself, but Christians have settled there. The German word *kreuzweg* means both the Way of the Cross, *Via Crucis*, as well as a crossroad. Rilke does not however explain what he means by the true or final destination, although it may simply refer directly to God. God's purpose is beyond the symbol and image we make of him. Christians keep returning to Christ but Rilke wanted to be usable for God, just the way he was with his works without 'his ray of light being refracted even in Christ'. He can go straight to God through his works, he doesn't need the word faith. He says 'I don't want to be worsened for Christ's sake but want to be good for God'.[108] Christians have made a job out of the Christian purpose; a bourgeois activity. We speak of God like we speak of love – with abandon – and deny them both the

---

[104] Rilke, *Letters*, 37–8.   [105] Macy and Barrows, *A Year*, 32.   [106] Wilde, *Selected Letters*, 204.
[107] Rilke, *Letters*, 71.   [108] Rilke, *Letters*, 88.

seriousness each deserves. Rilke writes with the an inner certainty that if he really reached out to God, 'What is this I feel falling now, falling on this parched earth, softly, like a spring rain?'[109] Everything in life is an unfolding, a letting go, an expectation of a prayer being answered. In a letter to Rudolf Zimmerman, Rilke wrote:

> In the last analysis, I have a completely indescribable passion for experiencing God, and this God is unquestionably closer to that of the Old Testament than He is to the Messiah's Gospels. I must admit that what I have most wanted in this life has been to discover within myself a temple to earth, and to dwell therein.[110]

God is a paradoxical constant for Rilke, embodying all that he cannot understand or resolve.

Rilke and Ghazali both wrote of struggle and suffering as they experienced it in their own lives and as the basis of the human condition. As a poet mystic, Rilke searched for and extolled solitude as the creative refuge for the artist and as a theologian mystic, Ghazali saw that remembering death, repentance and prayer were the secret to understanding the human condition. For Ghazali, the awareness that we take nothing into the next life other than our good deeds gave a new meaning to this life and his search for spiritual growth. The letter form gives their thoughts a more personal touch even though their advice is undoubtedly for a wider audience. Ghazali was a theologian and Rilke was a poet but their letters were fragments of advice to themselves as well as to their recipients. Both thinkers travelled in search of inner solace and for their own intellectual well-being. For Ghazali, the Qur'anic verse, 'the mercy of God is near to those who do good' (Q7:56) guided his writing. Humankind searches for meaning and repose everywhere but there is no meaning to life outside worship of God. Ghazali was a dedicated scholar; he admits that theory was easier for him than practice and yet he struggled with conventional scholasticism and the limits of the intellectual life. Theological sophistry was seductive but had failed to resolve the deeper yearning for truth and peace, and it is not clear whether he ever did find the inner peace for which he appears to have searched so desperately. But self-discipline is important for great thinkers and his writing, in which his philosophical reflections stayed largely within Sunni orthodoxy, still gave order to his life. His purpose was to convince his reader that the intellectual life was worthy but no substitute for the life of pious devotion; the remedy was worship and it was only through worship and prayer, the inner spirit, that one experienced God.

---

[109] Macy and Barrows, *A Year*, 181. [110] Macy and Barrows, *A Year*, 33.

Remembering the next life and working for one's salvation in the hereafter, are the themes which infuse his advice to his disciple. The future is inevitable, divine judgement is inevitable and if we forget that, we forget the only truth which matters in life. The very impermanence of life is proof that this life is no more than a preparation for the next and that it's sole purpose should be a turning to God. It is only because 'God is kind' that we humans become complacent. His advice in *Ayyuha* might be the succinct distillation of all his learning.

Yet Ghazali is also a writer of hope. While judgement in the afterlife is real and should be our ultimate concern, as believers, if we do not have hope, we do not have belief. There is no end to God's mercy because there is no end to God's goodness. In his writings, we find several traditions defining the importance of hope as a basis for human devotion and worship:

> It is related that there were two devotees equal in devotion. When they entered the garden, one of them was elevated to the highest degree over his companion. So he said, 'O Lord in what way did this man exceed me in devotion on the earth? Yet you have elevated him over me in the highest heaven'. So God says, 'Truly, while he was on this earth he was constantly asking for the highest degrees, while you were asking for salvation from the fire. So I have given every creature his request'. And this is a pointer to the fact that worship which is on account of hope is the more meritorious because love dominates the person who hopes more than it does the one who fears.[111]

But for Rilke, there was no salvation or hope outside the experience of this life. If suffering and pain drove us to a higher consciousness, physical desire and sensual experience were also a kind of pure knowledge. This desire has been granted to us so that we can know the world in its fullness. Pleasure is not a bad thing but what is bad is that 'almost all of us misuse the experience and waste it and apply it as a stimulus to the tired parts of our lives as distraction instead of as a concentration of ourselves'.[112]

The exploratory discursiveness of his writing articulates 'experiences of "disbelieving" and "unknowing" that tacitly destabilise normative concepts of belief and knowledge'.[113] His concern with human salvation casts his writing into the religio-philosophical realm but this search for the divine is a search for that reality which remains within and paradoxically beyond the grasp of human understanding; God is a mix of symbols and imagery. Life can be merciless but Rilke's advice to the young poet abounds with an optimism, even hope, which the artist must feel and project not loudly but

---

[111] William McKane, *Al-Ghazali's Book of Fear and Hope*, Leiden: Brill, 1962, 21–2.
[112] Rilke, *Letters*, 24–5.   [113] Castelvedere, 'Neither Religion', 134.

with delicacy and quiet. He could express this aspect of God for those for whom there is no God, no afterlife, no heaven or hell, no redemption or salvation; heaven and hell are here and now. Our earthly existence, brief, solitary and rarely happy, is still meaningful, because to have lived once, as he says in his *Ninth Elegy*, that cannot be taken away from us: 'Never again. But having been earthly, just this once even though it was only once, can never be taken back'.[114] Everything is transient, but human imagination and solitude recognise and give meaning to life's impermanence. Poetry is not a triumph over transience but a celebration of it: 'Poetry is not a separate enclosure, walled off from time and decay; poetry is existence'.[115]

Rilke's God may not have promised immortality in the next life but he was the metaphor for the most intensely conscious part of mankind. Rilke was explicit that he didn't care for the Christian concept of an afterlife because 'it makes us less present and earthy. As long as we are here, and cousin to tree, flower, soil, may all that is near at hand be real to us and enter fully our awarenes's.[116] For Rilke, like for other artists, darkness is the place of God's becoming; darkness is the matrix of artistic life when creativity is at its peak and all kinds of future worlds are possible. He writes, 'I cherish my mind's hours of the dark, in which the extended senses sink and deepen; there as in old letters recollected I find my daily life already lived, distant, quiescent, more as legends are. And from them I become aware that in me I build room for a second, time-wide life'.[117]

Both writers, with their vastly different backgrounds and religious and cultural contexts, still speak of the essential human search for truth and meaning. Their writings reveal their inner journeys and some of their inner contradictions as they dealt with the crisis of epistemology. As Ulrich Baer writes, 'In our age that is so hungry for spiritual sustenance and so easily seduced by the promise of salvation, Rilke proves relevant by defining love as modern man's equivalent of the prayer to our vanished gods'.[118] Rilke wanted his poet to search for meaning in the very questions of our lives. He urged the young poet to be patient in his search and not to measure his art in terms of time. Ghazali was frustrated with what he had studied and learnt. He wanted to know more, he wanted a faith which could possess him leaving no room for feelings of doubt, and he wanted answers to his perennial questioning.

---

[114] Good, *Rilke's Late*, 49. I have substituted 'can never be taken back' for 'irrevocable', as in Good's translation.

[115] Good, *Rilke's Late*, 17.   [116] Macy and Barrows, *A Year*, 292.

[117] Ben Hutchinson (ed.), *Rainer Maria Rilke's* The Book of Hours: *A New Translation with Commentary*, trans. by Susan Ranson, Woodbridge: Boydell and Brewer, 2008, 7.

[118] Baer, *The Wisdom*, xii.

Ghazali wanted to feel closer to God and was desperate that his faith and devotion would be the solution to his spiritual and intellectual dilemma. He was convinced of the truth of an afterlife which, for him, demanded turning away from the temptations and desire of an earthly existence. But he remained torn because human nature yields to both the earthly and the divine. Rilke, for his part, saw that all the happiness we seek in this world, in which we seek refuge, is not unworthy of desire, it is simply that it is transient. How we face death depends on how we choose to live. Rilke, despite his untimely death and his very real suffering, felt that life had to be lived with truth, imagination and recognition of our uniqueness. He found beauty and cruelty in almost everything but did not lose faith in life's greater meaning which lay beyond this life. We give and we take from life as he writes in the *Sonnets*:

> Don't be afraid to suffer: the burden,
> Give it back to the weight of the earth;
> heavy the mountains, heavy the seas.[119]

His poetry is scattered with images which speak of a desperate desire to experience the transcendence and goodness of God within the mystery of our earthly life. The poet breathes and imagines with dread and hope. Yet, Rilke is always grateful for life: that when all said and done, it is good to have made the passage here willingly, so that at the end one will be wonderfully prepared for the relationship with the divine.

[119] Good, *Rilke's Late*, 62.

3

Community and Divine Calling in Dietrich Bonhoeffer and Sayyid Qutb

*T*HROUGHOUT HISTORY, POLITICAL LIFE HAS OFTEN BEEN MARKED BY the struggle of individuals who wanted to take their societies in a different direction. This chapter looks at two giants of twentieth century theology and political theology, Dietrich Bonhoeffer (1906–45) and Sayyid Qutb (1906–66). Born in the same year, both men were products of their political environment, Qutb in the context of European colonial rule and Bonhoeffer in the context of the rise of Nazism and anti-Semitism in Germany. Their lives bear witness to what they thought their respective Muslim and Christian faith required from them as individuals and for their societies. At a time when the word *jihad*, is ingrained on our minds and conflates personal, social and militant struggle against the state, in some ways, these two people epitomise the complexities of keeping faith linked to an ethical and political purpose. They wrote about their faith and ethics as citizens and as prisoners and while they have left very different legacies, both men were eventually hanged on charges of conspiring against the state. Sayyid Qutb criticised the Muslim world for lapsing into a state of ignorance and unbelief (*jahiliyya*) alongside his condemnation of the West and America in particular for its violence, sexual freedoms and materialism. While he regarded Islam as the solution to the world's injustices, he remains a controversial figure, especially in the West where his writings are frequently associated with inspiring violence, Islamist ideologies and movements. Qutb argued that religion is not a mere theory, but also a programme, a reality and a movement for life. For him, any action that is not inspired by faith and divine law has no value. The struggle to realise divine law was not a temporary phase but rather an eternal state because 'truth and falsehood cannot co-exist on this Earth'. For Bonhoeffer, the accusation against his fellow Christians was not one of unbelief but still a critique of their less than Christ-like ways of being Christian. The political and theological struggle of the time focused on how

Christians were to act responsibly in the Church Struggle created by Hitler and Nazism. Bonhoeffer never ceased to believe in the church despite being disillusioned by its failures. He became a leading figure in the Confessing Church which stood in open conflict with the German Reich Church who supported the Nazi government. His writings focused on a Christ-centred spirituality in that one could not separate Jesus's commands from secular life; costly grace means obedience to the call of Jesus Christ. Both men went from believing in the state to ultimately seeing it as unjust and transgressing the law. In the end they both died at the hands of the state and their prison writings bear testimony to their character and their personal faith in the face of this complex struggle.

It is difficult to speak of Islam today without reference to political Islam. Political Islam is a polyvalent concept in both lay and academic debates. It is used loosely to refer to both twentieth-century revivalist and modernist movements and struggles across the Muslim world. Political Islam is often equated with Islamism and both share in their desire for the transformation of state and society. This may include overthrowing existing states and institutions, reinterpreting Islam for contemporary challenges as well as promoting particular notions of Islamic principles in society. In contrast to Muslims who wish to practice their faith indifferent to their political surroundings, Islamists are explicitly politically engaged in critiques of those institutions and practices which do not conform to their views of their ideal Islam. While they are heterogeneous and often overlap in their outlook, with inherent contradictions, Islamist movements are usually characterised by social conservatism, literal readings of the foundational texts, the Qur'an and *hadiths*, strong emphasis on Islamic ritual and dress and, most importantly, the notion that salvation is tied to participation in this world. Thus political Islam often calls for the implementation of *shari'a,* which is perhaps the defining feature of Islamist movements. The call to implement *shari'a* is held as the solution to modern ills. But this appeal to *shari'a* is premised on a break with the past. It is not a call or return to any classical intellectual heritage of legal schools and discursive interpretation. It is rather a reimagining of society where early precedents such as the Prophet's leadership in Medina, or the expansion of the Islamic empire under the early Muslim leaders, are held as historical proof of the social and spiritual superiority the Islamic faith over other systems of governance. The genealogy of Islamism lies in Salafi orientation. The Salafis claim strict adherence to the practices of Muslims of the first generations of Islam (*al-salaf al-salih*), either contemporaries or successors to the Prophet, who are regarded as exemplars of an authentic Islamic piety. While this vision of an earlier Islam may underpin the ideologies of Islamist groups, seldom do they articulate how and to what extent *shari'a* can be applied as a normative set of rules for the ordering of an Islamic state or society. Western observers often distinguish between Islamist groups and the personal piety, beliefs and practices of ordinary Muslims, which is considered simply Islam. Yet this distinction is anathema to Islamists themselves, who consider their political views a representation of 'true' and 'authentic' Islam.

Political Islam is an ambiguous but umbrella term encapsulating several movements of critique across much of the Islamic world in the early part of the twentieth century. The critiques are related to aspects of the good society, rightful authority and moral practice. There were many reasons behind the growing momentum in a call for action. The growth of urbanisation, industrialisation, increased literacy and disenchantment with the world order formed a general social malaise. But reaction to European colonialism, the struggle for freedom and the experiences of oppression under dictatorial secular regimes in the Arab world, continuing economic stagnation in many Muslim countries and the widespread sense of Arab humiliation after defeat in the Six-Day War with Israel in 1967, were the more prevalent factors. Thus, the discourse around political Islam and Islamism seeks to address popular grievances and restore a sense of Muslim empowerment as well as re-establishing divine sovereignty through the political implementation of its Islamic vision of divine commands.

Several key figures have been instrumental to the growth and worldview of political Islam. The Egyptian Hassan al-Banna (d.1949) was the founder of the Muslim Brotherhood. Under mottos such as 'the Qur'an is our constitution' and 'Islam is the solution', al-Banna sought Islamic revival through preaching and by providing basic services to his Egyptian community. Al-Banna believed in the gradual implementation of Islamic law in all areas of personal and public life, as a means of eliminating colonial influence in Egypt and the Muslim world. In South Asia, Sayyid Abu Ala Mawdudi (d.1979) held that Muslim society could not be truly Islamic without governance by *shari'a*. He accepted Western notions of universal human rights, which were being formulated and ratified during his time, insofar as they did not contradict Islamic law.

The democratic openings that emerged after the Arab uprisings of 2011 have ushered in a decisive period for Islamist movements. Across many countries, such as Libya and Tunisia, Islamist parties have risen to prominence as the primary beneficiaries of democratic elections. For movements that have spent most of their history in opposition, these successes create new possibilities but also unprecedented challenges. Many question the capacity of Islamist groups to address long-standing, systemic issues of poverty, unemployment, economic development, gender inequalities, corruption and illiteracy that plague much of the Muslim world. Perhaps their biggest challenge lies in the appeal of the modern Western world and whether any Islamic vision can offer a meaningful alternative.

Islamic thought has often been expressed through a political lens, refering to the complex relationship between the state, authority and the moral and legal framework of society. The colonial period proved to be one which stirred the imagination of many writers and thinkers who reflected on the situation of Muslims and Islam under Western political and intellectual hegemony. One of the most distinct and controversial voices of twentieth century Islamic revivalist thought was Sayyid Quṭb (1906–66). He is often described as the Egyptian Islamist ideologue and his legacy endures in the public imagination in multiple ways. His journey from a secular educator-writer to an outspoken political activist against the Egyptian state for which he was hanged, earned him the status of martyr in the eyes of many. He is regarded by some as the architect of the mind-set that inspired the 11 September 2001, hijackers, or as Paul Berman scathingly called him 'the Philosopher of Islamic Terror'.[1] His perceived influence upon groups which were motivated by an anti-Western ideology, such as al-Qaeda, means that Qutb has been widely described as the intellectual godfather of modern Islamist activism, Islamic radicalism, and militant *jihad*. In recent years, Qutb has attracted considerable attention in the West as the person who paved the way for 'Islamist terror'. This projection of encouraging violent activism onto Qutb's life and work is controversial and the connection is arguably not easily made. As his biographer John Calvert notes:

> In the aftermath of the 9/11 atrocity, commentators scrambled to piece together Al Qaeda's ideological genealogy ... Generally, in these studies, Qutb stands at the fore of the genealogical trail. A consensus has emerged that the 'road to 9/11' traces back to him ... One cannot deny Qutb's contribution to the contemporary tide of global jihad.[2]

While this perception gained huge traction, John Calvert has also reflected on the ambivalence in relation to violence which has defined some of Qutb's writings:

---

[1] Paul Berman, 'The Philosopher of Islamic Terror', *New York Times Magazine*, March 23, 2003.
[2] John Calvert, *Sayyid Qutb and the Origins of Radical Islamism*, London: Hurst & Company, 2010, 6–7. See also Giles Kepel, *Muslim Extremism in Egypt*, Berkeley: University of California Press, 1993; and Malise Ruthven, *A Fury for God: The Islamist Attack on America*, London & New York, Granta Books, 2006.

It's worth speculating about how Sayyid Qutb would have regarded the 9/11 attacks. Almost certainly, Qutb would not have sanctioned the extreme violence that the hijackers employed. As Qutb pointed out in his writings, the killing of innocents finds no justification in the Qur'an. In fact, it's a moot point whether he would have sanctioned violence, pre-emptive or otherwise, against state or military targets. Nor would Qutb have understood Al Qaeda's desire to attack Western targets. In his mind, the jihad against the purported idolatry at home was always paramount. Yet Qutb would have appreciated Al Qaeda's view of itself as knights under the Prophet's banner; in other words, as comprising a vanguard striving to change society from outside. And although he would have disagreed with the hijackers' purpose, he would have understood the substratum of their ideology: that the world, as it stands, constitutes a conceptual realm of irreligion, vice and exploitation that ought to be resisted in the name of God.[3]

Others see him as a persuasive writer and preacher committed to advancing a sociopolitical role for Islam as a complete system for life in opposition to Western colonialism and internal corruption and social injustices. His reputation balances between these views. He is both an influential architect of contemporary Islamist Sunni thinking, as well as a visionary who wanted to mobilise a gradual reformist movement amongst Muslims. As Calvert writes:

> What is clear, however, is that Qutb's adoption of the Islamist position was gradual and tended initially to buttress, rather than to supersede, the secular concept of national distinctiveness which had dominated his writings since the 1930s. Despite his strong appeal to scriptural and prophetic authority, Qutb's primary concern remained to enhance the identity of the virtuous national self against the different and competing alter ego of the West.[4]

He wrote a huge range of books, articles and letters as well as an extensive Qur'an commentary *In the Shade of the Qur'an (Fi Zilal al-Qur'an)*. Written in several drafts between his prison years 1954–66, this is Qutb's magnum opus and considered one of the most influential, widely read and translated Qur'an commentaries of recent times. The following excerpt from the commentary encapsulates much of his thinking on the nature of divine sovereignty and the divine–human relationship in reviving the true potential of Islam:

---

[3] John Calvert, https://foreignpolicy.com/2010/12/15/the-afterlife-of-sayyid-qutb/.
[4] John Calvert, 'The World Is an Undutiful Boy!': Sayyid Qutb's American Experience', in *Islam and Christian–Muslim Relations*, 11:1, 2000, 87–103.

> We may describe the Islamic faith as a declaration of the liberation of
> mankind from servitude to creatures, including man's own desires. It also
> declares that all Godhead and Lordship throughout the universe belong to
> God alone. This represents a challenge to all systems that assign sovereignty
> to human beings in any shape or form ... As a declaration of human
> liberation, Islam means returning God's authority to Him, rejecting the
> usurpers who rule over human communities according to man-made laws.[5]

This struggle to align the moral, social and political order through establishing divine law was the dominant sentiment behind much of his writing. This
was a particular feature of several writers who wished to posit a powerful
challenge to both the legitimacy of secular, modernising Middle Eastern
regimes and to the Western rationalist and imperialist ways of understanding and thus organising political life. Unlike John Rawls and other modern
theorists whose concern was that a well-ordered society need not presume
a metaphysical conception of the good, many of the Muslim thinkers of this
period were concerned with making divine law an imperative to the foundation of a moral society; that metaphysics was not an anachronism in the post-
Enlightenment world.[6] Thus, for Qutb, Islam was a total system and not just
a personal faith. In this respect, the political theorist Roxanne Euben offers
an interesting analysis of Qutb where she presents him as essentially a critic
of secular, Enlightenment rationalism. The singular insistence upon establishing divine law, or *shari'a*, that underpins much of Qutb's works, especially his prison writings, is, for Euben, an attempt to challenge modern
notions of political sovereignty and governance that have, since the
Enlightenment, excluded religious authority and transcendent truth from
the sociopolitical sphere. Rationalist discourse is lacking in the higher purpose of human life and yet dominates the governance of society. As Euben
writes:

> All of what we have come to call 'modern' forms of authority are premised
> upon the right of human beings – either through a leader or representative
> or directly – to rule the public sphere ... Qutb (thus) engages not just
> institutional and historical reality of secularism, but the epistemology and
> worldview upon which it is founded ... [that is] the claim that knowledge is
> ascertainable through human reason, and that a theory of legitimate

[5] Roxanne L. Euben and Muhammad Qasim Zaman (eds.), *Princeton Readings in Islamist Thought*, New Jersey: Princeton University Press, 2009, 146–47.

[6] Roxanne L. Euben, 'Comparative Political Theory: An Islamic Fundamentalist Critique of Rationalism', *The Journal of Politics*, 59:1, 1997, 28–55, 29. See also John Rawls, 'Justice as Fairness: Political not Metaphysical', *Philosophy and Public Affairs*, 1985, 22–51.

authority must be premised upon the right of humans to govern without the necessity of divine intervention.[7]

As early as his 1954 work, *The Future of This Religion*, Qutb heavily engages with the history of European Enlightenment and condemns the Western separation of religious from political authority. Qutb calls this a 'hideous schizophrenia' *(al-fasam al-nakd)*.[8] He writes:

> It is not in the nature of a religion that it be separated from worldly life, nor for the divine system to be confined to personal feelings, ethical rules and ritualistic worship. Nor is it in the nature of a religion to be kept restricted to one corner of human life and be called a 'personal affair'. No revealed religion can isolate just one small section of human life for God.[9]

Born in 1906 in the village of Musha in Upper Egypt, Qutb was the eldest child of a formerly well-to-do rural family that had fallen on hard times. According to Qutb's quasi-autobiographical novel, *A Child from the Village (Tifl min al-Qarya)* published in 1946, his schooling was both modern and traditional. The Westernisation process which had begun in the nineteenth century was evident in most areas of Egyptian society, including a secular education structure. Thus, while Qutb memorised the Qur'an as young boy, this tension between the triumph of modernity over traditional forms of religious culture stayed with him throughout this life. In the novel, Qutb portrays the intellectual and cultural tension his family faced when deciding what kind of education they wanted for him:

> One group wanted him to go to the *kuttab* to memorize the Qur'an and to obtain the *baraka* that comes with having learnt the Book of God by heart. The other group wanted him to go to the state primary school because it was cleaner and more progressive, and the Qur'an was taught there also, along with other subjects. The debate swirled on about him and he did not even know it.

In the end, Qutb attended the primary school but, not wishing to be out-performed by the students from the *kuttab* at memorising the Qur'an, he writes:

> He put a great strain on himself and his health, staying awake until mid-night each night going over everything he had previously memorized. And that was on top of his other studies. By the time the year had ended, he had

---

[7] Euben, 'Comparative', 51.   [8] Qutb, *Islam: The Religion of the Future*, 34–61.
[9] Qutb, *Islam*, 34.

memorized one third of the Qur'an excellently and would compete in
recitation with anyone who challenged him.[10]

Themes of tradition and modernisation in a rural environment infuse his
autobiography. This is summarised in the picture of an Egyptian village,
struggling with poverty and its associated hardships. These are the lives of
victims of politicians and landowners who control much of Egypt's wealth:

> The spectre of peasant indebtedness and loss of land haunts the pages of the
> autobiography, as does disease caused by unhygienic conditions and the
> peasants' recourse to folk remedies and barber surgeons rather than scien-
> tifically trained physicians. The joys of Ramadan, birth ceremonies, and
> other festive occasions are juxtaposed to death, tragedy and the laments of
> women whose families patiently endure hard lives.[11]

His father, al-Hajj Qutb Ibrahim, was a member of the National Party and
the family home was often a meeting place for the political elite of the region.
Being exposed to anti-British Egyptian nationalism, Qutb became politically
aware from an early age. It is said that his mother hoped that Qutb would
improve the family's material fortunes and wanted him to study at al-Azhar.
At the age of 15, he was sent Cairo to complete his education at the Dar al-
'Ulum teacher training college where his uncle introduced him to the
intellectual circles of the capital and to the Wafd Party. Qutb became
a member of this party, but while he was in Cairo, his father died and he
asked his mother to come and live with him.

It was during his early years in Cairo that, through his love of Arabic
language and literature, he began to compose poetry and write essays and
articles that appeared in Cairo's publications *The New Life* (*al-Jadida*) and
Proclamation (*al-Balagh*). He began to attack British policies and gradually
aligned himself to the influential Wafdist journalist and leader of the new
school of modern poetry, the Diwan School, ʿAbbas Mahmud al-ʿAqqad.[12]
The cornerstone of the Diwan School was that 'poetry is subjective,
a reflection of the heart and an interpreter of the soul, not merely
a description of outer things'.[13] It is said that Qutb saw poetry as preserving
him from pollution as he saw it as the fine art which links what is and what
ought to be, between reality and ideal. The poet stands at the threshold for he

[10] Sayyid Qutb, *A Child from the Village*, ed. and trans. by John Calvert and William Shepard,
   Syracuse, NY: Syracuse University Press, 2004, 8 and 21.
[11] Calvert and Shepard, *A Child*, xxx.
[12] Adnan A. Musallam, *From Secularism to Jihad: Sayyid Qutb and the Origins of Radical Islamism*,
   Connecticut: Westport, 2005, 35.
[13] Musallam, *From Secularism*, 36.

is at one with the people and yet possesses a higher sensibility and imagination. Qutb was heavily influenced by Al-'Aqqad's standards in politics and literature, which meant he ventured far beyond Arabic literature into all areas of Western political, social and scientific writings. Alongside his reform projects, he was a man of letters, a journalist and an astute literary and social critic. He himself had little literary success but was among the first champions of Naguib Mahfouz, a young modern novelist who, in 1988, would win the Nobel Prize for Literature.

In 1933, he received his BA in education and went on to work for the Egyptian Ministry of Education serving as an inspector for the Ministry between 1940 and 1948. From the late 1930s onwards, with his professional and personal interest in education, and his increasing despair of the social mores around him, Qutb began speaking about the moral decay of Egyptian society. This included criticism of popular songs on the radio, men and women bathing in public beaches and the demise of serious reading among the younger generation. He blamed the mass media for contributing to the deterioration of public morals and at one stage writes of his admiration for he more puritanical Wahhabi ideologies:

> Over there in the Nejd, poets who flirt with love poetry are whipped. Over here in Egypt they clap for those who guide boys and girls towards immorality (da'arah) and train them on shamelessness. God have mercy on you oh Muhammad ibn 'Abd al-Wahhab and God favor you oh 'Abd al-'Aziz ibn Sa'ud. We need only one day and one night in Egypt to whip those fools in the broadcasting service, cinema studios and in all Egyptian magazines.[14]

In the mid 1940s, Qutb's writings acquired clear political overtones. Egypt was completely independent in 1936. It was now a free kingdom but British culture and British money were everywhere. Mohammad Ma'mun El-Hudaibi (a contemporary leader of the Brotherhood) expressed the political and social situation:

> They came out of the age of imperialism with a weak social structure and a ruined economic system in which poverty, ignorance, disease, and backwardness prevailed. Consequently, the system of government became corrupt and weak. Tyrants seemed to be supported by forces of imperialism which withdrew their armies but retained their influence in various means.[15]

---

[14] For a longer account, see Musallam, *From Secularism*, 76.
[15] Muhammad M. Al-Hudaibi, *The Principles of Politics in Islam* (2nd ed.), Cairo: Islamic Inc. Publishing and Distribution, 2000, 11.

In this context, Qutb attacked the Egyptian elites who, instead of fighting the British occupation and the colonial carving up of the Middle East, only cared for their own interests. It was around this time that he also abandoned the Sa'dist Party, a breakaway faction of the Wafd named after party founder and former Prime Minister Sa'd Zaghlul, and started criticising the multiparty system. In July 1944, he was demoted to the post of inspector for primary education because of his political activities, but ten months later, he was reappointed to the General Culture Administration where he worked from 1945 to 1948. His writings shifted from literature to nationalism and political and social problems. He became increasingly concerned with wanting to offer practical Islamic solutions to the deteriorating social conditions of the country which he felt the state and intelligentsia ignored. Qutb and his colleagues wanted to 'articulate the views of the underprivileged masses who lived amid poverty and hunger in a society dominated by the big landowning ruling classes'.[16] This led to the emergence of a new journal entitled *New Thought, (al-Fikr al-Jadid)*. Under Qutb's editorship, the journal was an attempt by educated Egyptians to present alternative solutions to the problems of society. Qutb and his colleagues felt that social justice should be based on the comprehensive Islamic way of life. Islam offered a kind of social justice which was spiritually superior to that offered by the growing spread of communism. But the journal agitated the ruling classes and came to a demise in 1948, but by then, Qutb's ideas were consolidated in his major work, *Social Justice in Islam* ('Adala ijtima'iyya fi'l-Islam). In this work, Qutb argued that Islam was the only system that guarantees justice because it is based on equality and social solidarity. For Qutb, capitalism and communism were similar in that they both rest on a materialistic philosophy, and prophesied that the real battle would be between these materialistic doctrines and Islam'.[17] All other man-made systems were flawed whereas Islam was the closest to human nature or *fitra*. These ideas were similar to the ideas of the Muslim Brotherhood, the *Jama'at al-Ikhwan al-Muslimin*. Qutb had inherited from their founder, Hasan al-Banna, the idea of Islam as an 'integral' or 'total' system that controls all aspects of life and responds to all human needs. For Qutb, 'the *shari'a* is not limited to laws, but includes everything God has dictated to organise human life: creed, government, ethics, behaviour, knowledge'.[18]

[16] Adnan A. Musallam, 'Sayyid Qutb and Social Injustice, 1945–1948', *Journal of Islamic Studies*, 4:1, 1993, 52–70, 59–60.
[17] Ana Belén Soage, 'Islamism and Modernity: The Political Thought of Sayyid Qutb', *Totalitarian Movements and Political Religions*, 10:2, 2009, 189–203, 189.
[18] See Soage, 'Islamism', 192.

In November of that year, he acquired a professional scholarship to study in the United States, so as to become acquainted with the fundamentals of its educational curricula. His ideas for social reform based on Islamic law, and his criticisms of the West, had become a concern for some of this friends in the Ministry of Education. It is said that Qutb was gradually transitioning from being a fairly prominent member of the secular intellectual class in Cairo towards becoming an Islamic activist, increasingly vocal in his criticisms of Western influence and its complicity in Egyptian political affairs. His superiors hoped that a trip to the United States, the richest country in the world, would put an end to his increasing moralism and Islamist drift but in fact the exact opposite happened. He left for the USA at the age of 42, spent time in New York and Washington, DC and eventually obtained his MA from the University of Northern Colorado. Qutb was impressed by the scientific and technological advances in America but saw that these came at a cost. He wrote extensively on how hurried life was here; no-one seemed to have time to reflect on life, humanity and morality. He was troubled by American secularism and wrote scathingly about the racism, sexual permissiveness as well as the materialism he encountered. The following encapsulates the comprehensiveness of his criticisms:

> Its shaky religious convictions. Its harmful social, economic and ethical condition. Its notions of the Trinity, sin and sacrifice, which do not convince the mind nor the conscience. Its capitalism, with its monopolies, its usury and its ugly sombreness. Its selfish individualism, which lacks solidarity except when forced by law. Its materialist, trifling and dry conception of life. Its beastly freedom, which they call 'the mingling of the sexes'. Its white slavery, which they refer to as 'the emancipation of women'. Its stupid, clumsy, aberrant and unrealistic marriage and divorce laws. Its harsh and evil racial segregation.[19]

But as Belen writes, this move backfired, for Qutb viewed his stay in America 'through the lens of a stark division between an embattled Islam and a West he characterized as anti-Muslim, racist, sexually promiscuous, reflexively pro-Israeli, and morally and spiritually impoverished despite its material prosperity'.[20] Saeb Dajani, a student who knew Qutb during his time in the United States and who also saw him in Jordan several times after he returned to the Middle East, writes that there was a confusion amongst

[19] Soage, 'Islamism', 90. While most biographies of Qutb mention his stay in the USA, for an in-depth study of how it affected his thinking, see John Calvert, 'The World Is an Undutiful Boy: Sayyid Qutb's American Experience', *Islam and Christian–Muslim Relations* 11:1, 2000, 87–103.
[20] Euben and Zaman, *Princeton Readings*, 130.

many Middle Easterners because they loved the United States but were 'so damn mad at it' for supporting Israel and not Palestine – many simply felt not just disappointed but betrayed by America.[21]

In his analysis of Qutb's America trip, John Calvert writes:

> it would be easy to dismiss Qutb's characterizations of American society as being simply 'cartoonish', born of a mind incapable of appreciating the nuances of culture and the continuities which bind humanity together. Yet for all of its caricatures and gross generalizations, his discourse on the United States and its inhabitants is not without a certain logic.[22]

Qutb and others had recognised the uncomfortable truth that the Western-dominated elites would not push effectively for Egypt's full inde-pendence, rather they were complicit in keeping ordinary Egyptians in a desperate condition. Following Terry Eagleton's analysis of national strug-gles, Calvert continues that people are united around symbols for their political struggles and that 'men and women engaged in such conflicts do not live by theory alone'. The negative portrayals of America and the West facilitated the political struggle Qutb was seeking.[23]

And so, returning to Egypt with his Masters degree on 23 August 1950, Qutb was given a hero's welcome by the *Ikhwan*/Muslim Brotherhood's youth wing. He worked first as an assistant inspector in the education minister's office and then in the Southern Cairo School District in October 1951, and finally, in May 1952, he moved to the Office of Technical Research and Projects. But he resigned his ministerial post just six months later in October to protest what he claimed were the non-Islamic education policies of the new revolutionary government.

In July 1952, Egypt's pro-Western government was overthrown by the nationalist Free Officers Movement headed by Gamal Abdel Nasser. The coup d'etat against the monarchic government was welcomed by Qutb and the Muslim Brotherhood who hoped that Nasser would establish an Islamic government. The Nasserites and the Muslim Brotherhood shared social welfare concerns, they advocated pan-Arabism and anti-Western outlooks, and they both enjoyed a certain popularity both in Egypt and the wider Muslim world. However, the co-operation between the Brotherhood and

[21] James L. Nolan Jr, 'From Musha to New York: Qutb Encounters American *jahiliyya*', in *What They Saw in America: Alexis de Tocqueville, Max Weber, G.K. Chesterton and Sayyid Qutb*, Cambridge: Cambridge University Press, 2016, 168–9.

[22] Calvert, 'The World', 101.

[23] Calvert, 'The World', 101–2. See Terry Eagleton, *Ideology: An Introduction*, London: Verso, 1991, 190.

Free Officers which marked the revolution's success soon soured as it became clear that Nasser's secular nationalist ideology was incompatible with the Islamic agenda of the Brotherhood. For his part, Nasser began to resent their hostility and interference and in 1954, surviving an attempt on his life by a young Brother in Alexandria, he had the Muslim Brotherhood banned. Hundreds of supporters were tortured and imprisoned including Qutb who was condemned to fifteen years with hard labour. It is said that prison cemented the more militant expression of Qutb's writing. The change came not only from the effects of his own isolation and loneliness but by what he saw as the barbarism of the camp guards against the Muslim Brotherhood prisoners. Scholars refer to a particular incident at the end of May 1957 when, fearing for their lives, Muslim Brotherhood prisoners locked themselves in their cells. But 'armed soldiers broke into the cells and massacred twenty-one of them. The authorities said that they had put down a rebellion'.[24] These incidents had a profound effect on Qutb's view of political legitimacy and sovereignty. It was in prison where Qutb wrote many of his most famous and popular works. These include a thirty-volume commentary on the Qur'an, *In the Shade of the Qur'an* (*Fi Zilal al-Qur'an*), and his most controversial, Islamist writings such as *Signposts along the Road or Milestones* (*Ma'alim fi'l-tariq*).[25]

This was published in 1964, the year he was freed through the intercession of the Iraqi President, `Abd al-Salam `Azif. But after only eight months of freedom, Qutb was re-arrested, together with members of the Brotherhood and his brother and two sisters. Qutb spent most of the rest of his life in prison where his traumatic experience included further isolation and torture. The charges against all of them 'included planning an armed revolt, conspiring to kill public figures and plotting to blow up the Aswan Dam'. With these terrorism charges, Qutb was sentenced to death and executed in August 1966. As Soage writes 'The regime killed a man but inadvertently created a martyr. The next year, many saw the Arab defeat in the Six Days War as a divine punishment for Nasir's persecution of pious Muslims'.[26]

His most prolific prison work, *Milestones*, sealed Qutb's fate as a particular kind of Muslim thinker/activist in the Islamic world and later in the West. Qutb first developed the ideas for this book in dialogue with a small number of his fellow inmates, and then included them in notes that were smuggled

---

[24] Bergesen, *Sayyid Qutb*, 4.

[25] For English translation, see Sayyid Qutb, *In the Shade of the Qur'an*, trans. Adil Salahi and Ashur Shamis, Leicester, UK: The Islamic Foundation, 2003. Also, Sayyid Qutb, *Milestones Ma'alim fi'l-tariq*, New Delhi: Islamic Book Services, 2002.

[26] Soage, 'Islamism', 191.

out of jail to be read by members of his family and others close to them. These notes became the basis of *Milestones*, and began to be circulated underground in manuscript form for a couple of years before being pub-lished in Cairo where it was quickly banned. Consequently anyone caught with a copy would be charged with sedition. He wrote this book against the way he saw his own faith – a moral calling. For him, faith was compelling and it demanded action:

> Faith is not merely feelings in the heart or ideas in the mind, with no application in life, nor is faith merely rituals of worship, without action in society ... The Muslim, under the inspiration of the Islamic concept, feels personally responsible to be a witness to the universal and eternal *din* of Islam. He cannot rest, nor can his conscience be satisfied, nor does he feel that he has fully expressed his thanks to Allah Most High for His great favour in making him a Muslim, nor can he even hope to be saved from Allah's punishment here and in the Hereafter, unless he has given complete testimony to the truth of Islam through his life, effort and wealth.[27]

Thus, faith was action, a moral imperative to act and to struggle with all that one has to realise God's will. Qutb insists the Qur'an should be internalised as a lived experience, not engaged as a text for scholarly reflection only. His aim was to bring humankind back to Islam. The notion of struggle permeates Qutb's views of his faith and the Qur'an and the early Muslim community: 'What an amazing phenomenon in the history of mankind: a nation emer-ging from the text of a Book, living by it, and depending on its guidance as the prime sources!' In Qutb's eyes, it was the first generation of Muslims who moulded their lives according to the teachings of the Qur'an. As he writes, 'they led mankind in a manner unparalleled in history, either before or after ... later generations drifted away from the Qur'an ... [such that] today we see mankind in a miserable condition'.[28]

Qutb's prison writings are rooted in his conception of divine unity or *tawhid*. This has a strong political and legislative dimension and underpins Qutb's thought. The core doctrine of the oneness of God, he explains, cannot be limited to personal belief or ritual acts; it must underpin the social and political system. It is precisely this underpinning of *tawhid* which makes his writings powerful but problematic. The real meaning of 'no god but God', for Qutb, is that there is no sovereign or authority other than God. For Qutb, the

---

[27] Albert J. Bergsen, 'Qutb's core ideas' in Albert J. Bergsen (ed.), *The Sayyid Qutb Reader*, London: Routledge, 2008, 20. Sayyid Qutb, *The Islamic Concept and Its Characteristics*, Plainfield, IN: American Trust Publication, 1991, 156 & 157.

[28] Bergsen, 'Qutb's core ideas', 14. Qutb, *The Islamic Concept*, 3.

shahadah is not simply a theological creed but a political statement, a challenge to all other human authorities and forms of governance. Islam is not just a number of beliefs that our minds accept, nor a host of rituals and acts of worship, nor a worldly system which is separated from faith and worship. There can be no division between accepting God's unity and implementing the sovereignty of God.[29] From prison, Qutb proposed an Islamic alternative to the dominant political systems and ideologies of the West, such as capitalism, communism and nationalism – ideologies which have all failed to provide leadership for humankind. Belief in God is about a way of being in the personal, political and social dimensions of life.

As a mid-twentieth-century Muslim thinker, Qutb writes in an environment where Western political influence is pervasive. His prison works are set against the backdrop of the height of the Cold War, with the demise of fascism still in vivid memory. Against the prevailing political context of capitalism, communism and Islam, Qutb argued for the comprehensiveness of Islam. The religion of Islam, he writes, offers an independent and complete (*mutakamil*) system that is entirely distinct and not dependent upon any Western system or ideology.[30] He followed Hassan al-Banna's lead and argued for a direct, personal and intuitive understanding of divine revelation. Like al-Banna, he distrusted the capacity of reason to distinguish right from wrong and believed that true knowledge came only from God. From the 1950s, Qutb speaks of the rival blocs or camps of capitalism, communism and Islam.[31] The dramatic opening lines of *Milestones*, set the scene for how Qutb sees the world around him, a world desperately in need of salvation:

> Mankind today stands on the brink of a precipice, not because of the danger of complete annihilation which is hanging over its head – this being just a symptom and not the real disease – but because humanity is devoid of those values which are necessary not only for its healthy development but also for its real progress. Even the Western world realises that Western civilization is unable to present any healthy values for the guidance of mankind. It knows it does not possess anything which will satisfy its own conscience or justify its existence ... [I]t is essential for mankind to have new leadership![32]

His purpose in this book is to speak of the 'deep truths' and while his thoughts may seem 'random and disconnected' these 'thoughts are

[29] Sayyid, Qutb, *Fi zilal al-Qur'an*, 6 vols., Cairo: Dar al-Shuruq, 2004, 2/1110.
[30] Qutb. *Al-'Adala al-Ijtima'iyya fi'l-Islam*, Cairo: Dar al-Shuruq, 1993, 91–2 and 7.
[31] Qutb, *Al-'Adala*, 190, 214 & 216.   [32] Qutb. *Milestones, Ma'alim fi'l-tariq*, New Delhi: Islamic Book Services, 2002, 7.

milestones along the road, and it is the nature of signs along the road to be disconnected'.[33] The problem is that, for Qutb, 'the Muslim community vanished the moment the laws of God became suspended on earth'.[34]

In *Milestones*, Qutb recognises the 'creative genius' of Europe and its history of material invention, which according to him, has been lacking in the Islamic world, yet he sees no choice other than a revival of Islam. This is because Europe, despite its technological and material progress, no longer offers 'the life giving values which enable it to be the leader of mankind'.[35]

But Qutb also mentions the civilisations of the Islamic empire which were based on mutual cooperation and the ties of Islam:

> In this great Islamic society Arabs, Persians, Syrians, Egyptians, Moroccan, Turks, Chinese, Indians, Romans, Greeks, Indonesians, Africans were gathered together – in short, people of all nations and all races. Their various characteristics were united, and with mutual cooperation, harmony and unity they took part in the construction of the Islamic community and Islamic culture. This marvellous civilisation was not an 'Arabic civilisation' even for a single day; it was purely an 'Islamic civilisation'. It was never a nationality but always a 'community of belief'.[36]

Qutb recognises that the Muslim world is a fusion of civilisations but the Muslim community must still be returned to its original form:

> It is necessary to revive that Muslim community which is buried under the debris of manmade traditions of several generations, and which is crushed under the weight of those false laws and customs which are not even remotely related to the Islamic teachings, and which, in spite of all this, calls itself the 'world of Islam'.[37]

The nostalgia Qutb feels for what Muslims once were and what a truly Muslim polity and society could be, underpins his approach to *jahiliyya* – a term which normally refers to the state of ignorance of God in pre-Islamic Arabia – and became a central theme of his intellectual struggle. Following on from the famous Pakistani thinker and journalist, Maulana Mawdudi (1903–79), who was a pioneer in politicising Islamic thought, Qutb is also of the view that the *jahiliyya* is not specific period in time but a state that repeats itself every time humankind deviates from Islam. Qutb's concept of *jahiliyya* is a defining feature of his prison works and he has been called the 'exponent

[33] Qutb, *Milestones*, 13.   [34] Qutb, *Milestones*, 9.   [35] Qutb, *Milestones*, 9.
[36] Qutb, *Milestones*, 52.   [37] Qutb, *Milestones*, 9.

of *jahiliyya par excellence*.[38] For Qutb, the Western idea of a separation of institutional spheres leaving Caesar's sovereignty to Caesar and God's sovereignty to God, was a challenge to obeying God: *jahiliyya* is essentially a rebellion against divine sovereignty on earth.

While the word has been used in several ways in the Islamic thought, for Qutb, *jahiliyya* denotes a bleakness of the human condition, a state of being when the laws of God are suspended on earth. Qutb mentions *jahiliyya* numerous times but his thinking is essentially Manichaean – there are only two types of society: Islam, or *jahiliyya*.

> Islam knows only two kinds of societies, the Islamic and the *jahili*. The Islamic society is that which follows Islam in belief and ways of worship, in law and organisation, in morals and manners. The *jahili* society is that which does not follow Islam and in which neither the Islamic belief and concepts, nor Islamic values or standards, Islamic laws and regulations, or Islamic morals and manners are cared for.[39]

Qutb's zeal in constructing an Islam versus *jahiliyya* debate pervades his work:

> The requirement of Islamic belief is that it takes shape in living souls, in an active organisation, and in a viable community. It should take the form of a movement struggling against the *jahili* environment while also trying to remove the influences of *jahili* society in its followers.
>
> The function of the Divine system which is given to us – we, who are the callers to Islam – is to provide a certain style of thinking, purified from all those *jahili* styles and ways of thinking which are current in the world and which have poisoned our culture by depriving us of our mind.[40]

For Qutb, the purpose of Islam is to rid humankind of its servitude to other human beings and this meant that sovereignty (*hakimiyya*) belonged to God alone. While classical exegetes looked at divine sovereignty as God being the source of all things, Qutb went in a particular direction where divine sovereignty is clearly conceived on political and legislative terms. Thus, he rejects all man-made systems of governance; human sovereignty is, by definition, illegitimate. As Andrew March has argued, 'For Qutb, the most damaging legacy of Western imperialism for Muslims was that Islam had been relegated to a purely spiritual doctrine and deprived of jurisdiction over

---

[38] Giles Kepel, *Muslim Extremism in Egypt: The Prophet and the Pharoah* (2nd ed.), Berkeley: University of California Press, 2003, 46. See also Sayyed Khatab, *The Political Thought of Sayyid Qutb; The Theory of Jahiliyya*, London: Routledge, 2005.
[39] Qutb, *Milestones*, 101.   [40] Qutb, *Milestones*, 41 and 43.

all realms of this worldly life'.[41] There is no divide between the spiritual and the worldly.

The whole trajectory of thought for the *Ikhwan* was both anti-colonialist powers but also against the internal and political corruption of the Egyptian state. In his analysis of the *Ikhwan's* resentment of their political situation, William Guggenberger argues that their resentment arose also from the deeper sense of a spiritual and moral malaise, similar to that of the Catholic Church.

> After the dissolution of the Caliphate in 1924, many Muslims found themselves in a state of uncertainty. The question of to what extent society should be shaped according to Muslim standards had to be answered anew. This was a situation similar to that of the Catholic Church, after the loss of temporal power by the eradication of the Papal States and the collapse of the Holy Roman Empire. The Second Vatican Council found a new position for the Catholic Church, at least on a theoretical level, even if there are many practical questions still unresolved. However, this theoretical answer was arrived at only after more than a century of consideration and conflict.[42]

For Qutb, Islam was the answer, for he claimed its creed 'while concise, included the whole of life'. In *Milestones*, Qutb traces what he sees as the injustices of society during the time of Muhammad's call to prophecy. For him, this was a time when

> a small group monopolized all wealth and commerce, which increased through usury. The great majority of people were poor and hungry. The wealthy were also regarded as noble and distinguished, and the common people were not only deprived of wealth but also of dignity and honour.

Islam and the Prophetic call were a movement and struggle against this social injustice. Qutb's criticism of both his contemporary society and the injustices of seventh century Arabia both needed an awakening, which essentially meant abandoning *jahiliyya*. Again, Guggenberger likens this call to a religious awakening in the words of Pope Leo XIII and Catholic Social Teaching. Society cannot progress on economics and technology alone but needs a spiritual dimension to social problems:

> Even prosperous societies may be retarded to some degree if they lack a spiritual dimension. The result of this kind of partial development is the

---

[41] Andrew March, 'Taking People as They Are: Islam as a "Realistic Utopia" in the Political Theory of Sayyid Qutb', *The American Political Science Review*, 104:1, 2010, 189–207, 194.

[42] Wilhelm Guggenberger, 'Muslim Brotherhood, Social Justice and Resentment' in M. Kirwan and A. Achtar (eds.), *Mimetic Theory and Islam*, Cham: Palgrave Macmillan, 2019, 155.

continuance of injustice and social to imbalance, which leads to conflict and violence. To overcome this urgent state of affairs, humanity has to accept an authority which transcends immanent powers. Qutb and Catholic Social Teaching both formulate such an approach, which is in complete contrast to socialist and capitalist concepts.[43]

But it worth remembering that while many revivalists and activists spoke of Islam as a solution to what they saw as an oppressed society, there was no specific Islamic system which could be put in place. As John Calvert says, 'The attention of the jurists had focused on the affairs of the community (*umma*), not the state (*dawla*), which they conceived strictly as a custodial agent for the implementation of the Sharia. The chief duty of government was simply to allow the Muslim to lead a proper Muslim life'.[44] Furthermore, while Qutb spoke consistently of the Islamic way (*minhaj Islami*), exactly how believers act towards achieving practical ends is never demonstrated. As Shahrough Akhavi explains, Qutb writes about religion being a practical answer in the lives of Muslims, but 'he is forced simply to assert in ad hoc fashion that they act. We never see Qutb problematizing human action. It is within the bounds of his theory, elided'. Rather,

> Qutb's thought is thoroughly suffused with reifications. It is not Muslims who act in his worldview. Instead, he holds that 'Islam' believes, 'Islam' maintains, 'Islam' establishes, 'Islam' generates – in a word, that 'Islam' is the actor. Human agency is assumed somehow to operate, but in fact, his theory cannot accommodate human agency.[45]

And yet, it is in denouncing the whole of society around him that Qutb and his supporters are both radical and ordinary. But radical should not be interpreted as extreme or militant, as is so often the case in contemporary popular political use; rather radical connotes an idealisation. For while Qutb's ideas, like those of many revivalists, may seem revolutionary in their call for *shari'a* and social piety, these ideas are in essence quite prevalent amongst many Muslim societies for whom a particular understanding of *shari'a* informs the fundamentals of Islam and their piety. It is not radical but rather normative for many to project the ideal Muslim community back on to the early period of Islam. Many charismatic leaders or ideologues, as they

[43] Guggenberger, 'Muslim Brotherhood', 156.
[44] John Calvert, *Sayyid Qutb and the Origins of Radical Islamism*, New York: Oxford University Press, 2013, 135.
[45] Shahrough Akhavi, 'Syed Qutb' in John L. Esposito and Emad El-Din Shahin (eds.), *The Oxford Handbook of Islam and Politics*, New York: Oxford University Press, 2013, 164.

are often called, manage to rhetorically capture what ordinary communities understand as the desired goal of their faith. As Soage writes:

> Like all Islamist authors before and after him, Qutb's utopia was the state established by Muhammad and continued by his immediate followers, the 'Rightly-Guided Caliphs', in seventh-century Medina. He offered an extremely idealised picture of that first Islamic state, supposedly created by God to save men from their misfortunes and their corruption and show them the model to follow.[46]

Where Qutb differs is that in his eyes there no longer remained a Muslim community. Indeed, Muslims no longer live out the divine law he thought necessary for the flourishing of social justice and divine purpose. So integral for Qutb is the belief in God as divine ruler and lawgiver, that even if you were complying with God's law but you did not acknowledge the divine source, you could not enforce that law. God's kingdom was the essential Islamic state where people acknowledged God's sovereignty in all matters. Qutb saw Islam and Islamic law as the 'natural religion' (*din al-fitra*) and one which most aligned itself to human nature (*fitra*). For Qutb, it is both natural and rational for humans to obey God because divine law is perfectly suited to the needs, desires and inclinations of human beings. As March explains, 'a variation on this claim is that humans have an innate moral sense prior to an encounter with revelation that is congruent with the teachings of revelation, as well as a device for interpreting it'. Qutb's views reside in aligning Islamic law and human morality and while these points of doctrine have a long theological history, they are 'particularly ubiquitous across the ideological and political spectrum of modern Islamist writings on the suitability of Islamic law for all times and places, despite Islam's apparent setbacks since the rise of colonialism and postcolonial imperialism'.[47]

Therefore, in his writings, he returns to a past which is highly mythologised, where governance was in the hands of the Prophet and his companions, and where there was no conflict between civil and religious law. The fundamental problem however was that Qutb's understanding of *jahiliyya* was a mixture of many things, not just the godless Western science, the various legacies of Greek philosophy, Judaism and Christianity or the moral and social depravity of Western influence. In his analysis of *jahiliyya*, William Shepard summarises both earlier definitions as well as Qutb's own unique view:

> The sense of *jahiliyya* as the definitional opposite of Islam, as a transhistorical reality, and as a reality found among Muslims, he appears to

---

[46] Soage, 'Islamism', 196.   [47] March, 'Taking People', 189.

have gotten from Nadwi and Mawdudi in the early 1950s. The strong sense of dichotomy between truth and falsehood, good and evil is present in his early Islamist writings – indeed, even before – but is not usually attached to the idea of *jahiliyya*. Only in the latest writings, published in 1964 or after ... do we find the shift of focus from the moral to the theological, the extreme dichotomizing which excludes any mixture of Islam and *jahiliyya*, and the idea that *jahiliyya* has become so omnipresent that Islam no longer 'exists'. It is also only in these writings that *jahiliyya* becomes a central category of Qutb's thinking, a forceful symbol that pulls the various strands of this thinking together. These are precisely the novel elements in his theory.[48]

In the first few pages of *Milestones*, Qutb writes that he has written this book for a vanguard whose purpose it is to revive Islam and who with this determination 'keeps walking on the path, marching through the vast ocean of *jahiliyya* which has encompassed the entire world'.[49] The only way to realise divine law and rule is through struggle in the path of God or *jihad*. For Qutb, *jihad* is simply a name 'for striving to make this system of life [Islam] dominant in the world'.[50] *Jihad* is about a witness to faith, manifesting Islam, and a political tool only in releasing humankind from servitude to other human beings. And in this system, matters of belief will be left to the 'individual conscience'. His reasoning is that the purpose of *jihad* is to be a movement to establish divine sovereignty, a movement to restore a particular political system, but it is not about 'imposing belief on people's hearts'. As he writes:

> Islam does not force people to accept its belief, but it wants to provide a free environment in which they will have the choice of beliefs. What it wants is to abolish those oppressive political systems under which people are pre-vented from expressing their freedom to choose whatever beliefs they want, and after that, it gives them complete freedom to decide whether they will accept Islam or not.[51]

Throughout different Islamic civilisations, *jihad* has remained a contested concept, almost always on some spectrum of personal struggle versus violent struggle. For Qutb, *jihad* is not a temporary 'defensive movement' but rather a defence of human freedom and the Islamic system is the only one which will ensure freedom of religion.[52] And while he saw both the Torah and the

[48] William E. Shepard, 'Sayyid Qutb's Doctrine of "Jahiliyya"', *International Journal of Middle East Studies*, 35:4, 2003, 521–45, 534.
[49] Qutb, *Milestones*, 12–13.   [50] Qutb, *Milestones*, 81   [51] Qutb, *Milestones*, 59.
[52] Qutb, *Milestones*, 80–1.

gospels as 'distorted', no longer authentic books, he nevertheless felt that the concept of *jihad* lay also in the Old Testament in which 'there is much encouragement to the Jews to fight their pagan enemies in order to ensure the triumph of their faith'. While the gospels no longer carried the concept of *jihad*, this was simply distortion because in his view 'striving for God's cause, is a deal binding on everyone who believes in God'. He writes, 'But striving for God's cause does not mean rushing to fight the enemy. It is the practical translation of a principle of faith which influences the feelings, attitudes, behaviour and worship of the believers'.[53]

For Qutb and his followers, the state was neither ethically, politically nor socially Islamic and it was only the realisation of divine law and sovereignty in Islam which could deliver all the freedoms for the people living with poverty and in subjugation. But it remains unclear what he means by words such as *jihad* when Qutb speaks of the vision of his movement as 'one which does not confine itself to mere preaching to confront physical power, as it also does not use compulsion for changing the ideas of people'.[54] Qutb is not calling for active even violent resistance or civil unrest, but revolt against injustice is always implied. It seems unlikely that preaching alone could bring about the spirit of revolutionary change which he found so lacking in Nasser's regime. But Qutb seems insistent that those who speak of *jihad* by citing Qur'anic verses have distorted the Qur'anic message. As Bergesen writes of his prison writings:

> Sometimes what is clearly understood as revolutionary action is put in terms where the actor is somewhat generically 'Islam', and the opposition isn't so much Nasser, but the '*jahili* system' which could be both be a general condition of ignorance of the guidance of God or the specifics of the Egyptian government.[55]

Despite the shadow of excommunication (*takfir*) from the Muslim community, it is difficult to be precise about this concept in Qutb's works. In the editorial footnotes to a recent edition of *Ma'alim*, his Arabic biographer al-Khalidi writes:

> We need to remember that *jahiliyya* does not necessitate *kufr* ... Sayyid Qutb is often accused of declaring *takfir* over Muslims ... even though he did not think this way. (What Qutb means by *jahiliyya*) is that we simply have to purify our thoughts, cultures and sciences that all the errors of *jahiliyya* are linked to, that confuse us, and that narrow our path.[56]

---

[53] Bergesen, 'The Earth's Suffocating Expanse' in *Sayyid Qutb*, 122–3. [54] Qutb, *Milestones*, 58.
[55] Bergesen, *Sayyid Qutb*, 5. [56] See editorial footnotes in Qutb, *Ma'alim*, 37, n.1.

Yet it is this very notion of pronouncing *takfir* en masse and thereby justifying violence which has so often been associated with the legacy of Qutb. Nevertheless, it seems that this is a reductive view of *Milestones* which is purposefully ambiguous. One could argue that rather than project contemporary notions of 'radicalisation' onto this writings, this abstraction of theological and philosophical thinking is embedded within the larger re-adjustment of the Muslim world since the nineteenth century. The discourse fits 'broader webs of cultural framing that link terms and phrases to more clearly understood nationalist anti-colonial concerns'.[57] His perspectives should be understood alongside the political struggles of a diverse range of intellectual figures who found themselves caught between pan-Arabism and pan-Islamism, secular democracies or Islamic-based polity. He reflects and reinforces the grievances of all those who would see themselves as 'engaging in a permanent *jihad* on behalf of Islam and against a corrosive human arrogance inaugurated by Western powers that abetted corrupt Muslim leaders who no longer know what Islam really is'. His insistence on the undiluted supremacy of divine sovereignty is not so much a resurrection of a past historic ideal, as it is a visionary project in conversation with the phenomena of modernity such as Enlightenment philosophy, socialism and liberalism.

In addition, Qutb sees European secularity with a wider lens. He speaks of the Christian faith as being too Romanised, which resulted in the modification of Jesus's original message. He writes that 'Christianity was born in the shadow of the pagan Roman Empire. Later, when the Roman Empire adopted Christianity as the state religion, it did great violence to the teachings of Jesus, distorting them beyond recognition'.[58] Qutb surveys a steady decline in European Christianity. When the scientists clashed with the churches in the Middle Ages, the churches lost; God was no longer sovereign and Western Christianity become detached from its roots. All this meant the secularisation of knowledge and meaning. Interestingly, just a few decades later, Pope Benedict XVI spoke of Europe 'losing its soul'. His lament was for Europe's lost Christian heritage: 'Not only are we no longer Christian, we're anti-Christian; so we don't know who we are'. And despite his critique of Islam, Benedict notes that today 'Islam is capable of offering a valid spiritual basis for the life of the peoples, a basis that seems to have slipped out of the hands of old Europe, which thus notwithstanding its continued political and economic power, is increasingly viewed as a declining culture condemned to fade away'.[59]

---

[57] Bergesen, *Sayyid Qutb*, 5.   [58] Qutb, *The Islamic Concept*, 9.

[59] Russell Shorto quoting Pope Benedict in, 'The Anti-secularist: Can Pope Benedict XVI Re-Christianize Europe?' *The New York Times Magazine*, April 8, 2007.

Qutb's writings became an integral part of what is known as Islamic resurgence which draws much of its strength from the unmitigated failure of established Arab regimes to solve their pressing social, economic and political problems. His execution in 1966, for allegedly leading an underground organisation, only added a new 'martyr' to the contemporary Islamic movements in Egypt and the Muslim world. His writing and his struggle thus became the symbol of state oppression. But Qutb's appeal lies in the wider existential questions which have always challenged humankind. For Euben and Zaman, 'his appeal lies in the sense of loss and suffering, a conviction that a world defined by overwhelming confidence in human knowledge and laws has lost the capacity to answer the most profound questions of the human condition: why we are born, how we ought to live, and why we all die'.[60]

And today, as many analysts speak of the resurgence of religious faith in its more visible and even belligerent form, one senses that the real struggle for many is not the economic struggle but the struggle for truth and belief. In the West, Islam is always perceived as political Islam and political Islam has become contested as it is often aligned with a form of *jihadism*. But if a main purpose of religion is to provide a moral view of society and life, then that entails inescapable political implications. For Qutb, religious struggle was expressed as a reaction against cultural and political oppression because for him the politics of his age had to change. As Bergesen explains:

> In the West, the true spirit is that of the economic struggle: it is still capital vs. labour on a global scale. But for Qutb the struggle is between *jahiliyyah* and Islam; between the tyranny of man over man vs. the freedom of submission to God. Proletarian rule whether as socialism, or with a withered away state, as some ideal world of pure communism, is still the servitude of servants, still the tyranny of man over man, still the absence of the divine guidance in the organization of human affairs, still then, a system in need of opposition and transformation.[61]

Thus the possibility of a new theoretical foundation is seductive. Qutb is not alone in this. Wherever there is rising social and economic inequity, the politics of moral rage follows. Religion is often seen as either a refuge or a solution. As Mike Davies writes on the population explosion and the rapid growth of urban slums in third world cities, 'Everywhere the continuous accumulation of poverty undermines existential security and poses even more extraordinary challenges to the economic ingenuity of the poor'. The

---

[60] Euben and Zaman, *Princeton Readings*, 135.   [61] Bergesen, *Sayyid Qutb*, 30.

last few decades have seen a new momentum in peoples' search for meaning and dignity in their lives, a call for a new prophetic democracy and civilisational solidarity. Davies contends that religious passion occupies a social space 'analogous to that of early twentieth century socialism and anarchism' and that for the moment at least, Marx has yielded the stage to Mohammed and the Holy Ghost. If God died in the cities of the industrial revolution, he has risen again in the post-industrial cities of the developing world.[62]

Most of the twentieth-century Muslim reformers are actually modern, even though they distance themselves from what they regard as the idolatrous aspects of modernity. Their understanding of Islam is based upon the Qur'an – a Qur'an they claim to understand without the guidance of other religious authorities: a sort of *sola scriptura* principle, which Qutb had adopted in his extensive commentary *In the Shade of the Quran*. There is a sound spiritual impulse in the words and movements of many of these revivalists. For Qutb, the struggle was not temporary, it was eternal. This struggle was based on political activism as a projection of personal piety and arguably it pointed to a revolt of some kind. But whether his message was also one which extolled violence as a means of realising God's kingdom on earth, remains open to debate. For Qutb, the Kingdom of God, the sovereignty of God and the political order were one. Yet despite these structural flaws in his thinking, his idealisation and passion seem intellectual, faithful, dangerous to many and yet still naïve. Alongside all the interest in his life and legacy, for Guggenberger, Qutb 'especially in his last years in prison, seemed to have become an outstanding and exemplary believer'.[63]

In the opening paragraph to his masterful biography of Dietrich Bonhoeffer (1906–45), Charles Marsh writes that Bonhoeffer and his sister Sabine often lay awake at night trying to imagine eternity (*evikgeit*). He adds 'Sabine found the word "very long and gruesome". Dietrich found it majestic: an "awesome word", he called it'. It would seems that Bonhoeffer wanted to 'welcome death as an expected guest – he did not want to be taken by surprise'. Marsh writes that Bonhoeffer would often picture himself on his deathbed, knowing what his last words would be and 'reclining on the threshold of heaven'.[64] Death enthralled him more than it frightened him.

Dietrich Bonhoeffer (1906–45) remains one of the most famous and one of the most complex Christian theologians of the twentieth century. His leadership in the anti-Nazi Confessing Church make his works a unique source for

---

[62] Mike Davies, 'Planet of Slums', *New Left Review*, 26 March–April, 2004, 30 and 31.

[63] Guggenberger, 'Muslim Brotherhood', 156.

[64] Charles Marsh, *A Life of Dietrich Bonhoeffer, Strange Glory*, New York: A.A. Knopf, 2014, 3.

understanding the interaction of religion politics and culture during the 1930s. From the time the Nazis came to power in 1933, Bonhoeffer was involved in protests against the regime, especially its anti-Semitism, and became a leading spokesman for the Confessing Church, the centre of German Protestant resistance to the Nazi regime. His works such as *Discipleship* and the posthumously published *Letters and Papers from Prison* have become classics of Christian theological reflection. Because of his participation in the resistance against the Nazi regime and involvement in a plot to overthrow Adolf Hitler, Bonhoeffer was arrested and imprisoned in 1943 in Berlin. Following the failure of this plot, on 20 July 1944, the discovery of documents linking Bonhoeffer directly with this conspiracy led to his further interrogation and eventual execution. Hitler himself ordered him hanged in the concentration camp at Flossenberg on 9 April 1945, just a few weeks before the allied liberation of the camp. One of his brothers and two brothers-in-law were also killed, thus leaving ten fatherless children.

Stephen Plant writes 'Bonhoeffer is one of the best known theologians of the twentieth century but not often the best understood. Few theologians, of any century, are burdened by his celebrity status'.[65] Summing up why Bonhoeffer continues to be of such interest in diverse contemporary settings, Philip Kennedy sees his legacy invoked as a prescient forerunner of 'anti-apartheid struggles in South Africa; the civil rights movement in North America; late twentieth-century ecumenism; North-Atlantic Continental political theology; and Latin American liberation theology'.[66] And in his preface to the *Cambridge Companion to Dietrich Bonhoeffer*, John W.De Gruchy articulates the continuing attraction of Bonhoeffer as a thinker and theologian:

> He would also have shunned any attempt to turn theology into a trendy exercise which showed little respect for Christian tradition or which misused it in the pursuit of unfaithful 'relevance'. What attracts most of us to Bonhoeffer is precisely his endeavour to be faithful to the past and yet take risks for the future, his commitment to the gospel and yet his creativity in expressing its meaning, his passionate interest in theology and yet his love of learning in all its variety, and his being rooted in German culture while seeking to be a citizen of the world.[67]

---

[65] Stephen Plant, *Bonhoeffer*, London: Continuum, 2004,ix.

[66] Philip Kennedy, 'Review of *The Cambridge Companion to Dietrich Bonhoeffer*, edited by John W.De Gruchy', Cambridge: Cambridge University Press, 1999, in *Journal of Ecclesiastical History*, 52:1, 2001, 168–9.

[67] John W.De Gruchy (ed.), *The Cambridge Companion to Dietrich Bonhoeffer*, Cambridge: Cambridge University Press, 1999, online 2006, xviii–xix.

For several decades, the magnum opus of the life of Bonhoeffer has been the classic biography by his closest friend Eberhard Bethge, *Dietrich Bonhoeffer: Theologian, Man for His Times*. Indisputably, this account of Bonhoeffer's life still reigns supreme as the foundation for various biographical sketches of his life and is used for the following bibliographical material.

Dietrich and his twin sister Sabine Bonhoeffer were born on 4 February 1904, in Breslau, which became the Polish city of Wroclau after 1945. The family roots however were not in Breslau but in Swabia and Prussia. Bonhoeffer was the sixth of eight children and came from an upper-middle-class family that embodied the best traditions of German bourgeoisie. His father Karl Bonhoeffer was a psychiatrist at a time when psychiatry had only just started to become a required department in medical schools. The family moved to Berlin in 1912 when Karl Bonhoeffer became professor of psychiatry at the University of Berlin. In fact, he became the leading psychiatrist and neurologist from 1912 until his death in 1948. He was a powerful influence on the children's lives. His daughter Christine writes, 'He was not the kind of father whose beard one could stroke or whom one could call by a pet name, but when he was needed he was as firm as a rock. And how he always knew what was bothering us is a mystery to me to the present day'.[68]

Bonhoeffer's mother is described by Sabine as someone with a talent for teaching, a strong personality and social gifts. The city of Berlin, with its rich cultural heritage and intellectual life became Bonhoeffer's home. Bethge writes that of all the other places that were important in his life and influenced his formation – Breslau, Tubingen, Barcelona, New York, London, or Finkenwalde – it was Berlin which remained the decisive influence:

> The imperial and republican city that slowly succumbed to Nazism; the liberal and ecclesiastical, the conservative and the cosmopolitan Berlin, with its academic and working class sectors, its concert halls and museums; the Berlin of street brawls and political plots. . . . From the beginning to the end of his career, the ideas that drew recognition and conflict developed here. In Berlin, he enjoyed all the privileges of his sphere of life, and it was there that he eventually risked life and limb for their sake.[69]

His parents enjoyed a happy relationship and by all accounts the children were raised in an intellectually liberal but disciplined and stimulating

---

[68] Eberhard Bethge, *Dietrich Bonhoeffer, A Biography: Theologian, Christian, Man for His Times*, Minneapolis: Fortress Press, 2000, 15.

[69] Bethge, *Dietrich*, 23.

environment. The rich world of his ancestors on both sides set the standards for Bonhoeffer's own life. Bethge puts it succinctly: 'He grew up in a family that derived its real education not from school, but from a deeply-rooted sense of being guardians of a great historical heritage and intellectual tradition. To Dietrich Bonhoeffer this meant learning to understand and respect the ideas and actions of earlier generations'.[70]

The family was not overtly religious and seldom attended church but they had 'their own direct relationship with the Bible and the history and traditions of the church'.[71] The family offered grace before meals, participated in evening prayers and were baptised and confirmed in the faith. Family hymn singing was a regular and popular event around the piano, reflecting as much the musical talent of the family as it did their Christian heritage. Bonhoeffer's skill at the piano, in fact, led some in his family to believe he was headed for a career in music. Later on in life at the Finkenwalde Preachers' Seminary, Johannes Goebel, a seminarian recollects, seeing Bonhoeffer play the piano. Having 'cast out the passion' of playing the piano for a greater passion (i.e. his call to the church, Goebel writes of Bonhoeffer sitting erect at the piano:

> His playing was hard, he hammered away, too loud. I do not, unfortunately remember the musical style of his improvisation, probably because it fascinated me more to witness the native human quality breaking through his personality, than to pay attention to his music. And suddenly he stopped as abruptly as he had begun.

Goebel interprets Bonhoeffer's 'short, harsh, sharp overcoming of himself in the way he broke off his playing so suddenly' as a contribution to 'sanctification' and to 'discipleship'.[72] For Goebel, it remained a precious memory.

The shaping influence of the Bonhoeffer family persisted all through the years, even during his lonely months in Tegel Prison where, as F. Burton Nelson writes, 'His prison writings are permeated by references to family life, just as his drama and fiction pictured what life was like growing up in Berlin in the early twentieth century'.[73] Recreating his family setting gave him confidence and strength in his bleakest times. Bonhoeffer's life spanned three eras in German history and two wars. The world in which he was born was very different from the one in which he died. As Plant writes, in

---

[70] Bethge, *Dietrich*, 13.   [71] Bethge, *Dietrich*, 35.

[72] Johanes Goebel, 'When He Sat Down at the Piano' in Wolf-Dieter Zimmermann and Ronald Gregor Smith (eds.), *I Knew Dietrich Bonhoeffer*, trans. by Kathe Gregor Smith, London: Collins, 1966, 125.

[73] F. Burton Nelson, 'The Life of Dietrich Bonhoeffer' in De Gruchy (ed.), *Cambridge Companion*, 26.

1906 European society was highly ordered where people knew their place. Germany before the war was a 'patchwork quilt of former states each with its own culture, institutions and polity, gathered loosely into the Empire. But beneath this brittle exterior unity, tectonic plates of social and political life were shifting'.[74] Population explosion, industrial expansion and the changes in cities and towns were storing up problems for the future.

Living in the affluent suburbs of Berlin, enjoying the family holiday home in Friedrichsbrunn in the eastern Harz Mountains prior to 1914, Bonhoeffer was very conscious of the security which his parents provided and almost uneasily aware of his sheltered life. As a student, walking with his younger sister, he once told her:

> I should like to live an unsheltered life for once. We cannot understand the others. We always have our parents to help us over every difficulty. However far away we may be from them, this gives us such a blatant security.[75]

This sense of security was shattered by the death of his second eldest brother Walter on the war front in 1918. Bonhoeffer was eight and a half years old when World War I broke out, but, in 1918, Walter volunteered as an ensign. Sabine writes that the family took him to the station and as the train started, their mother ran alongside calling out to Walter "'Its only space that separates us", and for a long time these words moved us deeply'.[76] On hearing of his death a fortnight later, his mother was broken and while she eventually recovered, this tragedy left an indelible mark on Bonhoeffer. At Bonhoeffer's confirmation, his mother gave him the Bible which Walter had received at his confirmation and Bonhoeffer used it 'throughout his life for his personal meditations and his worship'.[77] It would appear that Bonhoeffer may have always wanted to be a minister and theologian. But he expressed his decision clearly around the age of fourteen, despite critical even contemptuous comments from his older brothers.

At the age of seventeen, Bonhoeffer went to Tübingen University, as was the family tradition, Tübingen being their father's *alma mater*. Bonhoeffer's primary interest was philosophy rather than the adoption of any particular theological direction. But he was drawn to the biblical work of the seventy-one-year-old Swiss Reformed-Church professor of New Testament studies, Adolf Schlatter (1852–1938). Schlatter conveyed a sense of the 'authority' of Scripture which diverged significantly from the prevailing liberal-Protestant

---

[74] Stephen Plant, *Bonhoeffer*, London: Continuum, 2004, 15.   [75] Bethge, *Dietrich*, 20.
[76] Sabine Leibholz, 'Childhood and Home' in Zimmermann and Smith (eds.), *I Knew*, 30.
[77] Bethge, *Dietrich*, 28.

view of the Bible as a 'source-book for religious ideas' to be found 'not *in* but *behind* the text'. Martin Rumscheidt explains that it was this 'naive biblicism' for which Schlatter was often denigrated, a 'firm sense that in all decisions in matters of faith and church he was accountable to the Bible alone', which influenced the young Bonhoeffer. He writes, 'Although Bonhoeffer learnt this understanding of faith from Martin Luther, it was this Reformed professor of New Testament who implanted it in the young student to the extent that it became an essential part of Bonhoeffer's epistemology and, finally, of his whole theological existence'.[78]

He was also drawn to travel and at eighteen went to Rome with his brother Klaus who had recently passed his bar exams. While Klaus was fascinated by classical antiquity and sense of adventure, Bonhoeffer 'succumbed to the spell of Catholic Rome, and found it difficult to tear himself away from St. Peters'.[79] The Roman expression of the universality of the church, the *ecclesia* and its liturgy had a huge impact on Bonhoeffer and influenced his thinking about dogmatics. For Bonhoeffer the meaning of 'church' had been forgotten. In July 1928, as a curate in Barcelona, he preached a sermon in which he said that when a Catholic hears the word 'church' it 'kindles all his feelings of love and bliss; it stirs the depth of his religious sensibility, from dread and awe of the Last Judgment to the sweetness of God's presence'. But when a Protestant hears this word, 'it has the sound of something infinitely commonplace, more or less indifferent and superfluous, that does not make their hearts beat faster; which they associate with a sense of boredom'.[80] In 1927, Bonhoeffer organised regular discussion groups for a group of Grunewald schoolboys. While still filled by his Rome experience, he questioned whether the Catholic world has really remained the church of Christ? He outlined the Protestant position to his pupils that while Catholics and Protestants make the same profession of faith, and share a number of practices, 'we do not want anything to be taken from us that we know to be the word of God. We are not concerned with the terms Catholic or Protestant, but with the word of God'.[81]

In their search for adventure, the brothers also travelled to Sicily and, unbeknownst to their parents, crossed the Mediterranean into Tripoli and the Libyan desert. Only towards the end of the African episode does Bonhoeffer write of his first encounter with the Muslim world:

[78] Martin Rumscheidt, 'The Formation of Bonhoeffer's Theology' in De Gruchy (ed.), *Cambridge Companion*, 52.

[79] Bethge, *Dietrich*, 57. Bethge writes that the diary does not give any details about where Bonhoeffer studied or worked in Rome (i.e. whether it was the German college, the Gregorian library or the state university).

[80] Bethge, *Dietrich*, 63.   [81] Bethge, *Dietrich*, 64–5.

In Islam everyday life and religion are not kept separate, as they are in the whole of the church including the Catholic church. With us one goes to church and when one comes back an entirely different kind of life begins again. . . . Islamic and Jewish piety must naturally be marked religions of law, when the national and ritual elements are so intermingled or actually identical.[82]

After his travels, Bonhoeffer returned to Berlin in 1924 to continue with his formal education. Bethge describes the atmosphere and legacy of the founders succinctly:

Berlin University was just over one hundred years old, but the influence of its theological faculty was worldwide. The influence of Schleiermacher, was as great as that of Adolf von Harnack, its controversial director in Bonhoeffer's day. When Bonhoeffer began his studies in 1924 the faculty's reputation was considerable. Of its great teachers, only Ernst Troeltsch was no longer there.[83]

Stephen Plant however writes that the discipline of theology was undergoing a 'crisis of its own arising from war and political bedlam'. Taking Karl Barth's 1919 commentary on Paul's letter to the Romans and his lecture at Tambach, Germany, on 'The Christian's Place in Society', Plant sees these two events as marking a new theological movement that would dominate Western theology in the twentieth century. Barth was not only shocked at the way leading German academic theologians had supported the war but also stood against the prevailing liberal scholarship of the time. The most distinguished member of the Berlin faculty was undoubtedly Adolf von Harnack (1851-1930), under whom Bonhoeffer studied over three terms.

The work of Adolf von Harnack is characterised as 'liberal theology at its height'. The term 'liberal' [when applied to theology] was a theology under the imperative of freedom: freedom of thought and the pursuit of truth on every path it took. . . . In theological terminology, liberal theology assumes the existence of a perfectly symmetrical relation between faith and what faith claims to be its subject or object'.[84]

For Rumscheidt, 'Liberal theology wanted to become a theology of the church, a church, however, which had also chosen to be a church in relation to modernity. The primary addressee was the cultured individual of modern times'.[85] Jesus's gospel of the kingdom of God was not directed to the church or any community, but to the individual: 'The kingdom of God comes by

[82] Bethge, *Dietrich*, 58–9.   [83] Bethge, *Dietrich*, 66.   [84] Rumscheidt, 'The Formation', 54.
[85] Rumscheidt, 'The Formation', 55.

coming to the individual, by entering into his soul and laying hold of it. True, the kingdom of God is the rule of God, but it is the rule of the holy God in the hearts of individuals'.[86]

For Barth, the Bible was not merely religious history but 'a witness to the Bible writers' encounter with a living God'.[87] Jesus Christ is the source of all theological knowledge, the one in whom God is both revealed and reconciled to humanity. As Paul Nimmo encapsulates, for Barth, human striving had lost all meaning and there was no human possibility of knowledge of God. Instead, 'Christian faith is a divine possibility, arising in an encounter with divine revelation, and theology exists only as human reflection upon that divine revelation'.[88] Christian doctrine had to be conclusively the doctrine of Jesus Christ where the essential task was to save the church from absorption into the culture in which it found itself.

Barth found the theology of the day inadequate for the service of the evils of a war he considered unjust and a war to which the churches had acquiesced in their inattentiveness to the gospel. Hegel had spoken of the history of the development of religious consciousness as an ascending and progressing series of divine revelations, the highest and ultimate of which is Christianity. The kingdom that Jesus came to teach is founded on a belief in the unity of the divine and the human. It is only because humans are spirit that they can grasp and comprehend the Spirit of God. For Barth, the Hegelian notion of Universal Reason culminating in Christianity eroded the very foundation of Christian theology:

> Indeed the history of the church had become the history of the Christian religion; the history of doctrine the history of the formation of religious ideas; the study of the Bible the history of literature and biblical theology the history of Israelite-Jewish or Christian religion. It was an enormous movement, interwoven with the general history of culture and the mind, subject to the unending, relativizing flow of becoming and ending, with no absolute value.

Barth's aim in his 'dialectical theology' 'was to make the message of the Holy God revealed in Jesus Christ the sole centre of Christian proclamation, in contrast to contemporary historical–relativistic, conservative–orthodox and pietistic–romantic understandings of the Bible'. One had to take seriously God and the reality of Christ. As Rumscheidt writes, 'This meant a decisive no! to all the forms of secular or sacral deification of the created that had

---

[86] Adolf von Harnack, *What Is Christianity*, London: Williams and Norgate, 1912, 57–8.
[87] Plant, *Bonhoeffer*, 18.
[88] Paul T. Nimmo, *Barth: A Guide for the Perplexed*, London: Bloomsbury T&T Clark, 2017, 7.

spread like a corrosive poison in empirical Christianity and its theological eudaemonism of culture and experience'.[89]

While influenced by Barth's critique of liberal theology, Bonhoeffer nevertheless completed his dissertation at the age of twenty-one under Reinhold Seeberg's tutelage. At times critical of Seeberg, Bonhoeffer did however learn from him how to make the Christian faith more concrete and appreciated his teaching that people exist in sociality. From Seeberg, he obtained an even deeper insight into nineteenth-century Protestant theology than he had in Tübingen and became acquainted with Hegel and his views on the nature of God's reconciliation with the world. According to Rumscheidt, Bonhoeffer took one concept in particular from Hegel's vocabulary, 'Christ existing in community', an adaptation of Hegel's 'God existing in community'. Seeberg had asserted in his 1924 *Dogmatics*: as the logos became flesh in Jesus, so the Holy Spirit becomes flesh in the community of Jesus Christ.[90] He spoke of Jesus as 'the inaugurator of a new humanity, the identification of Jesus and the community of the church'. Bonhoeffer was beginning to understand the concept of the church as community or congregation (*Gemeinde*). The question for him now was how the church is to be located theologically in the search for knowledge of God and the self. The Berlin Church historian Karl Holl (1866–1926) who was seen as one of the foremost interpreters of Luther at the time, had also joined the faculty as Harnack's colleague. Holl's Luther essays spoke strongly to a generation living with the ravages of World War I. Bonhoeffer disagreed with Holl's understanding of Luther's teaching as a 'religion of conscience' rooted in the uniqueness of Jesus. But Holl had implanted in Bonhoeffer, the 'doctrine of the *sola gratia* as the *articulus stantis et cadentis ecclesiae* [the place on which the church stands or falls], that [Bonhoeffer] never lost it again. He convinced him that even the devout are not able really to love God'. The challenge which Holl posed was 'how is the question of the church that exists today to be raised on the basis of the truth taught by the Reformation? A theological movement which drew its strength from the language of the past could no more help here and now than in the sixteenth century'.[91]

His dissertation, later published in 1930 as *The Communion of Saints*, (*Sanctorum Communio*), and his description of the church as 'Christ existing as community' proved to be formative for his subsequent theological perspectives. It would appear that until then, no one had attempted to relate

[89] Rumscheidt, 'The Formation',62.
[90] C. Gremmels and H. Pfeiffer, *Theologie und Biographie: Zum Beispiel Dietrich Bonhoeffers*, Munich: Chr. Kaiser Verlag, 1983, 32.
[91] Rumscheidt, 'The Formation', 57.

systematic theology to sociology. For Bonhoeffer, true community is composed of individuals participating in mutual ethical relationships. The 'theology of sociality' which characterises this early work was developed further in
his *Habilitation* published in 1931 as *Act and Being*, both works which,
according to John W. De Gruchy, have been neglected by those who have
been interested in Bonhoeffer's role in the Church Struggle or his theology in
prison. De Gruchy writes that his dissertation is 'an unprecedented attempt to
integrate theology and sociological theory in the development of an ecclesiology grounded in revelation yet rooted in reality'.[92] The climactic declaration
that 'Christ exists as church-community' (*Christus als Gemeinde existierend*),
reveals both an early interest in ecclesiology and also how Bonhoeffer's
theology was grounded in a social understanding of human existence interpreted in the light of God's revelation in Jesus Christ. As De Gruchy explains,
'Christ is undeniably *pro me*, yet this existential relationship is always located
within a broader framework, for my identity as a human person is inseparable
from "the other", and especially the ethical demands which "the other" makes
upon me'.[93] Clifford Green writes that for Bonhoeffer 'articulating a Christian
understanding of human sociality is an inner-theological task. What "person"
and "community" mean is a question of theological anthropology'. Thus,
a Christian concept of person could not be separate from Christian beliefs
about community. A theological focus on human sociality naturally entails
attention to the Christian community, the church; that is, being Christian is
life-in-church-community.[94] The church is established and real in Christ, the
social form of revelation, coming from God's action and presence. As Green
writes, 'the Christian church-community does not emerge from the
Volksgemeinschaft – it is a *Christusgemeinschaft*. It is not a community of
blood, but a community of water; it is constituted by baptism, not by race'.[95]
Yet Bonhoeffer's struggle was that the meaning of church could not be taken
for granted in Germany in the 1930s. The church had to be traced back to
Christology and Christology could not be complete without an ecclesiology:
'There the dispute over the meaning of 'church' was not confined to books and
journals; it was a political church struggle (*Kirchenkampf*) between the
Confessing Church and the majority "church" (*Reichskirche*) which tolerated
or, worse, enthusiastically supported National Socialism'.[96]

---

[92] John W. De Gruchy, 'Bonhoeffer' in Gareth Jones (ed.), *The Blackwell Companion to Modern
Theology*, Oxford: Blackwell Publishing, 2004, 358.

[93] De Gruchy, 'Bonhoeffer', 362.

[94] Clifford Green, 'Human Sociality and Christian Community' in de Gruchy (ed.), *Cambridge
Companion*, 114.

[95] Green, 'Human Sociality', 122.   [96] Green, 'Human Sociality', 114.

Franz Hildebrant, a professor and friend of Bonhoeffer since their student days at Berlin, speaks of their meeting at Reinhold's Seeberg's seminar:

> Having talked theology with him (and indeed not only theology) meant that one could never talk like that again to anyone else again, since he went . . . I did not know how many years, how many dimensions he was ahead of our generation . . . while we naively thought that all was more or less well with Church and state in the Weimar Republic, he had no illusions about the impending doom. The one thing that mattered in politics, while voting was still free, was to stem the Nazi tide; and when the worst had happened in 1933, Dietrich was ready for it.[97]

In 1928, Bonhoeffer served his initial pastoral ministry as a curate in a German-language United Protestant congregation in Barcelona and, in the autumn of 1930, he arrived at New York's Union Theological seminary for a year of post-doctoral studies. It would appear that Bonhoeffer was overwhelmed by the culture, poverty and racial segregation he witnessed in America. Union's reputation was at its height at the time and it was a favourite seminary for visitors from Europe who knew of its ecumenical ambitions. It was at Union where Bonhoeffer met and studied under Reinhold Niebuhr (1892–1971), the son of a Lutheran minister and one of the few faculty at Union for whom theology should be more concerned with a response to the contemporary social situation than doctrines. Bonhoeffer and Niebuhr became friends and corresponded until his imprisonment. When Bonhoeffer was to travel to America for a second time after the outbreak of war, Niebuhr writes of Bonhoeffer's sense of regret in coming to America and the remarkable spirit of his life. Even then, despite his admiration for his friend and now colleague, Bonhoeffer felt that while American theology had improved, even Niebuhr's work lacked an adequate Christology. He wrote:

> In American theology, Christianity is still essentially religion and ethics. But because of this, the person and work of Jesus Christ must, for theology, sink into the background and in the long run remain misunderstood, because it is not recognized as the sole ground of radical judgment and radical forgiveness.'[98]

Christian ethics, whether personal or social, should not be seen as a separate discipline, and it was alien to his way of doing theology in which one confessed Christ in the midst of the world. He faced a grave choice as he

---

[97] Franz Hildebrandt, 'An Oasis of Freedom' in Zimmermann and Smith (eds.), *I Knew*, 38.
[98] Dietrich Bonhoeffer, *Ethics*, New York: Macmillan, 1965, 115.

reflected on his country and his coreligionists. His dilemma was, 'The Christians of Germany would have to make a decision between wanting the victory of their nation, and the death of a Christian civilisation, or the defeat of their nation and the survival of a Christian civilisation'.[99] He could not stay in America when his fellow Christians were faced with such a momentous issue.

His experiences of Black churches, especially the Black Abyssinian Baptist church in Harlem, were very positive. And his friendship with Albert E. Fisher, an African American fellow student, helped him gain a more intimate knowledge of Harlem life. But Bonhoeffer noted with dismay the level of discrimination and racism in American society. When he wrote about this to his brother Karl-Friedrich, the latter replied from Frankfurt that this racial discrimination really was a problem 'for people with a conscience' and 'it seems impossible to see the right way to tackle the problem'. But Karl-Friedrich would not know the legacy that would one day be part of his own country when he wrote, 'In any case, our Jewish question is a joke by comparison: there won't be many people who claim they are oppressed here. At any rate, not in Frankfurt.'[100] Bonhoeffer's experience in America was mixed but he did not hide his disappointment at the theological atmosphere at Union:

> The theological atmosphere of the Union Theological Seminary is accelerating the process of the secularisation of Christianity in America … A seminary in which it can come about that a large number of students laugh out loud in a public lecture at the quoting of a passage from Luther's *De Servo Arbitrio* on sin and forgiveness because it seems to them to be comic has evidently completely forgotten what Christian theology by its very nature stands for.[101]

Aside from his friendship with Fisher, who asked him to speak of the sufferings of the African Americans when he returned to Germany, Bonhoeffer also became friends with a French theologian by the name of Jean Lasserre who had a deep impact on Bonhoeffer. In Lasserre, he found a man who spoke of the relationship between God's word and those who uphold it as citizens of the contemporary world and it was Lasserre who

---

[99] Reinhold Niebuhr, 'To America and Back' in Zimmermann and Smith (eds.), *I Knew*, 165.
[100] Bethge, *Dietrich*, 150.
[101] Nelson, 'Report on a Period of Study at the Union Theological Seminary in New York, 1930–31' in D. Bonhoeffer, *No Rusty Swords: Letters, Lectures and Notes, 1928–1936, Collected Works of Dietrich Bonhoeffer*', New York: Harper & Row, 1965, 91 in Nelson, 'The Life', 28.

'provided the initial impulse for Bonhoeffer's great book *Discipleship*'. As Bethge writes:

> Lasserre confronted him with an acceptance of Jesus' peace commandment that he had never encountered before. Not that Bonhoeffer immediately became a convinced pacifist – in fact he never did so – but after meeting Lasserre the question of the concrete reply to the biblical injunction of peace and of the concrete steps to be taken against warlike impulses never left him again'.[102]

Bonhoeffer's time at Union shaped his theology in several ways. His friend Paul Lehman writes of him as an 'un-German German', a man who demonstrated integrity and openness to everyone, 'utterly without obsequiousness, he was without a trace of status seeking or of pretence'. For Lehman, what Bonhoeffer demonstrated during his time at Union was the 'paradox of discipleship'. Commenting on both his aristocratic heritage and taste combined with his deep humanity and Christianity, he speculates,

> His pacifism may have been rooted in an inbred Lutheran disquiet about the anarchy to which revolutionary social change is prone. If so, it was due no less to his unwillingness to accept life in this world as a mere 'holding operation' until the triumph of the spirit in the second coming of Christ.[103]

At the age of twenty-four, Bonhoeffer was invited to join the faculty of the University of Berlin as a lecturer in systematic theology. This return marked the beginning of his academic life but also that of pastor and preacher. He felt strongly that there was more to life than academia and wanted to communicate the most profound ideas about God and the Bible to a wider audience through his preaching amongst informal student gatherings. This period was crucial to the way Bonhoeffer conveyed his own deepening commitment to the message of Scripture. Notable among the lectures were those on 'Creation and Sin', later published as *Creation and Fall* (1997), in which Bonhoeffer demonstrated his ability to interpret the Bible (in this case Genesis 1–3) in a way which spoke directly of the sinfulness of humanity to his time and context. The knowledge of good and evil at the heart of all ethics is a consequence of eating from the tree of knowledge; ethics is a symptom of loss from our original unity with God. As Plant writes, 'The ethical question "what is the right thing to do?" did not exist until the Fall because Adam and Eve simply knew and obeyed God's will for them'.[104] His lectures on 'Christology', which were subsequently reconstructed from students' notes,

---

[102] Bethge, *Dietrich*, 153.   [103] Paul Lehmann in Zimmermann and Smith (eds.), *I Knew*, 43–5.
[104] Plant, *Bonhoeffer*, 112.

became pivotal for understanding the development and shape of his theology from then on. In Bonhoeffer, the Christological foundation of Christian community is evident from the outset because for him scripture is more than just a collection of (culturally meaningful) texts. By grounding scripture in the domain of the triune God and his self-revelation, and more precisely in Jesus Christ, he is making a statement not only about the Bible but about all reality (*Wirklichkeit*). For Bonhoeffer, the presence of Christ attains its social concreteness in the Christian community. As Nadine Hamilton explains:

> In grounding the Bible within the *Wirklichkeit* of Jesus Christ, he binds together these human historical texts with the Word made flesh. More closely, he states clearly that the Bible is holy scripture, for in it God speaks just as the Spirit speaks in Jesus Christ. The Word made flesh is present and communicative precisely in these ancient texts.[105]

So despondent had been the German people after the defeat of World War I and the subsequent economic depression that the charismatic Adolf Hitler appeared to be the nation's answer to their prayer – at least to most Germans. Hitler rose in power, becoming chancellor of Germany in January 1933, and president a year and a half later. He was widely regarded as the leader or Führer who would rid Germany of the chaotic politics of the Weimar era and restore Germany's international prestige. Hitler's anti-Semitic rhetoric and actions also intensified. Bonhoeffer was appalled by the Nazi doctrine that the individual had to surrender his or her conscience to the Führer. He became involved in the early stages of the church opposition to Nazism, notably in drafting the Bethel Confession. His attention was dominated by the attempt of the Nazi 'German Christians' to take over control of the Evangelical Church (Lutheran and Reformed) and make it subservient to Nazi ideology. Though there were others who agreed with his outspoken position, noting the lack of decisiveness even in these circles made him leave Germany in October 1933, to become pastor of two small German-speaking congregations in London – one in Sydenham, the other in the East End. Despite being chided by Karl Barth for his absence from his motherland at such a politically momentous time, Bonhoeffer stayed in England. He enjoyed local church life and continued his involvement with the ecumenical movement to which he had been introduced through his friendship with George Bell, the Anglican Bishop of Chichester and chairman of the Council for Life and Work. It was in the aftermath of a conference in Fanö in Denmark when Bonhoeffer made an outspoken and uncompromising call for the churches 'to

---

[105] Nadine Hamilton, 'Dietrich Bonhoeffer and the Necessity of Kenosis for Scriptural Hermeneutics', *Scottish Journal of Theology*, 71:4, 2018, 441–59, 443.

declare together to the world God's concrete command of peace', that Bonhoeffer was co-opted to the council of Life and Work.[106] As a pastor of the Old Prussian Union in the 1930s, Bonhoeffer's participation in the ecumenical movement was significant and provocative. In 1935, he had written an essay which was published in *Evangelische Theologie*, 'The Confessing Church and the Ecumenical Movement'. The Church Struggle, he insisted, 'puts demands both on the ecumenical movement, to live up to the spirit of Fanö and so live up to its promise to be the church of Jesus Christ, and on the Confessing Church, to see the struggle as one for the very life of Christianity'.[107] As Nelson elaborates

> the struggle that was being waged for justice and truth by the Confessing Church was a vicarious struggle for the whole church of Jesus Christ. When Bonhoeffer realised by 1937 that the ecumenical leaders were not about to follow the clear counsel of the Fanö Conference, he requested that he be relieved of his task as a regional youth secretary. That decision, however, has not diminished his ongoing impact on the continuing ecumenical movement throughout the twentieth century.[108]

While he was in London, German church opposition to Nazism began to gather momentum and, in May 1934, the first Confessing Synod of the Evangelical Church was held at Barmen. As De Gruchy writes:

> This act of defiance against the official *Reichskirche* launched the Confessing Church. The Barmen Declaration, largely drafted by Barth, unequivocally affirmed the Lordship of Jesus Christ over against the ideological claims of Nazism, though it did not speak out on the 'Jewish Question'. Bonhoeffer, who was in constant contact with the situation in Germany, became an advocate of the Confessing Church within British circles and took a leading role in seeking to isolate the Nazi Christians from the ecumenical Church.[109]

At the centre of the Church Struggle in Germany was the challenge to Christians to identify with the plight of the Jews in German society. The suffering of Jews under Hitler had begun with the economic boycott of Jewish businesses with the infamous 'Aryan Clause'. This clause had the gradual effect of excluding all Jews from Germany's leading professions. Shortly after the passing of anti-Jewish legislation in April 1933, Bonhoeffer gave a controversial address on 'The Church and the Jewish Question'. Its primary thrust was to help determine a Christian response to the evolving anti-Semitic policies of the Nazi

---

[106] Keith Clements 'Ecumenical Witness for Peace' in De Gruchy (ed.), *Cambridge Companion*, 157.
[107] G. Kelly and F. B. Nelson, *A Testament to Freedom: The Essential Writings of Dietrich Bonhoeffer*, New York: Harper Collins, 1990, 140.
[108] Nelson, 'The Life', 35.   [109] De Gruchy, 'Bonhoeffer' in *Blackwell Companion*, 360.

government in which pastors of Jewish ancestry were to be immediately dismissed from their posts. Bonhoeffer was outspoken in his preaching on Jewish persecution even if his words were tempered by his Lutheran approach. The church has neither to praise nor to censure the laws of the state, but Christians had the right to accuse the state of offences against morality, for transgressing the law. While he acknowledged that the state had to deal with the Jewish question, it was also clear to him that it was necessary for the church, in the face of injustice, to take action against the state. For this reason, he insisted that Christians should pay attention to their plight while he himself assisted refugee Jews in England and encouraged others to intercede. There was to be no compromise with the Reich Church because he was convinced that Christianity and Nazism were completely incompatible. In his analysis of Bonhoeffer's pacifism, Keith Clements writes that 'it will always be asked how Bonhoeffer the conspirator can be reconciled with Bonhoeffer the pacifist'. His answer joins the threads of Bonhoeffer's Christian faith, witness to peace and ecumenical commitment, all of which were inseparable aspects of discipleship to Jesus Christ:

> The answer lies, first, in the fact that Bonhoeffer had never enjoined pacifism as an absolute requirement for all Christians. In refusing arms he was rejecting violence in an aggressive national cause, or in one's own individual interest. By the second year of the war the situation was quite different. He knew of the slaughter of countless Jews. The question was now, not that of preserving one's personal innocence in refusing to shed blood, but that of avoiding complicity in the greater guilt of allowing such genocide to continue. Secondly, the consistent thread in Bonhoeffer's pilgrimage from peace-worker to political resister lies in his ecumenism. In a time of peace threatened by war, he saw the ecumenical vocation as that of calling for peace among the nations.[110]

As Ruth Zerner writes, he was one of the first Christian theologians to sense the crucial centrality of Nazi anti-Semitism for Christian communities:

> Bonhoeffer clearly separated the Christian church's attitude towards the new political problems of Jews in general from the special problems of baptised Jews within the Christian church. Moreover he thrust the entire Jewish policy first against the backdrop of church-state relations and then against a wider historical and eschatological horizon. In neither framework are his arguments convincing or compatible with contemporary, post-Holocaust political and theological perspectives.[111]

---

[110] Clements, 'Ecumenical Witness', 158.
[111] Ruth Zerner, 'Church, State and the Jewish Question' in De Gruchy, (ed.) *Cambridge Companion*, 193.

It would be fair to conclude from some of his writings that while he rejected Nazism, he also reflected some of the anti-Jewish bias of centuries-old Christian teaching. Yet his own life story intersected with the tragic unfolding of the Nazis' growing persecution of the Jews. The Nazi legislation applied to his twin sister's husband, Gerhard Leibholz, and to his close friend and colleague, Pastor Franz Hildebrandt. Both of these men were baptised Christians of Jewish ancestry and both eventually fled to Great Britain.

Increasingly under the surveillance of the Gestapo, he was eventually forbidden to teach or preach in Berlin. He was appointed to direct a seminary, which had been established by his regional church, the Old Prussian Council of Brethren. In 1935, twenty-three pastoral candidates convened at Zingst on the beautiful coast of the Baltic Sea. A few weeks later in June they moved to an old manor house near a small rural town, Finkenwalde, near Stettin (now Szczecin in Poland), about 250 kilometres from Berlin. Finkenwalde was withdrawn from immediate involvement in the Church Struggle but it was an illegal seminary. Most of those who came to the seminary were well on their way to ordination and for six months they shared life together under the tutelage of 'Brother Bonhoeffer'. The Finkenwalde years were a particular experience for Bonhoeffer, a style of seminary entirely novel in the German Protestant tradition. It was based on a new kind of monasticism which involved sharing a common life together, unlike the traditional understanding of the parochial ministry, which for centuries had retained its individualistic character. Life comprised personal and group meditation, prayer, solitude and Bible study combined with singing and recreation, ministry and worship with the other seminarians. These years also provided the opportunity for Bonhoeffer and the seminarians to intermingle with a number of Confessing congregations. It was in the context of Finkenwalde that Bonhoeffer gave lectures on discipleship, lectures which were later published as *Nachfolge* (1937) with the popular English translation of *The Cost of Discipleship* (1949 and 1959). His other major work was *Life Together* (1939). In 1937, the Gestapo closed the seminary and many of the students were arrested and imprisoned. Perhaps the most significant event to take place during this time was his engagement to Maria von Wedemeyer, a romance which had considerable influence on Bonhoeffer's closing years.

When Bonhoeffer wrote about becoming a Christian, how reading the Bible and, in particular, the Sermon on the Mount liberated him from a sense of self-satisfaction, he realised that 'the life of a servant of Jesus Christ must belong to the church, and step by step it became clearer to me how far that must go'. He was already an activist pastor but as Haddon

Willmer writes, 'He became a Christian by submitting to God and becoming a disciple'.[112] Bonhoeffer called his book *Nachfolge* which means 'following' but Willmer explores why the English translation was called *The Cost of Discipleship*. He writes that 'Bishop George Bell began his Foreword to *The Cost Discipleship* (1958) by quoting Bonhoeffer's saying, "When Christ calls a man, he bids him come and die", thus reading the book in the memory of his final martyrdom'. Although Bonhoeffer was aware, when he wrote those words in 1937, that he might 'die a violent, shameful death, the prospect of achieving that kind of martyrdom did not inform or structure his book'. For Willmer, 'The dying to self, and of self, intrinsic to discipleship, occurred in many ways in life' and even though martyrdom and death are essential to the first chapter of the book, 'Martyrdom and death as costly suffering within discipleship do not, therefore, explain the language of cost in *The Cost of Discipleship*'.[113]

The book falls into two parts, with the first being largely an exegesis of passages from the Synoptic gospels, while in the second, Bonhoeffer turns to the Church. Bonhoeffer had been greatly influenced by Kierkegaard's study of Luther, *Der Einzelne und die Kirche: Uber Luther und den Protestantismus*, in which Kierkegaard mentions both the cheapness and costliness of faith in Luther's historical context and writings. Bonhoeffer's opening lines have an almost siren-like quality and are some of the most dramatic in modern Christian theology: 'Cheap grace is the mortal enemy of our church. Our struggle today is for costly grace'. Bonhoeffer explores the dialectic between cheap grace (*billige gnade*) and costly grace (*teure gnade*): Christian grace stands for the essence of the gospel, since it characterises the whole will, action and work of God for sinners. He saw that Luther's original sense of 'amazing, unexpected, undeserved and sufficient grace had excluded any reliance on human works for salvation and produced eventually a tradition in which God's grace was honoured in dishonourable ways'. Grace is made cheap when grace alone does everything, the world remains the same and the Christian makes no attempt to 'live an obedient life under the commandments of Jesus Christ'.[114] His famous lines defining cheap grace go to the

---

[112] Haddon Willmer, 'Costly Discipleship' in De Gruchy (ed.), *Cambridge Companion*, 173.

[113] Willmer, 'Costly', 176.

[114] Dietrich Bonhoeffer, *Discipleship, Dietrich Bonhoeffer Works*, English edition, Volume 4, (henceforth DBWE), John W. De Gruchy (ed.), Minneapolis: Fortress Press, 2003, 43 -4. This volume is part of the series of translations of the German, *Dietrich Bonhoeffer Werke* (1986–1999). Each of these definitive English translations in *DBWE* contains a very useful introduction and background. But for a helpful overview of the history of the Fortress Press project of translating and publishing Bonhoeffer's works in English, see John W. Matthews, 'The Dietrich Bonhoeffer Works English Edition,' *Word and World*, 34:4, 2014, 412–420.

heart of how he had begun to see his own life as a Christian and the whole book is framed around the one reality which matters to Bonhoeffer, which is that discipleship is commitment to Christ. For Bonhoeffer, Jesus' ethic is at its clearest in the Sermon on the Mount when we are witness to the differences between the disciple and the unbeliever. He writes, 'Cheap grace is grace without discipleship, grace without the cross, grace without the living, incarnate Jesus Christ'. In contrast, costly grace 'is the gospel which must be sought again and again . . . it is costly because it calls to discipleship; it is grace, because it calls us to follow Jesus Christ. It is costly, because it costs people their lives; it is grace because it thereby makes them live'.[115] Bonhoeffer called for real grace which cost God the death of his Son: 'Nothing can be cheap to us which is costly to God'. He writes that the 'life of God's Son was not too costly for God to give in order to make us live. God did, indeed give him up for us. Costly grace is the incarnation of God'.[116] Discipleship is the cost of grace, because it means following Jesus, breaking with the world, and being vulnerable to suffering. Bonhoeffer sees it as his duty to speak up at a time when cheap grace has made people cease to follow Christ and led to the collapse of the church; this lies at the centre of his own struggle. The extraordinary had to be done even if it led to all kinds of problems. He writes, 'we cannot deny that we no longer stand in true discipleship to Christ', and that 'Our Church's predicament is proving more and more clearly to be a question of how we are to live as Christians today'.[117]

In his analysis of the political dimensions of *Discipleship*, Willmer gives a detailed account of Bonhoeffer's rationale for his actions as a follower of Christ:

> In the end, it was discipleship which freed him from the command not to kill which inhibited resistance to Hitler – for the disciple is led by the call of Jesus Christ, who sets people free from the law for responsible action. Killing in war may be necessary to restore the authority of life, but even so, there is objective guilt for the breaking of the commandment. If this guilt is acknowledged, then the law may be hallowed even in its being broken. Acknowledging guilt involves more than churchly confession; it can be done by living before God, fully in the world, accepting that those who take the sword, even rightly, shall perish by the sword (Matthew 26:52).[118]

Bonhoeffer was ready to be responsible to God in all the complexities of his action knowing that:

---

[115] Bonhoeffer, *Discipleship, DBWE*, 4 45.   [116] Bonhoeffer, *Discipleship, DBWE*, 4 45.
[117] Bonhoeffer, *Discipleship, DBWE*, 4 55.   [118] Willmer, 'Costly', 186.

the disciple who uses force has to accept the perishing that comes upon the sword user . . . that the whole action takes place within the sphere of evil and as a playing out of evil, even though it is free and responsible action for the good, the sufferer overcomes evil finally. This victory is accomplished when the sufferer in penitence does not give an ounce of resistance to the effects of evil coming back upon himself, but accepts the truth of God's judgement in it. Evil is not overcome by virtue of the uncomplaining suffering, but by God's forgiveness of sins, which, in such circumstances, is certain but not cheap.[119]

Bonhoeffer knew what he was doing but was also aware that the disciple has to bear the sin in the realisation of forgiveness.

As the 1930s drew to a close, Bonhoeffer became increasingly disappointed and disillusioned about the Confessing Church's lack of assertiveness in the struggle against Nazism. The lowest point of the Confessing Church in 1938 coincided with the infamous *Kristallnacht* or Crystal Night on 9 November, when the Nazis 'destroyed more than seven thousand Jewish shops, burnt synagogues, desecrated Torah scrolls, murdered over ninety Jews and sent more than 20,000 to concentration camps'.[120] Scarcely any pastors or church leaders spoke out against these acts. Feelings of disillusionment deepened the following year on the occasion of Hitler's fiftieth birthday when the Minister for Church Affairs, Herr Werner, called on all pastors of the Reich to swear an oath of loyalty to Hitler. Again, it seemed that 'Neither from the leadership of the Confessing Church, nor from any other church in Germany, was there any significant resistance. Sadly, most of the Confessing Church pastors complied'.[121] Fearing that he might be drafted into Hitler's army, Bonhoeffer once again sought to travel to America at Reinhold Niebuhr's invitation to lecture. This was a short-lived four weeks' venture in 1939 as he wanted to return to Germany almost immediately. He had heard of those who had embarked on a risky, underground resistance movement to topple Hitler from power, though assassination if necessary; this included members of the wider Bonhoeffer family circle many of whom held high positions in the military and government. On his return to Germany, Bonhoeffer wanted to participate in this resistance movement.

The intellectual and emotional anguish that Bonhoeffer must have felt has been described by Willem Hooft who explains that 'It was unthinkable, and opposed to the very tradition of his Lutheran theology, that he should take up the fight against authority, and even help in a plot which aimed at abolishing that authority by force'.[122] Bonhoeffer had always fought for peace, impressed as he was by Mahatma Gandhi's approach to nonviolent peace and wishing to

---

[119] Willmer, 'Costly', 186.   [120] Nelson, 'The Life', 38.   [121] Nelson, 'The Life', 38.
[122] Willem A. Visser't Hooft, 'An Act of Penitence' in Zimmermann and Smith, *I Knew*, 193.

make a further trip to India. Yet all he had said about concrete discipleship meant that in the end, he could no longer remain in passive resistance alone. Until now, Bonhoeffer had tried to oppose the Nazis through religious action and moral persuasion. Now he signed up as a civilian member with the German Military Intelligence (*Abwehr*) which, ironically, was the centre of the conspiracy. Even though the Gestapo had suspicions, he was able to use his position to help smuggle Jews out of Germany and escape to Switzerland. It was during these years that he worked on *Ethics*, a manuscript he hoped would be his magnum opus. The work remained incomplete and was published posthumously. Bonhoeffer was arrested by the Gestapo in April 1943 on suspicion of aiding Jews to escape, and because he had 'evaded' conscription. He was placed in Tegel prison in Berlin. Here, he was condemned to isolation for a while but when it became known that he was related to the city commandant of Berlin, the attitude of the wardens changed. His star prisoner status was enhanced because, as Bethge writes, 'Bonhoeffer won the hearts some of the guards, who ended up doing everything for him, carrying out the most dangerous assignments as go-betweens on his behalf'.[123]

On 20 July 944, an assassination attempt was made on Hitler's life and while the plot failed, in October 1944, evidence came to light linking Bonhoeffer to the attempted assassination. All the conspirators implicated alongside him were arrested. After eighteen months in Tegel Prison, he was transferred in October 1944 to the Gestapo prison at Prinz-Albrecht-Strasse and his links with his family and friends ended. From February to April 1945, he was an inmate of the concentration camp in Buchenwald, then on to Regensberg and Schonberg. On 4 April 1945, the Gestapo, after relentless pursuit, had discovered secret diaries and papers which provided enough damning evidence against Bonhoeffer and Wilhelm Canaris, the head of the *Abwehr*. Hitler ordered the execution of all the conspirators and Himmler relayed the order directly to the Gestapo who coordinated the transfers. The SS transported Bonhoeffer by bus to the concentration camp at Flossenbürg in upper Bavaria. After a brief trial in the camp laundry-house by an SS court, a verdict of high treason was pronounced on Bonhoeffer and his co-partners. As Charles Marsh writes, 'No witness gave testimony, and the accused was allowed no defense counsel'. He was executed on 9 April 1945 at 6 a.m. in a small courtyard where, over the past year, more than a thousand people had been killed. This was just a few days before the camp was liberated by the Allies. In the same month, his brother Klaus and his two brothers-in-law, Hans von Dohnanyi and Rüdiger Schleicher, were also killed by a firing

---

[123] Bethge, *Dietrich*, 812.

squad. By late May 1945, Eberhard Bethge who had been released from prison, was able to confirm the prisoners' deaths and convey the news to the families.[124]

In a lecture in Göttingen on the 15 May 1957, George Bell speaks of these resistance years, the honour he felt at knowing Bonhoeffer, and his concerns about the Nazi state, the possibility of Europe making peace with Germany should Hitler and the Nazis be overthrown and the tragic failure of the Allies to make an adequate response. He writes:

> The driving force behind the Resistance movement was a moral force. I do not dispute that there were different elements in it, not all on the same level of moral and religious inspiration. But its leaders were men of high ideals, to whom Hitler and all his works were an abomination. Its finest spirit stood for a Germany purged of totalitarianism and the lust for aggression. It was of the very essence of the Resistance movement that it should aim at the building up of the national, economic and social life, both of Germany and Europe, on the fundamental principles of the Christian faith and life.[125]

At the time of Bonhoeffer's arrest in 1943, his writings, which would be collected under the title in English, *Letters and Papers from Prison*, were still scattered throughout his family.[126] The letters and other fragments had to be resurrected from all kinds of hiding places, and for the most part, carried or smuggled out of Tegel prison. The book itself was a gradual realisation once it was clear that Bonhoeffer was not going to survive. In exploring the emergence of his prison writings, Martin E. Marty quotes Bethge: 'it was only gradually that I became convinced that the fragments of his writings ought to be preserved and made available, and even more gradually that perhaps the contexts and relationships of these fragmentary works, deserved also to be recorded'.[127]

While Dietrich Bonhoeffer did not intend for his letters to be published or have a public readership, his friend and confidant Eberhard Bethge undertook this task to introduce his friend's extraordinary Christian life and work to a wider public. This volume of *DBWE* 8, is a completely fresh translation based on the enlarged and thoroughly revised critical German edition of *Widerstand und Ergebung* (*DBW* 8), first published in 1998. The English title is a translation of the German subtitle, *Briefe und Aufzeichnungen aus der*

---

[124] Marsh, *A Life*, 389–390.

[125] G. K. A. Bell, Bishop of Chichester, 'The Church and the Resistance Movement' in Zimmermann and Smith, *I Knew*, 210–11.

[126] See Marsh, *Strange*, 388–94.

[127] Martin E. Marty, *Dietrich Bonhoeffer's Letters and Papers from Prison*, Princeton: Princeton University Press, 2011, 35.

Haft. Bonhoeffer's struggle for justice and peace has been a source of inspiration to people from all backgrounds and walks of life. But the editor of this volume, John W. De Gruchy, writes that from all of his writings, 'none has contributed more to this wide ranging and global interest or to establishing Bonhoeffer's stature than his *Letters and Papers from Prison*'.[128]

This new translation contains letters from his aging parents, Karl and Paula Bonhoeffer, and from other members of Bonhoeffer's family as well as his fiancée Maria von Wedemeyer. De Gruchy explains that in the original compilation, 'Bethge modestly excluded much of his own correspondence which prevented the reader from discerning how much the letters between the two friends belong together and how much Bethge as partner in dialogue, contributed to the development of Bonhoeffer's theological explorations'. As his close friend, it is 'Bethge's role as posthumous interpreter of Bonhoeffer's prison experience and theology, which has shaped much of its reception'.[129] The letters, which are more theological in nature, are central to his prison writings but they are relatively small in number and only began towards the end of his imprisonment. The 'papers' contain a variety of writings including poetry, sermons, notes and prayers. So much of the content is about the hopes and fears of a man, a son, a friend, a fiancé and a pastor, awaiting trial with expectation and fortitude yet conscious of his own struggle as well as that of his fellow prisoners. Martin E. Marty speaks of the 'birthplace of this book' and writes 'from that cramped space designed to kill creativity and bury hope, however, there issued letters and papers that became the substance of one of the great testimonial books of the twentieth century'.[130] The letters reveal his requests for the mundane necessities of life which in prison become luxuries. His requests for certain clothes, books, as well as shoe laces and polish are often preceded or followed by the measured yet moving responses of his parents. The work is widely regarded as a classic of twentieth-century Christian literature.

Bonhoeffer writes: 'Ten years is a long time in the life of every human being'. He speaks of the gift of time and says 'time is lost when we have not lived, experienced things, learned, worked, enjoyed and suffered as human beings. Lost time is unfulfilled, empty time'.[131] Yet he himself does not feel that his own time was lost. He reflects on suffering and writes:

---

[128] Dietrich Bonhoeffer, *Letters and Papers from Prison, Dietrich Bonhoeffer Works*, English edition, Volume 8, John W. De Gruchy (ed.), Minneapolis: Fortress Press, 2010, 1. The first German edition was published in 1951 as *Widerstand und Ergebung, Resistance and Submission*.

[129] Bonhoeffer, *Letters and Papers, DBWE*, 8 7.

[130] Marty, *Dietrich Bonhoeffer's Letters and Papers from Prison*, 2.

[131] Bonhoeffer, *Letters and Papers, DBWE*, 8 37.

It is infinitely easier to suffer in community with others than in solitude. It is infinitely easier to suffer publicly and with honor than in the shadow and dishonor. It is infinitely easier to suffer through putting one's bodily life at stake than to suffer through the spirit. Christ suffered in freedom, in solitude, in the shadow, and in dishonor, in body and in spirit. Since then many Christians have suffered with him.[132]

On Easter Sunday, 25 April 1943, Bonhoeffer writes to his parents about 'celebrating a happy Easter' and says, 'What is so liberating about Good Friday and Easter is the fact that our thoughts are pulled far beyond our personal circumstances to the ultimate meaning of all life, suffering, and indeed everything that happens, and this gives us great hope'. He continues to reminisce about the joys of Easter spent with his parents.

By 5 May 1943, Bonhoeffer had been in prison for just over four weeks and in his letter to his brother-in-law Hans von Dohnanyi about what has happened to them, he writes, 'Such things come from God, and God alone . . . our response to God can only be submission, endurance, patience – and gratitude'.[133] Patience and gratitude are recurring themes in his prison writings but so understandably is the occasional sense of fear and unrest. In a letter to his parents on 15 May 1943, Bonhoeffer speaks of a particular emotion, (*anfechtung*), which 'includes the idea of being lured to act against God's will' but also connotes the sense of personal disintegration and meaningless. Bonhoeffer reflects from within his prison cell this feeling of being 'attacked from the outside':

However, I have never understood as clearly as I have here that the bible and Luther mean by 'temptation' [Anfechtung]. The peace and serenity by which one had been carried are suddenly shaken without any apparent physical or psychological reason, and the heart becomes, as Jeremiah very aptly put it, an obstinate and anxious thing that one is unable to fathom.[134]

His letters to his parents are interspersed with anecdotes about prison life, his physical and emotional health, his intellectual and theological journey and how he sought small joys during this period. On 4 June 1943, Ascension Day, Bonhoeffer speaks of this being 'a great day of joy for all those who are able to believe that Christ rules the world and our lives'. He laments causing his parents distress and speaks of how their letters make him feel:

It is as if the door of the prison cell opened for a moment, and I experienced with you a slice of life on the outside. The longing for joy in this sombre

---

[132] Bonhoeffer, *Letters and Papers, DBWE*, 8 49–50.
[133] Bonhoeffer, *Letters and Papers, DBWE*, 8 69.
[134] Bonhoeffer, *Letters and Papers, DBWE*, 8 79.

building is great. One never hears any laughter. Given what they witness, even the guards seem unable to laugh. One therefore makes the fullest use of all internal or external sources of joy.[135]

On 14 June 1943, Bonhoeffer speaks of his hopes of being free by Pentecost and despite this not happening, the need to continue being patient:

> Fritz Reuter puts it beautifully, 'No life flows so smoothly and gently that it would not at some point hit a dam and move in circles, or that people would not throw some stones in the clear water; well, mishaps happen to everyone – one just has to ensure that one's water remains clear, that it can mirror the reflection of heaven and earth – that basically says it all.'[136]

Many of the letters express gratitude for receiving letters, parcels and good wishes from his family and friends. His words juxtapose feelings of small joys and sadness as on hearing the sound of church bells and their haunting effect on him. 'All discontent, ingratitude and selfishness melt away. All at once you are surrounded by good memories, as if by benevolent spirits'.[137]

One is never far away from reading how night and darkness affect Bonhoeffer's thoughts about his own life and his family and friends. In a letter dated 5 September 1943, he realises that when thinking about those without whom 'one wouldn't want to live' one forgets about oneself. He writes, 'Only then does one sense how interwoven one's own life is with the life of other people, indeed how the center of one's own life lies outside oneself and how little on is an isolated individual.[138] Hope and despair run throughout his prison writings and in his letter dated 21 November 1943, he compares Advent to prison, 'a prison cell like this is a good analogy for Advent; one waits, hopes, does this or that – ultimately negligible things – the door is locked and can only be opened from the outside'.[139] But the reader is never far from detecting a yearning and anguish in his writing. An example of this is his letter dated 18 November 1943 to his friend Eberhard Bethge, when he laments not having access to a pastor but turning to him once again in his role as friend and pastor. Bonhoeffer speaks of the apathy and melancholy (*acedia/tristitia*) which he often feels: 'In the beginning the question also plagued me as to whether it is really the cause of Christ for whose sake I have inflicted such distress on all of you but soon enough I pushed this thought out of my head as a temptation (*anfechtung*)'.[140] As

---

[135] Bonhoeffer, *Letters and Papers*, *DBWE*, 8 97–8.
[136] Bonhoeffer, *Letters and Papers*, *DBWE*, 8 106.
[137] Bonhoeffer, *Letters and Papers*, *DBWE*, 8 113.
[138] Bonhoeffer, *Letters and Papers*, *DBWE*, 8 149.
[139] Bonhoeffer, *Letters and Papers*, *DBWE*, 8 188.
[140] Bonhoeffer, *Letters and Papers*, *DBWE*, 8 178–80.

Christmas approaches, we read a long letter dated 15 December 1943 in which he
is wondering whether he will be out for Christmas. While he mentions Maria in
many of his letters, in this letter, there is a particular frustration at having been
engaged for nearly a year but not having spent a single hour alone together:

> We have to consciously repress everything that is usually part of the
> engagement period; the sensual-erotic dimension ... month after month
> we sit next to each other for an hour as obediently as schoolchildren on
> their bench and are then torn away from each other again. We know next to
> nothing about each other.[141]

As he ponders being in prison over Christmas in December 1943, he feels that
it will be more meaningful in a prison cell than in 'places where it is
celebrated in name only'. Prison is a place of loneliness and misery but
'God turns towards the very places from which humans turn away'.[142] But
by 22 December 1943, Bonhoeffer thinks of his release in time for Christmas
and spending time with Maria and his family as a 'childish' question:

> To be sure these things matter to me very much, but I believe I could gladly
> give them up if I could do so 'in faith' and if I knew that it had to be so. 'In
> faith' I can bear everything (– I hope –), even a conviction, even the other
> dreaded consequences but an anxious outlook wears one down. ... I must
> be able to have the certainty that I am in God's hand and not in human
> hands. Then, everything will become easy, even the hardest privation.[143]

By 20 February 1944, as Bonhoeffer writes to his parents, he speaks of his 'inner
struggle', realising that his life may no longer be full but remain fragmentary
and unfinished. He writes poignantly, 'But precisely that which is fragmentary
may point to a higher fulfilment, which can no longer be achieved by human
effort. This is the only way I can think, especially when confronted with the
deaths of so many of my best former students'.[144] In many ways, he hid his
emotional anguish and his own struggle behind his profound gratitude for the
life and reflection he had. The flowers he often received, the beautiful sunlight
he comments on, the walks he could take; he wishes he could occasionally hear
a good sermon on Sundays but this was enough to keep him going.

The Christological concentration of his work which lay latent in
Sanctorum Communio and developed in his Christology lectures of 1933, is
made explicit once again in 1944 in his *Letters and Papers from Prison*. In his

---

[141] Bonhoeffer, *Letters and Papers, DBWE*, 8 221–2.
[142] Bonhoeffer, *Letters and Papers, DBWE*, 8 225.
[143] Bonhoeffer, *Letters and Papers, DBWE*, 8 235.
[144] Bonhoeffer, *Letters and Papers, DBWE*, 8 301.

famous letter of 30 April 1944 to Eberhard Bethge, he reflects, 'what keeps gnawing at me is the question, what is Christianity, or who is Christ actually for us today?' This question has been interpreted in several ways but Bethge writes that what lay behind this apparent question was how and where does one make faith real and true? His theological letters reveal the struggle he faces when thinking of the nature and purpose of Western Christianity when it seems to provoke so little reaction in the face of injustice and war. For Bonhoeffer, if this form of Christianity 'may be only a preliminary stage of a complete absence of religion', what does this mean for the church? He asks 'How can Christ become Lord of the religionless as well? Is there such a thing as a religionless Christian? If religion is only the garb in which Christianity is clothed – and this garb has looked very different in different ages – what then is religionless Christianity?'[145] Bonhoeffer's aim was not to say that the world was religionless but that people were no longer naturally inclined towards religion. While the church would have to face up to this, the church needed to live and practice the authenticity of the gospel in these changed circumstances. What was important was to think through what a Christian life meant in this world. What is the purpose of a Western form of Christianity which is gradually leading to a complete absence of religion. Reviewing the history of secularisation in the West since the Renaissance, Bonhoeffer asked whether humanity's increasing ability to cope with its problems without the hypothesis of God might not indicate the obsolescence of the 'religious premise' upon which Christianity had hitherto been based. He wanted the church to affirm man's maturity in a 'world come of age'. A preoccupation with personal salvation should be replaced by the Christian life sharing in God's sufferings in this world.

As Bethge explains, it was not his intention to try and convince the world of his thinking on this issue but 'he wanted his Church to see, in quite a new way, that there was a process of emancipation going on around her, and he wanted to enable her to grasp Christ as the Lord of this process'.[146] This was both a modest and revolutionary undertaking, but Bonhoeffer remained adamant that 'the church is church only when it is there for others'.[147]

In May 1944, Bonhoeffer, still imprisoned in Tegel, wrote his 'Thoughts on the Day of Baptism' of his great-nephew, Dietrich Bethge. It is a poignant yet curiously joyful expression of both his sadness at missing such an occasion but also his hopes for the new member of the family. It is a long reflection bringing together disparate thoughts on the contemporary situation and the

[145] Bonhoeffer, Letters and Papers, DBWE, 8 362–3.
[146] Eberhard Bethge, Bonhoeffer: Exile and Martyr, Collins: London, 1975, 140.
[147] Bonhoeffer, Letters and Papers, DBWE, 8 503.

responsibilities of a Christian life. The big cities which his generation had known and where life offered every pleasure have now 'brought death and dying upon themselves with every imaginable horror'. While parental advice had taught him to plan and shape life, Bonhoeffer laments that 'we have learned that we cannot even plan for the next day, that what we have built up is destroyed overnight'. Yet he does not wish that he lived in another age because the task of his age was to preserve one's soul and it is this preservation which is precisely the task of the newborn generation. The task of the new generation will be to 'relate thought and action in a new way' and to take responsibility. Quoting biblical verses throughout, Bonhoeffer realises that for his generation, for a greater part of their lives, 'pain was a stranger to us' and they lived in the vain hope that reason and justice would prevail influencing the course of history. But on the day of this precious baptism, he reflects on the joy and meaning of this important identity. He remarks that the great and ancient words of the Christian proclamation will be spoken over the baby without his understanding them. Yet, the church too is struggling to understand 'what it means to live in Christ and follow Christ'. All this is too difficult now and people have stopped speaking of it: 'The church has been fighting during these years only for its self preservation, as if that were an end in itself. It has become incapable of brining the word of reconciliation and redemption to humankind and to the world'.

Christians today can be Christian in two ways 'through prayer and in doing justice among human beings'. But he goes on nevertheless to speak in hope of the day when it will be possible to speak again the word of God, 'a new language, perhaps quite nonreligious language, but liberating and redeeming like Jesus's language . . . a language proclaiming that God makes peace with humankind and that God's kingdom is drawing near'. Until then, the Christian cause will be one a 'quiet and hidden one'. Till then, he prays that young Dietrich will live out his baptismal identity as one of those who prays and does justice and 'waits for God's own time'.[148]

For Bonhoeffer, the struggle which connected his inner life to the life of the church was how does one live and act in faith. This was a central question at a time when he felt 'God is being increasingly pushed out of a world come of age'.[149] In his letter of 21 July, written a day after the failed assassination attempt on Hitler's life, he explains what he means by learning to have faith where faith is not about living a saintly life or any ultimate quest for sanctity. Rather, as he writes, 'One learns to have faith by living in the full this-worldliness of this life'.

---

[148] Bonhoeffer, *Letters and Papers*, DBWE, 8 389–90.
[149] Bonhoeffer, *Letters and Papers*, DBWE, 8 450.

By this-worldliness he means 'living fully in the midst of life's tasks, questions, successes and failures, experiences and perplexities – then one takes seriously no longer one's own sufferings but rather the suffering of God in the world. Then one stays awake with Christ in Gethsamane'.[150] For Bonhoeffer, this was faith; this was how one became a human being and a Christian.

It was not long after his death that a debate about whether someone complicit in an attempt to assassinate the German Head of State could properly be designated a martyr. Peter Selby writes that 'Fifty years of knowing the evil Hitler represented should not prevent us from seeing the real force of that question'. However, he continues, Bonhoeffer has continued to 'attract admiration precisely because of, rather than despite, the recognised ambiguity of his actions'.[151] Indeed Haddon Willmer writes, 'Bonhoeffer's status in many circles as one of the few, perhaps the only, Protestant candidate for sanctity to come out of Nazi Germany, depends precisely on his willingness to incur guilt politically'.[152]

Both Bonhoeffer and Qutb were men of faith whose writings and activism left complex legacies. Their political and personal contexts were very different but each man felt called to preach and to write and most importantly to reflect on what had gone wrong with the inner life of their religious communities. The political turmoil within their respective countries forced a spiritual crisis of sorts and both men felt compelled to act even though they would have known that their words and actions might cost them their lives. They came from different religious, cultural and professional backgrounds but their controversial struggle to re-establish a faith in resistance which centred on following the commands of God seemingly makes them prime examples of the theologian-martyr.

It was in the 1940s when Qutb gravitated from a position of nationalism to one deeply engaged with the Qur'an as a potential blueprint for change. From around 1948, he seems to have turned from a cultural understanding of the role of Islam in society to one that saw in it a system that could respond to the political and economic needs of his context. Thus, while Qutb began his religious writings late in his life, the potency and urgency of his language had an impact, especially on the issue of an Islamic revival. He wrote passionately on how the Islamic world had plunged into ignorance and forgotten that it is only God's rule and law which should guide humankind towards a moral

---

[150] Bonhoeffer, *Letters and Papers*, DBWE, 8 486.
[151] Peter Selby, 'Christianity in a World Come of Age' in De Gruchy (ed.), *Cambridge Companion*,
[152] From the letter of 21 July 1944, quoted in Haddon Willmer, 'Bonhoeffer's Sanctity as a Problem for Bonhoeffer Studies', in *Celebrating Critical Awareness: Bonhoeffer and Bradford 60 Years On*, London: International Bonhoeffer Society, 1993, 10.

society. Islam was the solution to the ills of humankind but Muslims themselves no longer followed the true Islam which was God centred. In fact, much of *Milestones* is about Qutb's anger and frustration at the Muslims around him, notably when he writes that the Muslim community has been extinct for a few centuries. To enable such a restitution, it was imperative that God's sovereignty was thus put forward to indicate the exclusion of all systems of thought and government not derived from divine injunctions embodied in the Qur'an. For Qutb, Muslim societies were buried under 'the debris of man-made traditions' and he writes, 'I am aware that between the attempt at "revival" and the attainment of "leadership" there is a great distance as the Muslim community has long ago vanished from existence and from observation'.[153]

Qutb had risen to a position of relative prominence but he found himself observing an Egypt which was undergoing political change but remained socially stagnant. He felt compelled to speak on matters of social and political injustices as he began to see himself as a thinker who could be at the forefront of an Islamic revival. His *jihad* was to realise a more authentic Islam rooted in his view of God's oneness (*tawhid*), even though it's unclear how he hoped to achieve his vision beyond his political grievances. The call for a political revolution is clear but how that revolution was to realise a new Islamic dawn remains problematic. But if Bonhoeffer speaks of cheap grace, one could claim that Qutb speaks of cheap peace. He did not wish for the peace confined to the defence of Muslim lands but a call for a *jihad* where everyone should be free to submit to the will of God, away from oppressive legal systems. Nothing could be left to Caesar. Islam was the freedom of man from servitude to other men. His ideological call was that simply saying 'God is one' is not submission.

Bonhoeffer was well aware that he made his spiritual journey starting out from a position of privilege and relative stability. For all his various roles, he was pre-eminently a pastoral theologian and he retained his Lutheran heritage of Christ-centred transcendence. His orthodox Lutheranism equipped him to face the Nazi tyranny even as he became aware of his own vulnerability in the midst of this political nightmare. As Selby writes"

> His sacrifice was the loss of things he accounted good, but knew were not the supreme good, which was his understanding of and commitment to *Christ* for *us*. His surrender of life, and his call to the church to be prepared to do the same, was not the surrender of one who had hated his life, but one who had loved it.[154]

Bonhoeffer wanted discipleship, as such, which is the cost of grace; and discipleship involves suffering because it means following Jesus and breaking

---

[153] Qutb, *Milestones*, 9.   [154] Selby, 'Christianity', 242.

with the world, making oneself vulnerable to rejection by the world. As Willmer writes, 'Hitler's appeal lay partly in his command to disciples to follow'. Bonhoeffer opposed one discipleship for another but even though, for Bonhoeffer, Jesus Christ was a very different kind of Lord, it was 'a battle between Lords – not between an authoritarian conception of society and a liberal democratic one'.[155]

While the lives of both these men have captured the imagination of generations of believers, Qutb's legacy is seen as a more malign influence on Islamic thought and Muslim societies while Bonhoeffer has assumed the status of a saint for many, especially among Protestant Christians. Qutb's writings developed a binary between Islam and the West, and this seeming division is understood to be the intellectual inspiration and justification for violence in groups such as al-Qaeda. But in recent years, many who were close to him, argue that Qutb has been misunderstood. His appreciation of Qur'anic aesthetics and near mystical experiences in prison, gave a more nuanced texture to his writings than simply a call to revolt. His prison writings reveal a man who is disappointed but also angry with his government and his co-religionists. Not all revivalists were involved in an assassination attempt but the words of Wilfred Cantwell Smith reveal a particular dimension of modernist movements:

> The fundamental malaise of modern Islam is a sense that something has gone wrong with Islamic history. The fundamental problem of modern Muslims is how to rehabilitate that history, to get it going again in full vigour, so that Islamic society may once again flourish as a divinely guided society should and must. The fundamental spiritual crisis of Islam in the twentieth century stems from an awareness that something is awry between the religion which God has appointed and the historical development of the world which he controls.[156]

For Bonhoeffer, Christian ethics is also about obedience to the will of God and God demands responsible action. Bonhoeffer wanted to act as a Christian against the growing threat of Nazi ideologies. But maybe the biggest difference between the two men is that Bonhoeffer's prison letters are full of hope, not anger. They exude loyalty and joy despite flashes of sadness at his lonely and at times painful incarceration. Here is a man who wants to do right by his faith and by his country. He is also committed to peace which is intrinsic to his discipleship and to his faith in Jesus Christ. Around thirteen

---

[155] Willmer, 'Costly', 188.
[156] Wilfred Cantwell Smith, *Islam in Modern History*, New York: New American Library, 1957, 4.

years before his death, on 19 June 1932, Bonhoeffer had preached in a sermon at the Kaiser Wilhelm Memorial Church in Berlin:

> We must not be surprised if times return for our church, too, when the blood of martyrs will be called for. But this blood, if we really have the courage and fidelity to shed it, will not be so innocent and clear as that of the first witnesses. On our blood a great guilt would lie; that of the useless servant.[157]

Bonhoeffer's wrestled with his conscience but Clifford J. Green, in his analysis of Bonhoeffer's peace ethic rather than pacifism, argues that Bonhoeffer did not advocate violence despite his support for 'tyrannicide and the coup'. He writes that Bonhoeffer did not abandon his Christian peace ethic and it remained central to his theology where love of enemy is the very heart and substance of the gospel. This commitment to peace:

> 'has been overshadowed by his extraordinary, controversial, and sacrificial involvement in the conspiracy. But that unique undertaking was precisely the exception. His peace ethic has also frequently been confused by a narrow and uncritical definition of pacifism. Certainly nonviolence was Bonhoeffer's default position. But his Christian peace ethic cannot be reduced to the thin principle of nonviolence; rather it is defined by his thick commitment of faith in Christ with its manifold theological and ethical implications. The richness and boldness of that witness remains a critical challenge of Bonhoeffer's legacy to the church today in a deeply troubling time.[158]

Sayyid Qutb and Dietrich Bonhoeffer continue to be of scholarly interest and their lives and histories studied in new ways. Both men wrestled with their beliefs, and in the end, both men paid with their lives. Their faith may have taken them on different paths, but the moral question of what our faith demands from us in the face of injustices, remains as prescient as ever.

---

[157] Bethge, *Dietrich*, 236–7.
[158] Clifford J. Green, 'Pacifism and Tyrannicide: Bonhoeffer's Christian Peace Ethic', *Studies in Christian Ethics*, 2005, 31–47, 47.

4

Contemporary Islam and the Struggle for Beauty

*I*N THE PREFACE TO THE NEW EDITION OF THE SEARCH FOR BEAUTY in *Islam: A Conference of the Books*, the renowned American Muslim scholar Khaled Abou el Fadl writes:

> Today it is even more urgent and necessary that Muslims reconnect with what is beautiful in their tradition and reclaim what has been lost to the puritanical forces within their religion. It is nothing short of devastating to witness the persistence, severity, and uniformity of the ugliness that has been committed across the Muslim world. Rather than finding peace and tranquility in a shared understanding of beauty, today's Muslims find more shared commonality in bitter understandings of violence, hatred, ignorance, pain, and tragedy.[1]

Through a 'conference of the books', an imagined conference of Muslim intellects from centuries past, El Fadl speaks of the contemporary ugliness which he feels pervades the Islamic world and attempts to reclaim the moral value of beauty. El Fadl asks the question, 'What does God command other than *ihsan?* And, *ihsan* is derived from the word *hasan,* which means the good, proper, and beautiful'.[2] El Fadl is passionate about what he considers the current societal problems within the Islamic tradition which stem from an epistemological crisis. He writes that while many Muslims have been

---

[1] Khaled Abou El Fadl is a Professor at UCLA, a theorist of Islamic law and a fervent critic of the growing puritanical trends in Islam, especially the spread of Wahhabism. He is the author of several books on law and ethics but there are two works which form the primary analysis here. The first is Khaled Abou El Fadl, *The Search for Beauty in Islam: A Conference of the Books,* Lanham, MD: Rowman and Littlefield Publishers, 2005, 13 (online access). El Fadl informs the reader that the precursor to this book was a collection of essays published in 2001 under the title *The Conference of the Books: The Search for Beauty in Islam.* The second is his essay and the responses to his essay on tolerance published shortly after 9/11 in Khaled Abou El Fadl, *The Place of Tolerance in Islam,* Boston: Beacon Press, 2002.

[2] El Fadl, *The Conference,* 89.

touched by this book, for the non-Muslim, 'The Conference offered an opportunity to gain an insider's view to the struggles, problems, and pains of contemporary Muslims as well as to understand what the Islamic tradition had to offer humanity'. El Fadl sees that faith in God enables humankind to reach out for the transcendent and the beautiful and that we should seek the beautiful because God is beautiful. The need to reconnect with the beauty of Islam arises from the sense that Islamic thought and many parts of the Islamic world have been facing a cultural and political crisis over the last few decades. For El Fadl, the events of 9/11 tragically demonstrated the further importance and prescience of his book which had been written long before the events of 9/11, detailing 'the potential dangers, threats, and long-term effects of the ugliness of the puritanical Wahhabi movement upon Muslims and the world'.[3] For El Fadl, beauty is a source of hope for a better future and the challenge for contemporary Muslims is to 'discover beauty in the past that once was Islam'.[4]

The beauty which the writer refers to is not the beauty found in the arts and crafts of Islam, its architecture, literature or poetry. Rather it is about that which makes the Islamic tradition beautiful when the jurist tries to evoke the aesthetic appreciation of the good, and not just the lawful. El Fadl tries to articulate how the essential principles of Islamic law contain an inherent aesthetic sensitivity. For him, the legal and the spiritual are intertwined so that the search for knowledge and truth is also a search for beauty and reverence.

Many Muslim scholars in the broad field of Islamic Studies have written on the politico-ethical trajectory of Muslim societies and the ambiguities and challenges of definition:

> There is considerable contestation in many Muslim circles today on precisely what the 'crises' are that afflict Islam and Muslim societies, at whose doorsteps the blame for the provenance or persistence of these crises should be laid, what Islamic norms, institutions and practices need to be reformed, and on what authority such reform would take place.[5]

The debates which continue to exercise both the 'ulama and the contemporary Western scholar of Islam vary in tone and focus. But they normally weave in and out of issues of politics, gender and human rights, religious and social pluralism, authority and representation. These are just some of the topics which have been the focus of reformist ideas and internal critiques

---

[3] El Fadl, The Conference, 13.   [4] El Fadl, The Conference, 14.
[5] Muhammad Qasim Zaman, Modern Islamic Thought in a Radical Age, Cambridge: Cambridge University Press, 2012, 1.

among Muslim scholars for the last few decades. At the heart of these discussions lies the reading and interpretation of the Qur'an as fundamental to Muslim ethics. Over thirty years ago, the prominent Pakistani reformer of Islam, Fazlur Rahman (1919–88) wrote:

> The Qur'an is not a book of abstract ethics, but neither is it the legal document that Muslim lawyers have always made it out to be. It is a work of moral admonition through and through. A large part which deals with human relations (and which also includes many of the stories), is full of statements on the necessity of justice, fair play, goodness, kindness, forgiveness, guarding against moral peril and so on. It is clear that these are general directives, not specific rules.[6]

While the methodological complexities of the principles of Islamic law dominate much of contemporary scholarship, the relationship of law to ethics has also resurfaced as an urgent question and a variety of approaches to both scriptural text and human context. Rahman was of the view that the central concern of the Qur'an is the conduct of humankind. Yet, he argues, Muslim scholars have never attempted a systematic ethics of the Qur'an. For Rahman, ethics is the essence of the Qur'an linking theology and law, systematically or otherwise. He writes:

> It is true that the Qur'an tends to concretize the ethical, to clothe the general in a particular paradigm, and to translate the ethical into legal or quasi-legal commands. But it is precisely a sign of its moral fervour that it is not content only with generalizable ethical propositions but is keen on translating them into actual paradigms.[7]

In Rahman's view, Islamic law was not law in the modern sense, rather, material which could be used for modern legal systems but only some of it could actually ever be enforced in court. He explains that, from the beginning, the legal literature of Islam had a '"bookish" smell in contradistinction to the exigencies of everyday life: it is almost a theoretical effort'. This is because much of the legal literature is concerned with morality which is not 'enforceable in any court except of the human conscience'.[8] The law had to be *organically* related to morality'.[9] One could not insist on a literal interpretation of the rules of the Qur'an and ignore the social changes as this would be deliberately defeating the socio-moral message of the Qur'an. He argued that the Qur'an's message must be approached as a unity and not as

---

[6] Fazlur Rahman, 'Law and Ethics in Islam', 8.
[7] Fazlur Rahman, *Islam and Modernity*, Chicago: The University of Chicago Press, 1982, 154.
[8] Rahman, *Islam*, 29.   [9] Rahman, *Islam*, 155.

a series of isolated commands or injunctions. This must be the basis for the ethical framework rather than the atomistic and piecemeal approach of both medieval and even contemporary traditional exegesis. Rahman defines ethics as a 'theory of moral right and wrong' and stressed that a system of ethics must develop from the Qur'an. He argued for this not because Greek, Persian or any other ethical theories are necessarily 'antagonistic' to the Qur'an but because for Muslims, the Qur'an, as God's word, must be an infinite source for answers (i.e. the Qur'an must 'contain the answers potentially').[10]

Rahman claimed that if for Kant, no ideal knowledge is possible without the regulative idea of reason, in Qur'anic terms, 'no real morality is possible without the regulative ideas of God and the Last Judgment'. They exist for a religio-moral purpose and 'cannot be mere intellectual postulates to be "believed in"'. Rahman sees God as the 'transcendent anchoring point' of all moral values to which society must be subject if it is to prosper and this is a 'ceaseless struggle for the cause of the good . . . This constant struggle is the keynote of man's normative existence and constitutes the service (*ibada*) to God with which the Qur'an squarely and inexorably charges him'. But Rahman argues that in medieval Islam, 'what was regulative, namely God, was made the exclusive object of experience and thus, instead of men's seeking value from this experience, the experience became the end in itself'.[11]

What puzzled Rahman was why Muslim thinkers did not make the Qur'an the primary source for ethics in Islam. In several of his works, he explicated a Qur'an-based ethics set against his view that revelation was always mediated by the prevailing historical conditions. The divine origins of the Qur'an did not exclude the interface of revelation with the world. It was revelation itself which commented on the Prophet's personal behaviour and struggles and thus, concrete history matters in understanding the nature and movement of revelation. In his analysis of Rahman's approach, Ebrahim Moosa writes: 'The Qur'an explicitly states that Muhammad's speech was revelation (*wahy*) that descended on his heart. Revelation was entirely from God and at the same time the locus of revelation was the "heart" of the Prophet where it is vouchsafed in historical time'.[12]

What was imperative was the search for a new hermeneutical method in an age where Rahman argues, 'Islamic intellectualism has remained truncated'. For him, Muslims have either accepted aspects of modernity, rejected modernity or produced '"apologetic" literature that [endlessly] substitutes self-glorification

---

[10] Rahman, 'Law', 14.   [11] Rahman, *Islam*, 14.
[12] Ebrahim Moosa's 'Introduction' in Fazlur Rahman, *Revival and Reform in Islam*, Oxford: OneWorld Publications, 2000, 13.

for reform'. The search for a new Qur'anic hermeneutics of faith also demands an appreciation of aesthetics. Drawing upon the Sufi terminology of beauty and majesty (*jamal* and *jalal*), he writes that 'all revelation is a work of art and inspires a sense of the beautiful and a sense of awesome majesty'.[13]

For El Fadl, the relationship between God's law, ethics and authority remain central to his legal dynamics. His approach is frequently premised on the dialectic between Islamic law and its interpretation and the question of divine authority and authoritarianism:

> One of the most important issues confronting Islamic law today is how to balance the obligation to obey God against the fact that God's will is represented by human beings. In Islamic thought, God is the authoritative source of law, but what is the balance between God's authoritativeness and the potential for human authoritarianism?[14]

While it is important to distinguish between juristic discourses, Islamic law and Muslim law, El Fadl writes as a jurist trained in the classical Islamic sciences but also as a Western Muslim scholar of Islam, sensitive to the challenges Muslims face in living out their faith as diaspora communities. The studies presented in this book arose from his encounters, as a jurist and teacher, with Muslims in the United States and elsewhere. The essays, covering a broad range of topics, are written in response to actual problems and questions, directly relevant to the moral and ethical definition of Islam in the contemporary world. The topics include oppression, terrorism, women and equality, marriage, veiling and the dynamics between Islamic law and morality. While many would agree that the contemporary Muslim realities in parts of the Muslim world and in the West face various ethical and sociological dilemmas, El Fadl sees the recurring problems within Muslim societies as a kind of ugliness, in contrast to the beauty and diversity of a past and almost-forgotten Islamic intellectual heritage. Beauty therefore is about reconnecting meaningfully with that spiritual heritage and diversity of thought which has been somewhat lost in contemporary struggles which are directly relevant to the moral and ethical definition of Islam in the world today. El Fadl's use of the term 'beauty' occupies a place of critical importance in his work and is an established part of the classical methodology of Islamic law. The use of beauty as a marker for discerning the relevance of particular juristic formulations for specific practical occasions allows El Fadl to show flexibility in the law regarding contexts and particularities. As Angus

---

[13] Rahman, *Islam*, 4.
[14] Khaled Abou El Fadl, *Rebellion and Violence in Islamic Law*, Cambridge: Cambridge University Press, 2001, 1.

Slater explains, beauty in El Fadl's project is 'not an appreciation of logical clarity in argumentation, the satisfaction of having resolved a legal problem, or a static position, but rather a process of making and becoming beautiful'. In the same way that exercising beautiful practices, *ihsan*, based on scriptural commands and Prophetic examples, lead to the outward beautification of the believer as a *muhsin*, 'so the practice of picking the outcome of the law most in accord with the beauty of the Divine becomes a continuous practice of self-reflection and improvement'.[15] The law in its judgements and processes must mirror the internal beauty of the Divine. On his review of El Fadl's work, Reza Shah-Kazemi notes:

> [Abou] El-Fadl shows that the real beauty of this apparently arid dimension of the Islamic tradition arises out of the effort of the jurist to transcribe in legal terms his inner ethical sensibility – his 'aesthetic' appreciation of the good, which is inherently beautiful, and not merely the moral sense of right, based on what is lawful.[16]

Towards the end of *The Conference*, El Fadl writes in a tone of humility:

> I have been ugly and committed many, many sins, but I always believed in the beauty of God. I have transgressed, and been unjust to myself, but at the darkest moments I always longed for the light. If I lusted after this world, I always lusted in shame, and I never indulged my whims without the disruptions of a reproaching heart.[17]

In fact, for El Fadl, his faith and his search for knowledge lead him to conclude that the search for God is the search for beauty:

> I thank my Lord for teaching me that the omnipotence and immutability of the Divine means my utter humility. I thank my Lord for teaching me that the love of God will open the heart to its dormant sense of beauty. I thank the Lord, and remember my mother, father, teachers, books, and scholars who taught me that the heart and soul of Islam is the search for beauty.[18]

While not wishing to idealize the heritage of classical Islam, El Fadl admires it for being a more authentic expression of the Qur'an and the life of the Prophet where it's 'ethical and moral potential is far superior to anything that replaced it'.[19] He sees God's law or *shari'a* as a 'process, methodology, and

---

[15] Angus Slater, 'Khaled Abou el Fadl's Methodology of Reform, Law, Tradition and Resisting the State', *Journal of Law, Religion and State*, 4, 2016, 293–321, 306.

[16] Reza Shah-Kazemi, 'Review of *Conference of the Books* by Khaled Abou El Fadl', *Journal of Islamic Studies*, 15:2, 2004, 220, 221.

[17] El Fadl, *The Conference*, 341.   [18] El Fadl, *The Conference*, 347.

[19] El Fadl, *The Conference*, 18.

morality' and at the core of this morality is the value of beauty. However, he argues that, 'Positive commandments or rules delineate the outer boundaries of proper behavior, but they do not articulate the substance and soul of Islamic morality. The rules are at the fringe of Islamic morality; they are the external shell that do not express or create substance. The rules are about boundaries'.[20]

For El Fadl, rules do not create piety and he admits:

> I do not hide the fact that I see much ugliness in the reality of Muslims today, and that I think most Muslim discourses are either apologetic and dogmatic, or legalistic and formalistic. In contemporary Muslim discourses, legalism and the pursuit of pedantic rules have replaced the search for moral or normative values.[21]

Throughout the book, he shows through different examples how Muslim life is no longer under the influence of the 'Conference of Books, the citadel of knowledge', but rather defined by pain and injury:

> We are not defined by the Conference, our tradition, or religion – we are defined by our hurts, pains, and injuries. Our visions are blurred by the ceaseless flow of blood, and our ears are plugged by the thunderous clouds of agony encircling our world. Mercy and compassion, which we owe ourselves and others, have been buried under incrustations of salivations over power and obedience to the rules of obedience, but without the discipline of law.[22]

El Fadl speaks critically of the Muslims' lack of engagement with wider social and political discourse, that 'while the world discourses on Islam, Muslims exalt Islam and pretend the world does not exist'. Muslims, he argues do not heed the fact that whoever controls the flow of information, controls the discourse. He accuses the Muslim response:

> The Muslim response is to build Islamic centers, organize camps and conferences, and pretend that the mainstream does not exist. Although Islamic centers are necessary for generating a basic sense of community and identity, they are rarely a serious avenue for knowledge or discourse on Islam. As to the camps, conventions, and conferences, all too often they are no more than pep rallies or cheerleading events'.[23]

Yet, he is also critical of a certain construction of Muslims and Islam in wider society which does not engage with Muslims as subjects. This is especially so

---

[20] El Fadl, *The Conference*, 18.   [21] El Fadl, *The Conference*, 19.
[22] El Fadl, *The Conference*, 275.   [23] El Fadl, *The Conference*, 63.

in relation to terrorism and violence. El Fadl feels strongly that Muslims have become passive citizens and generally do not have the financial or intellectual power to reconstruct the image of the discourse; they are caught in an intellectual trap:

> Most of those who fund politicians, media organizations, schools, and Islamic studies programs are not Muslim and have no reason to cater to Muslim demands. Consequently, Muslims are powerless to direct the discourse or define the issues around which the discourse is to flow. Even more unfortunately, most Muslims do not appreciate or are not interested in the value of the discourse, the construction of an image, or the symbolic significance of a Conference of Books.[24]

For El Fadl, Islam was founded on a book and the religion is all about books and learning; yet this zeal for learning and deliberation seems to be lacking in contemporary Islam. An example of this is his chapter on 'Dial a Fatwa', in which he explains the seriousness and diligence a scholar had to historically show in issuing a fatwa or legal opinion. However, this process of learning, perseverance and humility has been undermined today, where the law of God is just a phone call away: 'But here in the United States, the comfort of a fatwa is right at your fingertips. As definite as a guaranteed-delivery pizza parlor, a fatwa is just a phone call away. With the sound reliability of a vending machine or the immediacy of an order of french fries, a fatwa is readily available'.[25]

The issue of authority within Islam is central to many of El Fadl's concerns. He narrates the case of a young man who spoke meticulous English and Arabic and gave a beautiful sermon (*khutba*) in a local mosque, explaining the importance of understanding and not simply reciting the Qur'an. On further inquiry about this young man, he discovered that people did not really approve of him because 'He does not fulfill the qualifications, brother; his appearance is not Islamic'. When asked why, the reply is 'He does not wear a beard, he tucks his shirt in, and, in addition, he is not married'. For El Fadl, this kind of response goes to the heart of a deeper problem with many Muslim communities whose acceptance of religious authority is dependent on particular traits and appearance rather than a person's religious understanding and ability to connect with the wider community. He writes, 'I felt the intellectual rigor mortis that follows insanity setting in; I felt the Conference distant and fading away'. He writes sorrowfully that the mosque got 'their married imam with his beard and untucked shirt. They got their

---

[24] El Fadl, *The Conference*, 65.   [25] El Fadl, *The Conference*, 60.

imam with the numbing rhetoric and incomprehensible broken English. But what they perpetuated is intellectual death'.[26]

El Fadl's lament at the demise of a certain kind of intellectualism and the social ills which accompany this phenomenon is reflected in many of his academic works. The crisis of religious authority and the relative stagnation of civic and economic life in many Muslim societies, has created a particular kind of spiritual malaise. This in turn has enabled jihadist organisations to fill in the political and social vacuum. In his short book *The Place of Tolerance in Islam*, written soon after the 9/11 attacks, he leads a debate in which he argues that Islam is a religion in which historically intolerant and fanatical sects have been marginalized; Islam is a deeply tolerant religion but is now being defined by intolerance. The book has a number of respondents who engage in varying debates with the author's thesis. El Fadl criticises the 'intolerant puritanism of the Wahhabi and Salafi creeds' which he claims 'rejected any attempt to interpret the divine law historically or contextually' and which 'treated the vast majority of Islamic history as a corruption of the true and authentic Islam'.[27] El Fadl does not go into any deeper explanation of the historical complexities of Salafism but Itzchak Weismann's analysis shows that while Salafism is often ill-defined and claimed and disclaimed by various movements and orientations, it has become 'the major ideology-cum-theology underlying modern Sunni Islamic thought'. Salafism reflects itself in various ways and there is a wide gap between the 'relatively liberal and open attitude of early modernist Salafism and the purist and xenophobic approach that characterizes its contemporary types' but as Weismann writes:

> For Jihadi-Salafis the West is the heinous enemy. Asked shortly after the terror attacks of 9/11 his opinion about Huntington's controversial paradigm of Clash of Civilizations, Bin Laden retorted, 'There is no doubt about it. This is a very clear matter, proven in the Qur'an and the traditions of the Prophet, and any true believer who claims to be faithful shouldn't doubt these truths'. Political Salafis are mostly concerned with the protection of Muslims from secular Western ideas and values. Quietist Salafis profess to ignore the infidel West altogether.[28]

A key theme which runs throughout his analysis is that those who engage in puritanical readings of the Qur'an regard moral ideas and historical contexts

---

[26] El Fadl, *The Conference*, 76.

[27] Khaled Abou El Fadl, *The Place of Tolerance in Islam*, Boston: Beacon Press, 2002, 8.

[28] Itzchack Weismann, 'A Perverted Balance: Modern Salafism between Reform and Jihad' in *Die Welt Des Islams*, 57, 2017, 33–66, 35.

as irrelevant. He insists on the Qur'anic recognition of human moral agency and a rich ethic of diversity and pluralism.

Taking a variety of Qur'anic verses such as 'if your enemy inclines towards peace, then you should seek peace and trust in God' (Q8:15), 'To each of you God has prescribed a Law and a Way. If God would have willed, He would have made you a single people. But God's purpose is to test you, in what he has given each of you' (Q5:49), 'O you who believe, stand firmly for justice, as witnesses for God, even if it means testifying against yourselves, or your parents, or your kin' (Q4:135), and others, El Fadl, tries to situate these verses in past and present contexts. Like many scholars who wish to revive an intellectual and sociological dynamism in Islamic cultures, El Fadl argues that the Qur'an, or any other text, speaks through the reader. The human ability to interpret a sacred scripture is both a blessing and a burden: 'It is a blessing because it provides us with the flexibility to adapt texts to changing circumstances, it is a burden because the reader must take responsibility for the normative value he or she brings to the text'.[29] El Fadl does not explore why puritanical ideas, especially those which construct intolerant theologies, become attractive in the first place. Nor does he distinguish between the puritanical aspects of religious thought, namely Wahhabism, and the more recent expressions of violence and militancy which have become increasingly global and visible. For him, as for many others, Saudi state funding is mainly responsible for the spread of particular exclusionary ideologies, thereby inducing an almost intellectual paralysis in many parts of the Islamic world. Yet, this still does not explain the relative appeal of puritanical ideas to a wider public at the expense of more open, discursive, even liberal understanding of Islam. Even though liberalism and liberal ideas may themselves be contested, understanding this particular trajectory is a real challenge for understanding the conflict of ideas and the internal struggle within the Muslim world. He concludes his essay with a note of cautious optimism:

> If we assess the moral trajectory of a civilisation in light of its past record, then we have ample reason to be optimistic about the future. But the burden and blessing of sustaining that moral trajectory – of accentuating the Qur'anic message of tolerance and openness to the other- falls squarely on the shoulder of contemporary Muslim interpreters of the tradition.[30]

In his response to El Fadl's essay, the American journalist, Milton Viorst writes that the open, tolerant Islam has never found a place in the hearts of believers, and that Islam's 'rejection of humanist values in favour of

---

[29] El Fadl, *The Place*, 22.   [30] El Fadl, *The Place*, 23.

otherworldiness long predated the Saudis'. Viorst argues, as an example, that the Mu'tazilites, the rationalist school of Islamic theology which flourished in Basra and Baghdad during the eight to tenth centuries, were ultimately rejected by the leading jurists of the time:

> It is an irony of this history that what the Muslims called 'Greek wisdom', the Mu'tazlite heritage, passed on to the West, where it gave birth to the Renaissance. Under this influence, the West humanized its values, while in Islam, scholars imbued with a 'sense of self-sufficient confidence', as Abou El Fadl puts it, rejected 'diversity and cross cultural intercourse'.[31]

Many of the essays are critical of El Fadl, arguing that insufficient tolerance within Muslim societies, Islam or Islamic ideologies is not the cause of the world's most pressing problems. Rather, 'the problem is the perpetuation of international systems of oppression and injustice'.[32] Terrorism on American soil focused public attention on Muslim theology, distracting attention from the 'real geopolitical struggle'. Mashhood Rizvi criticises the Western media for dismissing the links between the 9/11 attacks and the 'horrific legacies of U.S. foreign policy on millions of Muslims across the planet'. For Rizvi, all kinds of global injustices perpetuate the struggle, and the real challenge is not about simplistic questions such as tolerance in Islam but the vision of justice for all:

> The struggle between justice and tyranny cannot and should not be reduced to rich vs poor, white vs black or, for that matter, Islam vs the West. Such dichotomies stand in the way of serious discussion, and distract us from the specific cultural and economic mechanisms that subjugate and bewilder our moral instincts.[33]

In his response, the social anthropologist Stanley Kurtz writes that the real tension is between tradition and modernity so that only when 'some greater reconciliation between tradition and modernity on the level of fundamental social practice occurs can an ideological reformation succeed'. For Kurtz, the traditional patterns and structures of Islamic thought and society have been severely challenged by modernity:

> This is the crisis that has pushed so many educated but unemployed Muslim men into the arms of the fundamentalists. The same challenge of modernity has spurred a turn to veiling and fundamentalism among women torn between their commitment to education and employment

---

[31] Milton Viorst in El Fadl, *The Place*, 29.   [32] Mashhood Rizvi in El Fadl, *The Place*, 69.
[33] Rizvi in El Fadl, *The Place*, 70-1.

on the one hand, and the need to uphold the reputation and social position of their families, on the other.[34]

He argues that the reformation that is needed will not be brought about 'by innovative textual interpretation as much as it will depend upon fundamental social change'.[35]

Despite several critical responses to his essay, a couple of writers, including John L. Esposito, see what El Fadl is attempting to describe as a 'religious struggle for the soul of Islam between "puritanism" and modern Islam'. The struggle creates a political divide between a majority that may be conservative or reformist and a minority that may be fanatical, even violent, but which dominate the media news. Esposito argues that even if Western powers need to rethink and reassess foreign policies, mainstream Muslim still need to reject extremist elements in their desire of renewal and openness: 'The struggle for reform faces formidable obstacles: the conservatism of many (though not all) *ulama*; the traditional training of religious scholars and leaders; and the power of more puritanical, exclusivist Wahhabi or Salafi brands of Islam'.[36]

For El Fadl, despite the various critiques touching on issues of tradition, modernity, education and geo politics, theology also matters. He writes that as a believer, 'I would go further and assert that a just and good life is not possible without acknowledging the company and participation of God'.[37] Millions of people acknowledge God as part of their moral universe and this is why theology matters. El Fadl identifies the obligation of divine moral trust at the heart of the intellectual and interpretative struggle. Humankind cannot ignore that it has always had a duty to discharge this moral trust.

While El Fadl looks carefully at both the spread of puritanical thought in Muslim societies and the need to retrieve beauty from the interpretative legal processes, the late Mohammed Arkoun (1928–2010) who grew up on the fringes of the Arab, Islamic and European worlds, sought a new epistemology, new thinking for Muslim societies. In his 2003 article, 'Rethinking Islam Today', Arkoun writes that the issue is that Islamic revival and epistemologies have failed to recognise the overwhelming majority of ordinary Muslims. He accuses social scientists of having 'failed to liberate Islamic studies from pro- and anti-Orientalism cliches. Islam is still imagined as inferior (to Jewish and Christian traditions), unchanging, and militant by the West; and superior, dynamic, and peace loving by Muslims'. Arkoun argues for:

---

[34] Stanley Kurtz in El Fadl, *The Place*, 54.   [35] Kurtz in El Fadl, *The Place*, 54–55.
[36] John L. Esposito in El Fadl, *The Place*, 78–79.   [37] El Fadl, *The Place*, 104.

[a] new ijtihad for Muslim as well as non Muslim scholars to initiate a process of new thinking on Islam with tools such as history of thought rather than political events or fixed parameters; to make unthinkable notions-a historical rather than a religious postulate-thinkable; and to relate secularism, religion, and culture to contemporary challenges rather than substituting one for the other.[38]

Arkoun claims that it is not possible today to rethink any religious tradition without making a careful distinction between the mythical dimension linked to oral cultures and the official ideological functions of the religion.

Religious tradition is one of the major problems we should rethink today. First, religions are mythical, symbolic, ritualistic ways of being, thinking, and knowing. They were conceived in and addressed to societies still dominated by oral and not written cultures. Scriptural religions based on a revealed Book contributed to a decisive change with far-reaching effects on the nature and functions of religion itself. Christianity and Islam (more than Judaism, until the creation of the Israeli state) became official ideologies used by a centralizing state which created written historiography and archives.[39]

Aside from this necessary distinction, there is also a need to rethink tradition and orthodoxy. Tradition and orthodoxy are 'also unthought, unelaborated concepts in traditional Islamic thought' with tradition being largely reduced to a collection of 'authentic' texts. As for orthodoxy, he writes:

There has been no effort (*ijtihad*) to separate orthodoxy as a militant ideological endeavor, a tool of legitimation for the state and the 'values' enforced by this state, from religion as a way proposed to man to discover the Absolute. This is another task for our modern project of rethinking Islam, and other religions.[40]

For Arkoun, there is an 'Islamic framework' which remains constantly 'valid, transcendent, authentic, and universal in which all human activities and initiatives ought to be controlled and correctly integrated'. This framework is also part of the Islamic legacy and therefore one always looks back to time in search for the Truth. This might be orthodoxy for millions of Muslims, but it is also at the same time 'a methodology, an epistemology, and a theory of history'.[41]

His project is that of rethinking this operational, intellectual framework of Islam. This rethinking is a response to two major needs. One is the 'need of

---

[38] Mohammed Arkoun, 'Rethinking Islam Today' in *Annals of the American Academy of Political and Social Science*, 588, Islam: Enduring Myths and Changing Realities, 2003, 18–39, 18.
[39] Arkoun, 'Rethinking', 21.   [40] Arkoun, 'Rethinking', 22.   [41] Arkoun, 'Rethinking', 23.

Muslim societies to think, for the first time, about their own problems which had been made unthinkable by the triumph of orthodox scholastic thought' and the second is for 'contemporary thought in general to open new fields and discover new horizons of knowledge, through a systematic cross cultural approach to the fundamental problems of human existence'.[42] Arkoun identifies a particular issue in the study and definition of Islam which has been historically determined. So often Islam is presented and lived as a system of beliefs and non-beliefs which cannot be submitted to any critical inquiry. This, he argues, 'divides the space of thinking into two parts: the unthinkable and the thinkable'. He gives the example of Shafi'is systemization of the concept of sunna or Prophetic words and actions. After this systemization, many aspects of Islamic thought simply became unthinkable; Shafi'i's theory triumphed and this meant that there was no further thinking to be done on this issue.

The struggle between the inherited thinkable and the not yet thought has become more intense in Muslim societies since the violent introduction of intellectual modernity; but, as we have seen, the same struggle between the paradigms of knowledge and action started in Western societies in the sixteenth century. It was then that a process of a secularized culture began in Europe, a process which did not really touch the Muslim world. Yet Arkoun sees this historical divergence as central to the struggle in Muslim societies and Islamic thought. On the one hand, he argues, we cannot accept the concept of secularization or laïcité as it has been historically elaborated and used in Western societies. This is because there is a 'political and social dimension of this concept represented by the struggle for power and the tools of legitimization between the church and the bourgeoisie'. But nor can we 'interpret religion merely as positivist historicism and secularism did in the nineteenth century'. Religion is not the lot of those people who have as yet not received the 'light of rational knowledge'.[43] Muslim societies should and must be able to think about their own problems, something which had been made unthinkable by the triumph of orthodox scholastic thought.

What Arkoun promulgates is creating 'an intellectual and cultural framework in which all historical, sociological, anthropological, and psychological presentations of revealed religions could be integrated into a system of thought and evolving knowledge'. This is a bold task and one which must be accompanied by the concept of social *imaginaire* and the 'related notions of myth, symbol, sign, or metaphor'. Whereas reason is always referred to as the faculty of true knowledge, Arkoun calls for 'knowledge based on the

---

[42] Arkoun, 'Rethinking', 28.   [43] Arkoun, 'Rethinking', 28.

representations of the imagination'.[44] Appeals to the imagination is an ethic in itself where information is conveyed intuitively rather than analytically. Poetic information adds to the general intuitive grasp of life that human beings hold as humankind has always had an immediate intuition of the nature of the whole, an awareness to which storytellers, poets, and other artists contributed.

For Arkoun, however limited the influence of intellectual writers might be in injecting new dynamism into Islamic thought, where traditions have a long and deeply rooted history, this enterprise is necessary. Furthermore, it must be the project of thinkers, writers, artists and scholars and economic producers. They must all be committed to the idea that 'thoughts have their own force and life. Some, at least, could survive and break through the wall of uncontrolled beliefs and dominating ideologies'.[45] For Arkoun, the study of Islam today suffers particularly from the ideological obstacles created, since the nineteenth century, by the decay of the Muslim intellectual tradition, as it had developed from the first to the fifth century. But Muslim societies themselves seem to have struggled with economic pressures of the West, demographic changes and the general trend of positivist rationalism and material civilization.

Whereas El Fadl speaks of the moral trust placed in man, Arkoun claims that 'we should not forget that man agrees to obey, to be devoted, and to obligate his life when he feels a "debt of meaning" to a natural or a supernatural being'. If humankind acknowledges transcendent authority, then we are indebted to this authority to search for meaning. He writes of the experience of the Algerian war of liberation through which he learned 'how all revolutionary movements need to be backed by a struggle for meaning'. Yet he concludes that it is the conflict between meaning and power which 'has been and will be the permanent condition through which man tries to emerge as a thinking being'.[46]

Much has happened since the tragedy of 9/11 but El Fadl and Arkoun represent two of the scholars of the twentieth century who have wrestled with the question of how Islam, as a religious, cultural, political, and ethical heritage, can deal with the changes brought by a modernizing world. The onset of modernity, post-colonialism, globalisation and migration has challenged almost every single aspect of our lives. Alongside these transnational changes, new technologies have created problems and opportunities. If modernity brought scientific and technological benefits, it also had consequences for the Islamic faith and its diverse cultural

---

[44] Arkoun, 'Rethinking', 31–2.   [45] Arkoun, 'Rethinking', 21–4.   [46] Arkoun, 'Rethinking', 39.

values. They build their arguments acknowledging that the injuries wrought by colonialism and despotism have left many Muslims alienated and torn from the depth and beauty of their religious history and tradition. Some societies adopted modernity in a pragmatic manner that resulted in certain unforeseen discontinuities with the historical intellectual tradition. But for Muslims in the West who often struggle with issues of authority and ethics in more pluralist societies, Islam can mean and be many different things. Despite a wide ideological spectrum among modernist Muslim scholars in the nineteenth and twentieth centuries, most shared a common desire to fuse the present with the past in different ways. Their intellectual enterprise was to retain some much-needed continuity and to give Western Muslims in particular a sense of belonging to a tradition. The social, intellectual and epistemological struggle is not over, even though in recent years, it has been somewhat obscured by issues of global militancy and violence. There are no easy answers to ethical questions but nor can there be. Lived faith is complex, often socially and politically charged. Studied as an intellectual discipline which still speaks to the faithful, it can open new horizons for reflection but the moral challenge between knowledge and practice remains.

For Rahman, El Fadl and Arkoun, many Muslims, especially in the West, are caught in a tension which has probably always existed in the lives of the faithful but has in recent times assumed a particular focus. With so many competing sources of knowledge and ways of being, how can one live a life that is faithful, humane, generous, intellectually open and beautiful? Faith can be challenging and it can be a struggle, but for it to have any meaning, it must continue to inspire hope. Knowledge has traditionally been associated with practising piety and seeking religious knowledge but the life of the mind has its own way of breaking out – it has no boundaries. Knowledge is a form of travel and in whatever form, invites us to escape the intellectual and emotional limitations of our lives. In his work on spatiality and ritual prayer, Simon O'Meara states that 'ritual prayer is a type of travel' and the turning towards the direction of prayer (*qibla*) is the turning to God, a utopian travel. Ritual prayer promotes virtue and well-being in this life and the next. He cites Walid Saleh who stresses the importance of orientation in the Qur'an, what Saleh calls the 'theology of orientation':

> The Qur'an weaves a matrix of words around the concept of journeying, guidance, path, and destination. It speaks of finding one's way, of getting lost, of roaming the earth, of straight paths and crooked paths (Q 7:86); it speaks of lurking near highways to ambush, it speaks of stampeding on

a highway; it speaks of darkness lit by lightning through which one attempts to walk, only to halt again as the skies darken, thus recreating day and night in an instant, guidance and bewilderment in the flash of a moment, while the believers have their light guiding them on the way. ... Indeed the vocabulary is so rich and so varied, the imagery so complex and adroit that one has to take this imagery as fundamental in the message of the Qur'an as to how it understands guidance, and hence salvation.[47]

For those with a religious faith, faith can hold several competing claims on our lives. For some it is truth, history and fact told in multiple narratives, through multiple voices. Religion is God and goodness, poetry and prophecy told and retold in worship, stories and artistic renditions over the centuries. For others, despite the imaginative impulse behind all religion, religious faith has been confined largely to doctrines and dogmas, rituals and practices, many of which struggle to remain meaningful in peoples' lives today. As El Fadl laments, there is a tendency amongst contemporary Muslims to ignore contexts and contingencies:

> Instead of dealing with the full complexity and richness of life and with challenges on their own terms, the religious-imaginary limits what are considered to be the relevant facts in such a way as to avoid having to deal with challenges in the first place. In this situation, life is not experienced and studied in its full richness and diversity; rather, the process of living itself is conceptualized in highly stereotyped forms that have little to do with material culture or lived experience.[48]

An ethical imagination must lie at the centre of Islamic thought. Imagination is about seeing and understanding the world and this is inherently a moral activity. It is through observation that we become aware of human freedom to think and act, of our relational existence, of a moral impulse to make things better for all. Yet in our increasingly pluralist societies, faith in God should be a vessel for a shared imagination. This requires thinking beyond our personal struggle and beyond our personal salvation. It is a different engagement with faith which invites a different collective struggle where we retain a reverence for the desires and truths of others alongside our own

---

[47] Simon O'Meara, 'The Space between Here and There: The Prophet's Night Journey as an Allegory of Islamic Ritual Prayer', in *Middle-Eastern Literatures: incorporating Edebiyat*, 15:3, 2012, 232–29. Citation from Walid A. Saleh, 'The Etymological Fallacy and Qur'anic Studies: Muhammad, Paradise, and Late Antiquity', in Angelika Neuwirth, Michael Marx and Nicolai Sinai (eds.), *The Qur'ān in Context: Historical and Literary Investigations into the Qur'ānic Milieu*,Leiden: Brill, 2010, 666.

[48] Khaled Abou El Fadl, 'When Happiness Fails: An Islamic Perspective', *The Journal of Law and Religion*, 29:1, 2014, 109–23, 122.

hopes. Thus, the transcendent and the human social are intertwined. In the modern world, we stand at the *dhiliz*, a word common to many of the Islamicate languages such as Arabic, Persian Urdu and Turkish meaning threshold, passage and a corridor connecting and disconnecting spaces and places. When one is standing at the threshold, one is simultaneously inside and outside the broader frameworks of life and knowledge and reflecting whether to stay still or walk in either direction from the threshold. It is a challenge to our intellectual and moral life and most importantly, it is a metaphor to explain where many Muslim scholars as well as Muslim societies often find themselves.

5

The Struggle for Hope in an Age of Uncertainty

*T*ODAY WE LIVE IN AN AGE OF UNCERTAINTY. UNCERTAINTY IS NO longer a philosophical concern, a struggle, which for the stoics and epicureans of the classical world, was a way to find means of living well rather than seek knowledge or wisdom for their own sake. Nor is it about the torments of religious questions and the awkwardness of human existence, which for Søren Kierkegaard, ultimately meant taking a leap of faith into the arms of God. The anguish of a bygone philosophical age is today apparent in the anxieties of uncertainty everywhere, in our relationships, in our professional lives, in our health, in our politics. Uncertainty is also more than personal and societal distrust in our political and public institutions, rather it points to a kind of fragmentation in society where our struggle for meaning has become more acute.

There are a deluge of self-help books which encourage readers to look after their physical and mental well-being for a more fulfilled life, but there seem to be few meta narratives about how to lead the good life. As far back as the mid twentieth century, a time which seems both distant and very present, the German philosopher and psychologist, Theodor W. Adorno maintained that a good, honest life is no longer possible, because we live in an inhuman society. The book's epigram 'Life does not live', opens a series of reflections and aphorisms beginning with Adorno's famous reflection that what was once the true field of philosophy, the 'teaching of the good life' has now lapsed into an intellectual neglect.[1] For Adorno, 'what the philosophers once knew as life has become the sphere of private existence and now of mere consumption, dragged along as an appendage of the process of material production, without autonomy or substance of its own'.[2] Indeed what seemingly preoccupies many thinkers is whether life holds any meaning in the first place.

---

[1] Theodor W. Adorno, *Minima Moralia, Reflections on a Damaged Life*, trans. by E. F. N. Jephcott, Verso: London, 2005, 15.
[2] Adorno, *Minima*, 15.

This theme of uncertainty has been approached from a variety of angles and disciplines. However much of the literature vacillates between a nostalgic sense of loss and the human struggle for a just and more healing vision of society. For many social and cultural theorists, there is a certain malaise of contemporary culture in which, as Charles Taylor writes, 'people experience as a loss or decline even as our civilisation develops'.[3] Taylor's view is that our modern freedoms have been won by our breaking loose from older moral horizons, the cosmic order, 'the great chain of being' in which, as he says, humans figured in their proper place along with 'angels, heavenly bodies and our fellow earthly creatures'. The hierarchies of human society have been discredited and, while modernity is characterised by both grandeur as well as misère, to quote Pascal, the real challenge for us is the 'dark side of individualism centering on the self'.[4] The focus on the self has brought new freedoms and enriched our lives in many ways but the dominant contemporary narrative is that individualism has also flattened and narrowed our lives. Alongside this phenomenon, the rise of technology is all too often regarded as a solution to all of life's problems, when in reality, for Taylor, the relationship between human life and the cosmos need a new conversation, a search for a deeper mode of authenticity. He writes, 'what our situation calls for is a complex, many-levelled struggle, intellectual, spiritual and political, in which the debates in the public arena interlink with those in a host of institutional settings, like hospitals and schools, where the issues of enframing technology are being lived through in concrete form'.[5] Taylor's view is not that individualism be negatively reduced to self-centredness but that we use our modern freedoms to reimagine the meaning of identity, personhood and community.

In the West, cultural theorists have tended to advance their narratives against the political language of liberalism. While liberalism can be defined in many ways, Craig Hovey approaches it through the Rawlsian concepts of maximum justice and opportunity for all people:

> Liberalism is a political philosophy that seeks societal stability and unity in the absence of shared conceptions of the common good. It is therefore regularly associated with contemporary discussions of religious and other pluralisms and especially, in our day, is connected to the anxieties that set in when moral convictions previously thought to be self evidently true and binding lose their obviousness. How then will a society composed of diverse

---

[3] Charles Taylor, *The Ethics of Authenticity*, Cambridge, MA: Harvard University Press, 2018 (first paperback edition).
[4] Taylor, *Ethics*, 3–5 and 121.   [5] Taylor, *Ethics*, 120.

individuals – people of various faiths and traditions- function for its betterment?[6]

Liberalism conceives of humans as individuals who enjoy relative freedom to organise their common lives. Beyond the definitions and limits of the nation state, law and governance, liberalism's value lies in relating concepts of human dignity to happiness and human empowerment, integral to human flourishing; this has captured our imagination and immersed itself in the global political and legal discourse. But among the many critiques of political liberalism is the recurrent issue that liberalism posits the doctrine of the 'unencumbered self', that the individual must remain 'free and untrammelled' whose autonomy is its supreme and inalienable right. The theologian David Fergusson echoes the tension faced in freedom and rootedness in some form of religious worldview:

> It presents the individual as already valuing its autonomy prior to any other
> substantive moral commitments. In doing so, it denudes the self of the
> necessary resources for moral reasoning and decision-making. The indivi-
> dual of political liberalism is thus deracinated. She or he is no longer
> situated in a community or tradition of moral enquiry in terms of which
> judgements can be understood and practised. The shared goods and ends of
> human life are no longer built into the liberal individual's initial moral
> situation. These can be selected and endorsed by an act of freedom, but for
> the unencumbered self it is hard to see on what basis reasons favouring one
> decision over another could be offered.[7]

The struggle for individual rights differs from self-mastery. But the rights-based discourse that both frames and advances the cause of liberal societies, is often presented as the point in history where freedom has finally arrived. Yet liberal democracies, for all their strengths, have not led to coherent and peaceful narratives, the prophetic end of history or the Hegelian fullness of history. They have not been able to satisfy human longing and restlessness for something more. It may be that liberal democracies have lulled us into thinking that we in the West are now living in the best of all possible worlds as such democracies have gained almost universal legitimacy. This is Francis Fukuyama's thesis that the liberal *idea* rather than liberal practice has become universal. He argues that no ideology is in a position to challenge liberal democracy and argues that although Islam constitutes a coherent

---

[6] Craig Hovey, 'Liberalism and Democracy' in Craig Hovey and Elizabeth Phillips (eds.), *The Cambridge Companion to Political Theology*, New York: Cambridge University Press, 2015, 197.

[7] David Fergusson, *Church, State and Civil Society*, Cambridge: Cambridge University Press, 2004, 59-60. See also, Michael Sandel, *Liberalism and Its Critics*, Oxford: Blackwell, 1984.

ideology with its own code of morality and political rule, 'this religion has virtually no appeal outside those areas that were culturally Islamic to begin with'. Yet as Fukuyama contends, we may want peaceful lives but as individuals we are mostly restless and passionate beings, in search for causes. Our primordial instincts for struggle, our restlessness, is captured in his bold assertions:

> Supposing that the world has become 'filled up' so to speak, with liberal democracies, such that there exist no tyranny and oppression worth of the name against which to struggle? Experience suggests that if men cannot struggle on behalf of a just cause because that just cause was victorious in an earlier generation, then they will struggle *against* that just cause. They will struggle for the sake of struggle. They will struggle, in other words, out of a certain boredom: for they cannot imagine living in a world without struggle. And if the greater part of the world in which they live is characterized by peaceful and prosperous liberal democracy, then they will struggle *against* that peace and prosperity, and against democracy. [emphasis original][8]

Liberal societies have also allowed for an individualisation of religion, not as a transcendent experience but as value-laden normative ethics. The socioethical frameworks of the world order are being shaped by a technological connectivity that sees no limits to globalisation. The advances in sciences and medicine, an increased awareness of world poverty, the growing ecological concerns around climate justice and the associated economic issues, the shift in gender roles and the changes to the nature of family life, the social and political impact of personal and political expression, and the demise of structured and more formal modes of religious allegiance, are just a few examples exemplifying the shift in human consciousness. Within these multivalent ways of thinking and being, religious structures in the West have somewhat lost their pre-eminence and public hold. Religion may still have its connective and collective attraction binding people together as Charles Taylor states, but society is now one in which 'faith, even for the staunchest believer, is one possibility among others'.[9] In his analysis of Taylor's thesis, Philip Goodchild explores the place of God and theology in an era of capitalism, global growth and wealth creation. He argues, like many others, that free markets and the pursuit of profit has reordered society

---

[8] Francis Fukuyama, *The End of History and the Last Man*, London: Hamish Hamilton, 1992, 330 and 45-6.
[9] Charles Taylor, *A Secular Age*, Cambridge, Massachusetts: Beelknap Press of Harvard University Press, 2007, 3.

around an instrumental rationality. Traditional religious cultures ordered around rituals and customs have been undermined so that 'only the rational pursuit of profit and growth counts, while other forms of belief and behaviour fade into relative insignificance – they do not grow'.[10] Similarly, D. Stephen Long writes:

> The problem in the modern world is not that people no longer desire theological truths but that theology does not matter. I mean that in the most literal sense. Theology has no flesh, no embodiment in daily existence. Instead it is forced to the margins of everyday life to some sacred noumenal realm which is neither rational nor irrational.[11]

But these claims go deeper. Modernity is marked by a gradual turning away from seeing value and learning in traditional scriptural foundations for the daily order of society. An example by Jonathan Burnside is the place and paradox of biblical law on Western civilisation. Burnside writes that despite the Bible's deep influence on Western civilisation, our assumptions are very hostile to its having any influence on the modern world at all. He writes:

> From a modern perspective, biblical law is a spent moral force. We do not see its value as 'law', and so the subject has hardly any traction in modern law schools. Nor the picture any better in other disciplines. It seems irrelevant to the study of anthropology, economics, politics and psychology, as presently conceived. The sole exception is theology and religious studies. Yet, even here, few curricula focus on biblical law. Usually, it is submerged within more general studies of Judaism and the Hebrew Bible. It is largely ignored in courses on Christian ethics.[12]

Secularity has been a gradual process, having both flattening and also liberating modes on civilisation. For Goodchild, the secular age where religion is at best an option is a stark contrast to a society where 'it was inconceivable that people could reason, desire, and trust without grounding their hopes in an anticipated unity of metaphysical, moral and social aspirations: a personal God'. But today commitment to God is no longer required for science, economics or the state since 'science provides the basis for theoretical knowledge, the market for the practical aspirations of producers and consumers, and the state upholds society with law and the enforcement

[10] Philip Goodchild, 'Capitalism and Global Economics' in Craig Hovey and Elizabeth Phillips (eds.), *The Cambridge Companion to Political Theology*, New York: Cambridge University Press, 2015, 219.

[11] D. Stephen Long and Nancy Ruth Fox, with York Tripp, *Calculated Futures*, Waco, TX: Baylor University Press, 2007, 72.

[12] Jonathan Burnside, 'The Spirit of Biblical Law', *Oxford Journal of Law and Religion*, 1:1, 2012, 127–150, 127.

of contracts'.[13] Looking beyond Christianity in his exploration of secularity, Harvey Cox talks of a fundamental change in the 'nature of religiousness'. Cox states that in age of globalisation, religions are becoming less regional and less hierarchical and religious people are looking more for ethical guidelines than complex doctrines. Here also women are assuming positions of scholarly authority and leadership:

> As these changes gain momentum, they invoke an almost point for-point fundamentalist reaction. Some Shinto leaders retort by emphasizing the sacredness of Japan, while the Barata Janata party seeks to 'Hinduize' India. Radical Islamists dream of reestablishing a caliphate that encompasses all of Allah's land. Some Isreali settlers on the West Bank want to establish a 'Torah state', a holy land governed by scriptural law. The religious Right in the United States insists that America is a 'Christian nation'. Literalist bishops in Africa and their American allies threaten to split the world wide Anglican Communion over the ordination of gays and women. Indeed, a core conviction of all fundamentalist movements is that women must be kept in their place. All these, however, are in the true sense of the word 'reactionary' efforts. They are attempting to stem an inexorable movement of the human spirit whose hour has come.[14]

The overlapping debates on these social and political realities rest to some extent on the secularisation thesis. Broadly speaking, early social scientists such as Emile Durkheim and Max Weber argued that in the modern age religions would struggle to provide universal world views and that the products of modernity such as industrialisation, globalisation and individualism would inevitably impact on religious institutions and the vitality of religious practices and convictions. The ongoing presence of faith and the rise of various forms of religious fundamentalisms, including the more violent expressions, have challenged this narrative, but this cultural change has become a defining feature of many Western societies.

Yet alongside this perspective is the claim that the relationship between the secular and the Christian should not be regarded as two separate spheres. In 1953, Friedrich Gogarten advanced the thesis that secularisation, as an historical process, is 'not only not inimical to the Christian faith but has been made possible by it and is demanded by it'. A perceptive analysis of this relationship was coined by Marcel Gauchet who argues, 'Christianity proves to have been a religion for departing from religion'.[15] Assessing how the

---

[13] Goodchild, 'Capitalism', 220.
[14] Harvey Cox, *The Future of Faith*, New York: HarperCollins Publishers, 2009, 223.
[15] Marcel Gauchet, *The Disenchantment of the World: A Political History of Religion*, translated by Oscar Burge, Princeton: Princeton University Press, 1997, 4.

Christian faith has adapted to changing circumstances to preserve gospel values, the Indian Catholic priest Madathikunnel writes:

> What we see in the west today is a culture that began with religious determinations, but which has now become free of these, possessing two dimensions, namely, that of departing and liberating from the religious bond. The individual is important and everything turns around the individual. This has given a new model of freedom to society, along with a new social order and a dethroning of religion from its former elevated position in society. The rise of democratic rule, the concept of civil society, the consciousness of human rights, and individual freedom, have all accelerated the growth of secularism.[16]

But there are other philosophers and theologians for whom the secular societies of the modern West are the legacy of Christianity. While a controversial figure, Don Cupitt writes, 'This radical humanist world – the world of everyday life, the world of the novel – is simply Christianity itself realized, or objectified. God has, at last, fully become human and only human'. For Cupitt, Christ is 'all there is of God; and now that Jesus Christ is dead and gone he in turn remains and acts in the world only in and through the lives of his followers'.[17] Cupitt rejects the struggle to reconcile Church Christianity and the modern world for he sees in modern Western culture the human and Christian values that we will need to proclaim and defend in the future. Arguably, secularity has become an integrative feature of religion itself, emphasising that faith in God is not about the negation of this world but participation in this world, the moral imperative to make things better in the here and now, irrespective of hopes of salvation or redemption. Exploring the social significance of churches and the widely held view of the decline of Christian Britain, David Fergusson speaks of a particular paradox. Even with the relative demise of Christian consciousness, there is no alternative morally coherent viewpoint. If secular liberalism cannot provide a coherent moral framework, this provides new opportunities for Christians. Following on from Stanley Hauerwas, for whom the mission of the church is to be located primarily in faithfulness of its witness to Christ, Fergusson affirms that 'our core business is neither the takeover of the world nor the maximising'. He writes that this decline has contributed to a greater self-confidence amongst Christian theologians and ethicists. For Fergusson:

[16] Sabu George Maddathikunnel, 'Secularism and the Crisis of Secularization in India: A Taylorian Response', *A Journal of Religion, Education and the Arts*, 7, 2011, 4.

[17] Don Cupitt, *The Meaning of the West*, London: SCM Press, 2008, 19.

There is a sense of liberation in the realisation that the church no longer speaks for society, exercising a central role in promoting consensus and achieving social stability. This frees the representatives of the community to speak on distinctively Christian grounds, to fulfil the fundamental task of bearing witness to the faith, and to set aside the burden of being the state's major partner within civil society.[18]

For Fergusson, the question is always one of what sets the Christian faith apart from the values and progress already present within diverse civil societies. His conclusion is both faithfully and unsurprisingly that it is 'neither its particular set of virtues nor its doctrines but only the irreplaceable centrality of Jesus for faith and life'.[19]

For many Western theorists, the loss of the sacred, the emphasis on individualism and personal freedoms are complex and overlapping features of Western modernity. For Taylor, while self determining freedom holds enormous power in our political life, so does the moral ideal which 'accords crucial moral importance to a kind of contact with myself, with my own inner nature'; a search for individual fulfilment.[20] The rights and hopes of the individual frame much of our moral and political discourse over the last 100 years. Human rights are not easily won; they are a constant struggle. For some in the West, modernity has brought about a kind of cultural and moral relativism, which, in turn, has seen a rise in various forms of religious expressions and fundamentalisms. For others, the changes to our social and moral climate stemming from a greater emphasis on the autonomy of the individual are welcome because they are liberating for the whole of society. However, individual rights demand that our common humanity and mutual responsibilities and loyalties are not eclipsed by the drive for personal satisfaction alone. The danger then would be that there is no higher loyalty outside of oneself, no greater cause than one's emotional even intellectual needs. The challenge is to find modes of living which demand ties with others, the realisation that life is more than an exercise of personal choice and freedom, that there are horizons beyond the immediate and the self. Taylor points to an extreme form of anthropocentricism:

Anthropocentricism, by abolishing all horizons of significance, threatens us with a loss of meaning and hence a trivialization of our predicament. At one moment, we understand our situation as one of high tragedy, alone in a silent universe, without intrinsic meaning, condemned to create value. But at a later moment, the same doctrine, by its own inherent bent, yields

---

[18] Fergusson, *Church*, 98.   [19] Fergusson, *Church*, 113.   [20] Taylor, *Ethics*, 29.

a flattened world, in which there aren't very meaningful choices because there aren't any crucial issues.[21]

While Taylor is keen to emphasise that he is not condemning the ethic of self-fulfilment, his main concern is 'a continuing struggle to realize higher and fuller modes of authenticity against the resistance of the flatter and shallower forms'.[22] This is a complex struggle often mired in nostalgia and romantic ideals of a simpler preindustrial age. Such longings can obscure the challenges individuals and groups have faced to win even basic societal rights and semblances of justice.

The search to find meaning in the largely prosperous societies of the West, has been approached in several different ways. The American psychotherapist and former monk Thomas Moore rose to prominence with his hugely successful 1992 book, *Care of the Soul*.[23] Moore lists emptiness, a loss of core values and the general malaise of meaninglessness as hallmarks of our culture. He draws on his fifteen years of experience as a psychotherapist and begins with a simple claim: that 'the great malady of the twentieth century implicated in all of our troubles and affecting us individually and socially is "loss of soul"'.[24] While Moore accepts that it is impossible to define precisely what the soul is, he writes that definition is an intellectual exercise while the 'soul prefers to imagine'. The soul has to do with depth, a genuineness, 'life in all its particulars'.[25] Moore follows the approach of Carl Jung for whom religion helps to explain the psychological processes of man; there is no separation of psychology from religion. For Jung, the healthiest spiritual aim, the one of most benefit to the individual, is that of individuation – of trying to become more and more fully and truly who we essentially are. Yet, today, the powerful experience of the numinous that speaks of the mystery of life has been seemingly traded for a variety of substitutes that no longer speak to the depths of our humanity or serve our spiritual yearning. Moore is conscious that one should be more accepting of human frailties and foibles, rather than offering spiritual guidance which strives to transcend the human condition in search for perfection or salvation. What is required is 'concrete ways we can foster soulfulness in our everyday lives'. The soul, unlike the intellect, presents images that are not immediately intelligible to the mind because 'it insinuates, offers fleeting impressions, persuades more with desire than with reasonableness'.[26] Borrowing from the terminology of Christianity, although pointing out

---

[21] Taylor, *Ethics*, 68.   [22] Taylor, *Ethics*, 94.
[23] Thomas Moore, *Care of the Soul*, London: Piatkus, 1992.   [24] Moore, *Care*, ix.
[25] Moore, *Care*, ix.   [26] Moore, *Care*, 122.

that his proposal is not tied to any particular religious tradition, Moore calls his care of the soul a 'sacred art'. Psychology as 'modern, secular and ego-centred' must be reimagined bringing psychology and spirituality together.[27] While he speaks of care as ongoing attention rather than cure or fixing of a problem, Moore's basic premise is that our real struggle is that the soul craves:

> We yearn excessively for entertainment, power, intimacy, sexual fulfilment, and material things, and we think we can find these things if we discover the right relationship or job, the right church or therapy. But without soul, whatever we find will be unsatisfying, for what we truly long for is the soul in each of these areas.[28]

Moore draws on Michel Foucault's seminal work, *Technologies of the Self*, an exploration of what are the practices required for the 'care of the self/soul'. The term *technologies* refers simply to practices, or exercises, which affect both identity formation and spiritual transformation.[29] As Deborah Saxon writes, 'Foucault argues that since Descartes, the modern history of philosophy has typically focused on the Greco-Roman love of knowledge and assumed it to be the primary emphasis of the ancients. However, Foucault proposes that it is actually the care of the soul which is the main interest of the philosophers of antiquity'.[30] For the ancient Greek and Roman philosophers, the emphasis on 'knowing oneself' is actually subsumed within the broader notion of the care of the self/soul. Foucault's argument is that, in the modern period, historians of philosophy have simply assumed that the phasis was on knowledge. He feels this assumption is a result of what he terms the 'Cartesian moment', that is, 'the moment "when [it came to be thought that] knowledge itself and knowledge alone gives access to the truth"'.[31] Philosophy as a discourse about knowledge had been disassociated from philosophy as a discourse revolving around the care of the soul. While Foucault used 'care of the self' and 'care of the soul' interchangeably, both refer to the primary activity of looking after oneself. For Moore, care of the soul is about seeing another reality altogether. He writes:

---

[27] Moore, *Care*, xii–xiii.   [28] Moore, *Care*, xiv.

[29] Michel Foucault, 'Technologies of the Self' in Luther H. Martin, Huck Gutman and Patrick H. Hutton (eds.), *Technologies of the Self: A Seminar with Michel Foucault*, Amherst: University of Massachusetts Press, 1988, 16–49.

[30] Deborah Ann Niederer Saxon, *Representations of the Care of the Soul in Early Christian Texts*, PhD Thesis, Faculty of the University of Denver, Iliff School of Theology, 2013, 3.

[31] I am grateful to Deborah Saxon for this reference. Michel Foucault, *The Hermeneutics of the Subject*, Lectures at the Collège de France 1981–82, ed. by Frédéric Glos and trans. by Graham Burchell, New York: Picador, 2001.

[Care of the soul] appreciates the mystery of human suffering and does not offer the illusion of a problem free life. It sees every fall into ignorance and confusion as an opportunity to discover that the beast residing at the centre of the labyrinth is also an angel. The uniqueness of a person is made up of the insane and the twisted as much as it is of the rational and normal.[32]

Moore sees the family as the 'nest in which the soul is born'. The word family invokes complex emotions and images, 'secret transgressions and follies'. Family ties and memories are complex even as the family is experienced as 'the façade of happiness and normality, and the behind-the-scenes reality of craziness and abuse'.[33] But for Moore, family life is an enrichment of identity, its matrix of images forms us even as we appreciate its 'shadow as well as its virtue'.[34] Yet when people struggle emotionally and psychologically, the family influence is often seen as the formative factor. Moore challenges this: 'What if we thought of the family less as the determining influence by which we are formed and more the raw material from which we can make a life?' The argument is that the family is always what we imagine it to be because family history is invariably 'transformed into myth'.[35]

So much of the human search for meaning and fulfilment in life is connected with the human search for love and Moore writes with a particular sensitivity on this theme. He states that 'our love of love and our high expectations that it will make life complete seem to be an integral part of the experience'. But love is painful even as it promises 'that life's gaping wounds will close up and heal'. While acknowledging that we learn something from the suffering associated with love, Moore wants the reader to appreciate that 'emptiness is part of love's heritage and therefore its very nature'.[36] Love is not only about relationship but it is also an affair of the soul: 'Disappointments in love, even betrayals and losses, serve the soul at the very moment they seem in life to be tragedies. The soul is partly in time and partly in eternity'.[37] In Moore's analysis, for the soul, the ordinary is the sacred and the everyday is the primary source of religion. Suffering can only be lived in faith because 'suffering forces our attention toward places we would normally neglect'. Moore's conclusion is that caring for the soul is not a self-improvement project or even releasing oneself from the 'troubles and pains of human existence'. For the soul 'memory is more important than planning, art more compelling than reason, and love more fulfilling than understanding'.[38] Throughout his book, Moore is careful to emphasise that he cannot explain precisely what soul is but that care for the soul demands we

---

[32] Moore, *Care*, 20.   [33] Moore, *Care*, 28.   [34] Moore, *Care*, 29.   [35] Moore, *Care*, 32.
[36] Moore, *Care*, 78.   [37] Moore, *Care*, 96.   [38] Moore, *Care*, 304.

remain concerned about the suffering around us as well as the aesthetics of our own lives. Caring for the soul means being aware of how we learn from the past and relate to the past, present and future, whereas modernity is biased toward only living for the day:

> Soul loves the past and doesn't merely learn from history, it thrives on the stories and vestiges of what has been. Prophecy described by Plato and the Renaissance Platonists as one of the powers of soul, is a vision of life that embraces, past, present, and future in a way that transcends ordinary awareness . . . A soul sensibility awakens an appreciation for old ways and ancient wisdom, for buildings that hold in their architecture and design the tastes and style of another era.

Our sense of who we are as people and communities has also changed in the face of more globalised and moving societies. One of the most eloquent expressions of uncertainty and insecurity as facets of human struggle was coined in the phrase 'liquid modernity' by the renowned Polish Jewish philosopher and sociologist Zygmunt Bauman (1925–2017). Bauman was born into a Jewish family in Poland. He escaped to the Soviet Union at the beginning of World War II and, allying himself to the Red Army by joining the Polish army, he fought Nazism. He began his studies in sociology when he returned to Warsaw. But when his works were banned by the Communist Party, he moved to England and taught for most of his academic life at the University of Leeds.

Bauman's writings on liquid modernity present the narratives of endemic uncertainty, the collapse of traditional frames of reference and the deepening of personal and social anxieties. Ranging from personal relationships to societal bonds, his work defines modernity as a struggle on all fronts. The metaphor of liquidity effectively defines the essence of the world we live in where social and political stability of the past is partly being nullified because of the very progress of knowledge and technological progress that modernity itself had endorsed. A nation was once about territory, culture and language. But in the age of Facebook, a nation seems to be an 'ensemble of mobile individuals' and the question of how engaged you are with the debates and problems of your country depends on whether 'you are online or offline'. Bauman writes that 'modernity always was and continues to be, obsessed with how to get as much control over the human body and soul as possible without physically exterminating people'.[39] The modern state acts to protect its citizens but, in so doing, relies on human vulnerability and uncertainty.

---

[39] Zygmunt Bauman and Leonidas Donskis, *Moral Blindness*, Cambridge: Polity Press, 2013, 30.

Human beings are hostages of political doctrines. His interloctuer expands this view by claiming that human beings have been reduced to statistical units and little more than a workforce. It is purchasing ability that determines power on the global stage:

> The question of whether you are a democracy becomes relevant only when you have no power and therefore have to be controlled by means of rhetorical or political sticks. If you are oil rich or if you can consume or invest a great deal, it absolves you from your failure to respect modern political and moral sensibilities or to stay committed to civil liberties and human rights.[40]

Bauman writes of the new human narrative which is being created in virtual space. Technology no longer allows anyone to remain on the sidelines because it has overtaken politics and created a moral vacuum. Technology means that politicians have to be on social media, everywhere, otherwise they do not exist. A refusal to participate in technological innovation and social networks can result in one being removed to the margins of society. Technology has outpaced politics and we live in fear on so many fronts. As Bauman's conversation partner Leonidas Donskis writes, 'the fear of unimportance; the fear of vanishing in the air leaving no trace of visibility and presence; fear of being like others, fear of being beyond the TV and media world, which is tantamount to becoming a nonentity or the end of one's existence'.[41] For Bauman, progress, the manifestation of radical optimism, universally shared aspirations and happiness, has now moved to a dystopian world. Progress now 'stands for the threat of a relentless and inescapable change that instead of auguring peace and respite portends nothing but continuous crisis and strain and forbids a moment of rest'.[42] We are all too afraid of being left behind.

The huge effect of the Internet on our lives has created a kind of addiction to virtual communities, made us even more anxious as we lose more traditional frames of reference and bonds. An astute observer of the contemporary cultural scene, Andy Hargreaves writes:

> In airports and other public spaces, people with mobile phone headset attachments walk around, talking aloud and alone, like paranoid schizophrenics, oblivious to their immediate surroundings. Introspection is a disappearing act. Faced with moments alone in their cars, on the street or at the supermarket checkouts, more and more people do not collect their

---

[40] Bauman and Donskis, *Moral*, 53.   [41] Bauman and Donskis, *Moral*, 94.
[42] Zygmunt Bauman, *Liquid Times, Living in an Age of Uncertainty*, Cambridge: Polity Press, 2007, 10–11.

thoughts, but scan their mobile phone messages for shreds of evidence that someone, somewhere, may want or need them.[43]

Technology has created all kinds of connections, a quickening of society, and yet he links this greed for more financial and political power to evil which lurks in the banality of mundane life. He argues that evil is weak and invisible but lurking in each of us. We continue to speak of evil as residing in religious stories and mythologies when in fact, it lies within us; we fail to acknowledge it because it is too painful, 'unbearably difficult and completely overturns the logic of an ordinary person's everyday life'. Furthermore, 'evil is not confined to war or totalitarian ideologies, Today it more frequently reveals itself in failing to react to someone else's suffering, in refusing to understand others, in insensitivity and in eyes turned away from a silent ethical gaze'.[44]

The power of market forces is everywhere. Contemporary philosophers such as Michael Sandel explore how we are drifting from having a market economy to being a market society. The question Sandel asks is whether we want a society where everything is up for sale? He states that 'a market economy is a tool – a valuable and effective tool – for organizing productive activity. A market society is a way of life in which market values seep into every aspect of human endeavour. It's a place where social relations are made over in the image of the market'.[45] For Sandel, morality and spiritual concerns about the common good have been crowded out by free-market ethics but he argues that this recent phenomenon where money can buy almost anything, is good for neither democracy nor human welfare.

Bauman defines our modern societies as fractured where people are struggling to find ways of recreating familiarity, a sense of belonging to something and a sense of community. The anxiety of needing to belong has created a strange paradox on social media. Most people use social media not to unite, not to open their horizons wider, but on the contrary, cut themselves a comfort zone where the only sounds they hear are the echoes of their own voice, where the only things they see are the reflections of their own face. Social media are very useful and they provide pleasure, but they are a trap, not necessarily providing the hope or security that people are searching for. Similarly, our search hope for love and relationships has been

[43] Andy Hargreaves, *Teaching in the Knowledge Society: Education in the Age of Insecurity*, Open University Press, 2003, 25.

[44] Bauman and Donskis, *Moral*, 5–7 and 9.

[45] Michael Sandel, *What Money Can't Buy: The Moral Limits of Markets*, London: Allen Lane, Penguin Books, 2012, 10–11.

affected by the isolation of sex from love and this most fundamental change which defines our liquid societies:

> Sex is now expected to be self sustained and self sufficient, to 'stand on its own feet', to be judged solely by the satisfaction it may bring on its own (even if it stops as a rule well short of the expectations beefed up by the media). No wonder that its capacity to spawn frustration, and to exacerbate the very same sensation of estrangement it was hoped to heal, has also grown enormously. Sex's victory in the great war of independence has been, in the best of circumstances, pyrrhic. The wonder drug appears to produce ailments and sufferings no less numerous and arguably more acute than those it promised to cure.[46]

The physical aspect of globalisation, mass migration and the more general flow of people attracted to city dwelling away from the seeming monotony of rural life, are defining features of our liquid modern setting. Cities and urban spaces, marked by a high density of population and interaction, induce fear and insecurity. City life both attracts and repels as the confusing variety of lives and lifestyles is a source of fear and angst for many. People fear strangers, they fear immigrants and they are reluctant to be in proximity with those that arouse anxiety in them. Thus, we have gated communities, spatial segregation and homogenised areas, all of which may seem to lower anxiety but actually lower tolerance to difference.[47] The most harrowing contemporary fears are born of existential uncertainty. Sharing space with strangers is an escapable reality of city life and yet remains one of the most difficult. The polyvocality and cultural variation that has become a defining feature of most cities leads to a 'mixophobia'. Bauman describes this as 'a highly predictable and widespread reaction to the mind-boggling, and spine-chilling and nerve-breaking variety of human types and lifestyles that meet and rub elbows and shoulders in the streets of contemporary cities'.[48] But the roots of mixophobia are banal, based on not wishing to understand others, the refusal to compromise that living with others requires. As the sociologist Richard Sennett writes:

> Innate to the process of forming a coherent image of community is the desire to avoid actual participation. Feeling common bonds without common experience occurs in the first place because men are afraid of participation, afraid of the dangers and challenges of it, afraid of its pain.[49]

---

[46] Zygmunt Bauman, *Liquid Love*, Cambridge: Polity Press, 2003, 45–6.

[47] Bauman, *Liquid*, 89–91.   [48] Bauman, *Liquid*, 86.

[49] Richard Sennett, *The Uses of Disorder: Personal Identity and City Life*, London: Faber, 1996, 39 and 42.

Sennett speaks of indifference and complacency as fundamental features of alienation in modern life. We are in danger of becoming indifferent to the destiny of others. The individualised withdrawal 'seems the perfect recipe for complacency. You take for granted people like yourself and simply don't care about those who aren't like you. More, whatever their problems are, it's their problem. Individualism and indifference become twins'.[50]

The individualist model increases the need for control. Rowan Williams explains Sennett's arguments further through our growing unease with things we are unable to control:

> The best place to be is a place where you can never be surprised. We want to control what's strange, and we want to control what doesn't fall under our immediate power. We're uneasy with limits that we can't get beyond because limits, of whatever kind, remind us that there are some things that are just going to be strange and difficult wherever we are and however hard we work at them.[51]

The struggle for individual rights demands giving attention to universal rights. Our environment is created by the way we interact with others, our engagements to the people around us; there is no turning away from mutual recognition of others. Globalisation has now reached the point of no return and we are all dependent on one another. To some, globalisation may have seemed like a curse but it could turn out to be a blessing in that for the first time in human history, 'everybody's self interest and ethical principles of mutual respect and care point in the same direction and demand the same strategy'.[52] For Bauman, we do not lie at the end of history but rather at the 'threshold of another great transformation: the global forces let loose'.[53]

Bauman sees cities today as 'dumping grounds for globally produced troubles' but they are also 'laboratories' in which we need to learn how to live together. This is where hope lies. In such times, friendship as a mode of hospitality is a human trait and helps to define humanity. These encounters reveal complexities and sensitivities of being human. Using Hans Gadamer's phrase 'fusion of horizons', Bauman calls for conflict to be translated into 'benign, and often deeply gratifying and enjoyable daily encounters with the humanity hiding behind the frighteningly unfamiliar scenic masks of different and mutually alien races, nationalities, gods and liturgies'.[54] If we are to cultivate shared experiences as a human and social good, then we need

---

[50] Richard Sennett, *Together: The Rituals, Pleasures and Politics of Cooperation*, London: Allen Lane, 2012, 188.

[51] Rowan Williams, *Being Human: Bodies, Minds, Persons*, London: SPCK, 2018, 42.

[52] Bauman, *Identity*, 88.   [53] Bauman, *Identity*, 88–9.   [54] Bauman, *Liquid* Times, 91–2.

shared spaces. In our globalised world where different cultures, races and religions are coming together, even colliding in private and public spaces, friendship assumes a new significance and more importantly, gives new hope. A fundamental question of the modern era is who are our friends in fragmented and divided communities? There may well be emotional and psychological risks involved in the cultivation of new friendships, especially intercultural relationships. For some, this becomes a political question of self-identity but for many, the ambiguity of otherness does not create tension but rich opportunities of care and concern for those with whom friendships may not have been possible only a few years ago.

One of his central arguments within liquid modernity is the question of identity. Having left Poland and made Britain his home, then in the 'brutal awakening of March 1968 when my Polishness was publicly cast in doubt', Bauman speaks of his personal as well as the global issue of identity and nationality. He shares with millions of migrants and refugees who, even when they make another place home always feel 'out of place'. Bauman writes of the ambivalence of identity:

> To be wholly or in part 'out of place' everywhere (that is without qualifications and caveats, without some aspects of oneself 'sticking out' and seen by others as looking odd), not to be completely anywhere may be an upsetting, sometimes annoying experience. There is always something to explain, to apologize for, to hide or on the contrary to boldly display, to negotiate, to bid for and to bargain for.[55]

One can master the skills of negotiation and even feel that everywhere is home, but 'the price to be paid is to accept that nowhere will one be fully and truly at home'.[56]

Bauman writes of his puzzlement that a few decades ago, the issue of identity was more a philosophical than a sociological concern but today, identity has become a central concern for sociologists. Identity might be an ambiguous concept but Bauman sees it as a word that is most used when there is a battle going on; a battle between smaller and larger groups fighting over the extent to which difference is important and whether it should be preserved or whether there are higher calls of allegiance. There is an ebb and flow to how relevant it is in society, 'A battlefield is identity's natural home. Identity comes to life only in the tumult of battle; it falls asleep and silent the moment the noise of the battle dies down'. We may try but it is impossible to

---

[55] Zygmunt Bauman, *Identity, Conversations with Benedetto Vecchi*, Cambridge: Polity Press, 2004, 13.
[56] Bauman, *Identity*, 14.

ignore the issue because 'identity is a simultaneous struggle against dissolution and fragmentation; an intention to devour and at the same time a stout refusal to be eaten'.[57]

But amongst all the theories on identity, a particular issue is that of choice. Identities are part of the classification within societies and they can be imposed on us irrespective of whether or not we want to be defined in certain ways. But alongside the problematics of self-imposed or imposed identities lies the issue of those dubbed the 'underclass'. These are people who are seemingly denied a legitimate place in wider society. Bauman argues that once you have been assigned to the underclass because 'you are a school drop-out, or a single mother on welfare, or a current or former drug addict, or homeless or a beggar', any other identity you might aspire to or struggle to attain is a priori denied. This is an absence of identity, 'the effacement of denial of individuality' which then places you outside the social space in which rights and identities as well as moral care is negotiated.[58] Then there are those labelled refugee or asylum seeker who are placed in camps and spaces away from where 'normal' people live their lives. In his capitalist critique, Bauman sees that the expansion of the West and relentless globalisation has led to the notion of 'wasted humans'. This he defines as people 'no longer necessary for the completion of the economic cycle and thus impossible to accommodate within a social framework resonant with the capitalist economy'. Whereas Marx had spoken of human exploitation, today it is exclusion which underlies the malfunctioning of capitalism, human inequality and misery.[59]

In a critical review of *Identity*, Richard Mullender writes that while the topic of 'liquid modernity (i.e. postmodernity and the crisis of belonging), features in many of Bauman's works, he does not give an adequately nuanced account of this phenomenon. Mullender writes, 'For example, Bauman assumes that all those who live in the "unmapped land" that is liquid modernity are deeply uncomfortable with the experience. This seems too sweeping'. Furthermore, if there are few social anchors in society today, why should that be seen as a problem? Mullender may be right in saying that the narrative of 'liquid modernity' is overblown; even in an age of globalisation sources of identity have yet to evaporate.[60] But Bauman's incorporation of philosophy and other disciplines in his social critique made him a strong moral voice for the poor and dispossessed. Globalisation was not only

---

[57] Bauman, *Identity*, 77.   [58] Bauman, *Identity*, 39.   [59] Bauman, *Identity*, 40–1.

[60] Richard Mullender, review of 'Zygmunt Bauman, Identity: Conversations with Benedetto Vecchi', *History of Political Thought*, 28:2, 2007, 368–71, 269.

a numbers game, a story of people on the move. The real issue is how do people continue to find meaning and emotional strength when traditional forms of social cohesion have been somewhat eroded or left behind.

Bauman's observations can be situated in a long trajectory of therapeutic analyses of contemporary societies. Around four decades ago, Christopher Lasch's book, *The Culture of Narcissism*, became a bestseller for its perceptive observations on what was happening to American society in the wake of the decline of the family. Lasch was born in Omaha in 1932, and died at the relatively young age of sixty-one. During this time – the period from the early Cold War to the fall of the Soviet Union – he had become one of the most famous intellectuals in the world. Lasch's distinctive voice pierced through the din of the nation's noisy political and cultural debates. The historian Jackson Lears recalled, in particular, the 'spell that Lasch cast over a generation of historians and cultural critics who came of age in the 1960s and 1970s'.[61] He too had become a prophetic voice, an intellectual surveying the cultural and political issues of his time who concluded that humankind needed to be rooted. What was happening now was a certain deracination from family ties, community and sense of place. A product and one-time devotee of the American Left, Lasch later solidified his standing as a commanding figure in American letters as a trenchant and at times brutal critic of American liberalism.[62] Lasch's interest in religion and specifically in Christianity was the result of his desire to seek moral idealism and his awareness that leftist ideologies could never strike deep popular roots. Lasch's work remains both powerful and controversial for a number of reasons as he took what was still mainly a narrowly clinical term and used it to diagnose a pathology that seemed to have spread to all corners of American life. Narcissism is the metaphor of contemporary life. Asking the question, 'Who now reads Christopher Lasch?' Richard Kilminster recognises that many still do:

> Lasch still continues to find a resonance in contemporary debates about the problems of society. Rightly or wrongly, he is still one of the basic points of departure for framing social criticism, in particular. His targets included many features of the earlier period that are still widely regarded as the primary sources of society's ills to this day – hyper-individualism, selfishness, managerialism, hedonism and rampant consumerism.[63]

---

[61] Jackson Lears, 'The Grim Optimism of Christopher Lasch', *New Republic*, October 2, 1995.

[62] Jon K. Lauck, 'Christopher Lasch and Prairie Populism', *Great Plains Quarterly*, 32:3, 183–205, 183.

[63] Richard Kilminster, 'Narcissism or Informalization: Christopher Lasch, Norbert Elias and Social Diagnosis', in *Theory, Culture and Society*, 25:3, 2008, 131–51, 131.

However, Kilminster says, 'when social critics draw on Lasch they mostly assume narcissism to mean excessive egoism or selfishness, in a pejorative sense. But few have appreciated the way in which, for rhetorical effect, Lasch plays off this popular meaning of the term against the technical, psychoanalytic meaning – or otherwise elides them'.[64] Drawing from Freud, Lasch's definition of the narcissist is one who is driven by repressed rage and uses other people as instruments of gratification even while craving their love and approval. Freud's original idea, dependent on his libido theory, was that narcissism was a stage in the development of the ego in which the person chooses only themselves as a love object. Later modifications conclude that rather than narcissism being instinctually rooted, it was now seen to be related to the ways in which individuals cope with themselves and with their relationships with others. Narcissism was not about self-esteem but rather self-inflation.[65] Kilminster succinctly summarises the essential thesis which is that 'Lasch's diagnosis of the problems of contemporary Western societies is essentially a nostalgic lament for the passing of a society in which there were clearer social divisions, associated with the propertied bourgeois classes of the 19th century'.[66] For Lasch, this society has now been replaced by the rise of a new ruling class of managers, professionals, technicians and experts. It is this old order which has now been replaced by the narcissistic culture of our time.

Jan de Vos explains how Lasch critiques the dynamics of academisation and psychologisation as well as the bureaucratisation and instrumentalisation of our life-world so as to create 'a theoretical safe haven for the "besieged family"'.[67] The family cannot be just another contingent social unit as a victim for both the state and the capitalist market. In this context, Lasch uses psychoanalytic theory to bolster the status of the family and, thus, to safeguard it from colonisation. He begins his book by elaborating on the current malaise of American culture but also a critique of liberalism more widely. Much of this rests on the 'prevailing passion', which is to live for the moment; not to live for others but only for yourself. For Lasch humankind is losing its concern for posterity: 'We are fast losing a sense of historical continuity, the sense of belonging to a succession of generations originating in the past and stretching into the future'.[68]

For Lasch, liberalism is now both politically and intellectually bankrupt and 'economic man has given way to the psychological man of our times – the final

---

[64] Kilminster, 'Narcissism', 131.   [65] Kilminster, 'Narcissism', 136.

[66] Kilminster, 'Narcissism', 138.

[67] Jan de Vos, 'Christopher Lasch's *The Culture of Narcissism*', *Theory and Psychology*, 20:4, 2010, 528–48, 532.

[68] Christopher Lasch, *The Culture of Narcissism*, New York: W.W. Norton& Company, 1979, 5.

product of bourgeois individualism'.[69] Lasch's nostalgia is a nostalgia for the pre-psychologised individual and pre-therapeutic society. His writing portrays the 'struggle to maintain psychic equilibrium'. In the sixties, radical politics 'filled empty lives' but today: 'The contemporary climate is therapeutic, not religious. People today hunger not for personal salvation, let alone for the restoration of an earlier golden age, but for the feeling, the momentary illusion of personal wellbeing, health, and psychic security'.[70]

The inner emptiness that most feel means that people are searching for peace of mind even as society evolves to take that very peace away from them. People look for therapists not priests because we adhere to scientific methods of healing in a society 'which gives no thought to anything beyond its immediate needs'.[71] Our desperation is borne of weakness, fear or despair. We often feel that we are lost in life or that we don't know how to live in more meaningful ways. As Erich Fromm explains, despite so much potentially within our reach for the first time in history:

> Modern man feels uneasy and more and more bewildered. He works and strives, but he is dimly aware of futility with regard to his activities. While his power over matter grows, he feels powerless in his individual life and society. While creating new and better means of mastering nature, he has become enmeshed in a network of those means and has lost the vision of the end which alone gives them significance- man himself.[72]

Today the search is a search for authenticity, to find something real beyond bourgeois life. Larsh writes: 'Twentieth-century peoples have erected so many psychological barriers against strong emotions, and have invested those defenses with so much of the energy derived from forbidden impulse, that they can no longer remember what it feels like to be inundated by desire'. He elaborates:

> Today, Americans are overcome not by the sense of endless possibility but by the banality of the social order they have erected against it. Having internalized the social restraints by means of which they formerly sought to keep possibility within civilized limits, they feel themselves overwhelmed by an annihilating boredom, like animals whose instincts have withered in captivity ... people nowadays complain of an inability to feel. They seek more vivid experiences, seek to beat sluggish flesh to life, attempt to revive jaded appetites.[73]

---

[69] Lasch, *Culture*, xvii.   [70] Lasch, *Culture*, 7.   [71] Lasch, *Culture*, 13.
[72] Erich Fromm, *Man for Himself*, London: Routledge & Kegan Paul, 1949, 4.
[73] Lasch, *Culture*, 11.

Lasch's evocative and powerful language tries to persuade the reader that society is in a moral and psychological crisis. It is true that in much of the discussion surrounding Lasch's thesis it is tacitly assumed that people are, empirically, becoming increasingly narcissistic although this is never clearly specified. The empirical veracity of the thesis is either taken for granted or the empirical question avoided. But as Kilminster writes, Lasch is a historian and thus his interest is not sociological. Rather, Lasch is still drawn to the Freudian model 'because it fitted well with his prior moral and political views and his religious convictions about the "fallen" state of human beings'.[74]

The break with history means that Lasch sees crisis everywhere. He despairs of the growth of bureaucracy and the cult of consumption. The pursuit of gain and wealth have been replaced by a search for psychic revival. When it comes to sex and sexuality, in modern societies where women and men of all backgrounds enjoy a much greater array of freedoms but less commitment, cultural theorists analyse the effects of our changed lifestyles and expectations.

Lasch refers to the manner in which our yearning for meaningful relationships has increased. Desire is everywhere but fulfilment so often eludes us. Men and women find it difficult to put their relationships in perspective. When sex is valued purely for its own sake 'it loses all reference to the future and brings no hope of permanent relationships'.

> The demystification of womanhood goes hand in hand with the desublimation of sexuality ... Institutionalised sexual segregation has given way to arrangements that promote the intermingling of the sexes at every stage of life. Efficient contraceptives, legalised abortion, and a 'realistic and 'healthy' acceptance of the body have weakened the links that once tied sex to love, marriage, and procreation. Men and women now pursue sexual pleasure as an end in itself, unmediated even by the conventional trappings of romance.[75]

While we may long for emotional intimacy, sex and our physical world have become loaded with too many expectations for human fulfilment. Sex is divested of emotional intensity even though 'the degradation of work and the impoverishment of communal life force people to turn to sexual excitement to satisfy all their emotional needs'.[76] Yet as he explores the struggles of feminism, the battles against male domination, the disappointment so many women feel in marriages and relationships in their desire for sexual

---

[74] Christopher Lasch, *The Minimal Self: Psychic Survival in Troubled Times*, London and New York: W.W. Norton, 1984, 259.
[75] Lasch, *Culture*, 191.   [76] Lasch, *Culture*, 195.

fulfilment and tenderness, Lasch concludes that the driving impulse in sexual relationships is the 'flight from feeling' where people, through fear of being hurt and vulnerable, long for emotional detachment: 'For many reasons, personal relations have become increasingly risky – most obviously, because they no longer carry any assurance of permanence. Men and women make extravagant demands on each other and experience irrational rage and hatred when their demands are not met'.[77]

De Vos critiques Lasch's work for its essentialism but argues that the modern world carries an intrinsic emptiness which is separate from the primitive feudal world.

> One can argue that with the Enlightenment, the antagonism changed decisively: science and technology dramatically accelerated the encroaching on the other world by the positive term of the antagonism; the pre-modern and un-enlightened world shrivelled away. The last grand antagonism to dissolve was that between the West and the Communist world. With the fall of the Berlin Wall, we have lost the other world as such; there is no longer a world outside capitalism. And is this not precisely the source of the insecurity that Lasch describes?[78]

Lasch both praises and raises doubt about human ingenuity. Modern technology has made dazzling breakthroughs so that 'the secret of life itself is within our grasp, according to those who predict a revolution in genetics'. He writes that 'the impending triumph over old age and death, we are told, is the ultimate tribute to humanity's power to master its surroundings'.[79] Such thinking dreams of subjugating nature and presents itself as the ultimate utopian possibility.

Lasch's work explores all kinds of questions centred on the fragility and emptiness inherent in the malaise of modern life where 'reality is experienced as an unstable environment of flickering images'. This is a society where success is measured in public approval and acclaim and people do not want respect but crave envy from others. But his conclusion emphasises the need to accept human limitations. Meaningful relationships and mutual dependency are a reflection of emotional maturity:

> The best hope of emotional maturity, then, appears to lie in a recognition of our need for and dependence on people who nevertheless remain separate from ourselves and effuse to submit tour whims. It lies in a recognition of others not as projections of our own desires but independent beings with desire of their own. More broadly, it lies in acceptance of our limits . . .

---

[77] Lasch, *Culture*, 199.   [78] De Vos, 'Christopher', 540.   [79] Lasch, *Culture*, 244.

> Psychoanalysis confirms the ancient religious insight that the only way to achieve happiness is to accept limitations in a spirit of gratitude and contrition instead of attempting to annul those limitations or bitterly resenting them.[80]

Kilminster stresses that Lasch fails to provide any systematic empirical evidence for his critiques and evaluation of society, because 'right from the start he was not testing a sociological theory as such. Rather, he was engaged in persuading us, by whatever literary means at his disposal, to accept his ideological vision of a capitalist society in a moral and political crisis'.[81] The book remains a wholesale indictment of American culture.

Alongside these writers, who reflect on the cultural and social malaise of our times, are those whose work has pivoted on particular struggles even as they speak of wider political and societal anxieties. For many of these writers, struggle is in essence the search for justice. The struggle for racial justice is everywhere and its associated evils have never been far from our political consciousness. But the African American experience resulting from centuries of slavery, carries a distinct history and narrative. The Civil War (1861–5) had officially abolished slavery, but it didn't end discrimination against Black Americans. They continued to endure the devastating effects of racism, especially in the South. The civil rights movement was a struggle for social justice that took place mainly during the 1950s and 1960s for Blacks to gain equal rights under the law in the United States. While the United States has made significant progress in recent decades, there is still much to be done to combat all forms of racism and racial discrimination from its civic and institutional systems.

Born in Oklahoma in 1953, and currently teaching at Harvard University, Cornel West is one of America's most famous African American public intellectuals, often described as one of the great prophetic voices of our time. It is often claimed that his writings do not fall into any neat academic categories in that much of West's work is concerned with exploring what it is to be human and a citizen in America. While often hailed as a writer on issues of race and democracy, West himself says, 'My efforts to understand myself are inseparable from understanding what it means to be human, modern, American, black, male and straight in global and local contexts'.[82]

In one of his most famous works, *The American Evasion of Philosophy*, West praises American pragmatist thinkers precisely because they were able to avoid the narrow epistemological focus of European philosophy and

---

[80] Lasch, *Culture*, 249 and 242.   [81] Kilminster, 'Narcissism', 147.
[82] Cornel West, 'Preface' to *The Cornel West Reader*, Basic Civitas Books: New York, 1999.

engage instead in a 'future-oriented instrumentalism that tries to deploy thought as a weapon to enable more effective action'.[83] As he analyses a line of thinkers from Emerson and Du Bois to Rorty, West argues that, in America, philosophical thinking becomes 'a continuous cultural commentary or set of interpretations that attempt to explain America to itself at a particular historical moment'.[84] This swerve from epistemology or abstract pure philosophy did not lead to a radical dismissal of philosophy but to its reconception as a form of cultural criticism that is politically engaged. West places his own thinking in this lineage and sees himself as engaged in a similar, intensely practical effort at national self-understanding. For West, philosophy has slowly but steadily turned into a kind of cultural criticism in which the meaning of America is continually questioned and debated.

West's work is immersed in America and its meanings. As James Conlon writes:

> 'At least 10 of his books refer to America somewhere in their title or subtitle. In these books, he does not just analyze America's social and cultural environment but utilizes its character traits in his ethical explorations. His ideals are developed in agonistic dialogue with American values and directed specifically at challenging American citizens to a more complete humanity'.[85]

Conlon sees West as one of America's greatest critics but also one of its profoundest lovers and cites the following as a testament to West's devotion for his homeland:

> To understand your country you must love it. To love it you must, in a sense, accept it. To accept it as it is, however, is to betray it. To accept your country without betraying it, you must love it for that in it which shows what it might become. America ... needs citizens who love it enough to reimagine and remake it.[86]

Democracy, questions of race and human struggle feature throughout his work. Calling himself a 'prophetic Christian freedom fighter', his writings 'constitute a perennial struggle between my African and American identities,

---

[83] Cornel West, *The American Evasion of Philosophy*, Madison: University of Wisconsin Press, 1989, 5.

[84] West, *The American*, 4.

[85] James Conlon, 'Cornel West's Pragmatic Understanding of America', *Journal of Black Studies*, 28:1, 2017, 26–42, 27.

[86] R. M. Unger and Cornel West, *The Future of American Progressivism*, Boston, MA: Beacon Press, 1998.

my democratic socialist convictions and my Christian sense of the profound tragedy and triumph in life and history'.[87] West's prophetic pragmatism presents itself as a philosophy of struggle, a philosophy of praxis. He writes, 'Human struggle sits at the center of prophetic pragmatism, a struggle guided by a democratic and libertarian vision, sustained by moral courage and existential integrity, and tempered by the recognition of human finitude and frailty'.[88] In speaking of the American social and political vision, in which there were a hybrid of peoples and colours, West critiques how white America's national image continues to be. If America had nurtured a welcoming image as a beacon of opportunity for white European peoples, tragically this image was inextricable from 'its degradation and exploitation of darker skins'.[89] In two separate works, West speaks of the evil of slavery and the continuing divide in American society on the issue of colour:

> Like other indescribable evils of the recent past, the centuries long slave trade forces us to wrestle with levels of unjustified anguish and unmerited pain that are difficult to fathom. Most of us would prefer to turn our heads and hearts from this ghastly past and dream of a better future. Yet the pernicious effects and insidious consequences of New World slavery still linger in our perceptions and inform our sensibilities in regard to black people. The vicious legacy of institutionalized hatred of Africans is still with us (even if its raw forms are a bit out of fashion at the moment).[90]

While slavery may be as old as human civilisation itself, the distinctive feature of New World slavery was its racial character. The racialisation of American slavery was 'rooted in economic calculations and psychocultural anxieties that targeted black bodies'.[91] He writes:

> What made America distinctly American for them [Irish, Italians, Poles, Welsh] was not simply the presence of unprecedented opportunities, but the struggle for seizing those opportunities in a new land in which black slavery and racial caste served as the floor upon which white class, ethnic and gender struggles could be diffused and diverted . . . From 1776 to 1964 – 188 years of our 218-year history – this racial divide would serve as a basic presupposition.[92]

As Conlon explains:

> In other words, African Americans were not just one ethnic group among the many who made up America, albeit one that failed to become as well

---

[87] West, *The Cornel West*, 13.   [88] Cornel West, *American Evasion*, 229.
[89] Conlon, 'Cornel West', 30.   [90] West, *The Cornel West*, 51   [91] West, *The Cornel West*, 51.
[92] Cornel West, *Race Matters*, New York: Vintage Books, 1994, 156–7.

integrated into the dominant culture as, say, Irish Americans or Polish Americans had. Rather, African Americans functioned as the 'Other' against whom the European and lighter-skinned ethnicities were unified into an American culture'.[93]

In the making of America's grand narrative, Kelly Brown Douglas traces how America's democracy was conceived of as an expression of Anglo-Saxon character. For Douglas, the way in which the early Americans, as well as America's founding fathers, especially Thomas Jefferson, constructed the identity of the nation is consequential. Liberty and freedom were only for her white citizens because Anglo-Saxonism had become the civil religion; Anglo-Saxonism was sacred so that 'if one is alienated from Anglo-Saxon exceptionalism, one is alienated from God'. This myth of exceptionalism has had a devastating impact on America's cultural values. For Douglas, America is a land held captive to sin and she sees America's identity of Anglo-Saxon exceptionalism as sinful. She writes: 'There have been those who have considered the inhumane treatment of Native Americans as America's original sin. Others have claimed it to be the enslavement of African Americans. Both are the sins that sin produced'.[94] For Douglas, America's grand narrative is a web of sin. It is a narrative which has taken away the goodness and sacredness of people's humanity. America is still a nation 'divided by stand-your-ground-culture war' and will continue to be like this until the original sin of America's Anglo-Saxon exceptionalism is eliminated.[95] Douglas laments that Black people have struggled against Anglo-Saxon exceptionalism but this myth has distorted both notions of democracy and an understanding of Christianity throughout history. Many white Churches have been complicit in Black suffering. Douglas writes that the cross has been a 'stumbling block' for many churches when it comes to matters of race. Many churches 'stumble' when it comes to 'recognizing the face of the crucified Jesus that is not white'. Whiteness opposes the freedom of God which is love for all of God's creation.[96] In a similar vein, Willie Jennings writes 'Christianity in the western world lives and moves within a diseased social imagination'. For Jennings, the history of Christian theological imagination was woven into 'processes of colonial dominance'. As he writes: 'Indeed it is as though Christianity, wherever it went in the modern colonies, inverted its sense of hospitality. It claimed to be the host, the owner

---

[93] Conlon, 'Cornel West', 30.

[94] Kelly Brown Douglas, *Stand Your Ground: Black Bodies and the Justice of God*, Maryknoll, New York: Orbis Books, 2015, 196.

[95] Douglas, *Stand*, 196–7.   [96] Douglas, *Stand*, 200–1.

of the spaces it entered, and demanded native peoples enter its cultural logics, its way of being in the world and its conceptualities'.[97]

In an interview with the African American philosopher, George Yancy, West is asked what the 'black experience has to offer American philosophy that is of philosophical value'. West's reply is 'a profound sense of the tragic and the comic rooted in heroic efforts to preserve human dignity on the night side, the underside of modernity'.[98] For West, race is the dominating discourse in the United States for he says that 'modern Christianity is thoroughly shot through with white supremacy like every other institution in modernity'.[99] For West, the truth is stark: 'The notion that black people are human beings is a relatively new discovery in the modern West. The idea of black equality in beauty, culture and intellectual capacity remains problematic and controversial within prestigious halls of learning and sophisticated intellectual circles'.[100]

The African American encounter has been shaped by the doctrine of white supremacy. But West also regrets the absence of quality Black leadership. In his seminal work, *Race Matters*, he writes that to bring about strong leadership, what is needed is 'a vibrant tradition of resistance passed on to new generations' and that effective leadership is borne within a 'credible sense of political struggle'. Yet political leadership today is too genteel; passion and poignancy have been replaced by sentiment and sensation: 'In stark contrast, most present day black political leaders appear too hungry for status to be angry, too eager for acceptance to be bold, too self-invested in advancement to be defiant'.[101]

Where West finds hope is in his love for his country. This also allows West to speak of the significance of music, specifically blues and jazz, in American life. Since they are, he argues, America's most distinctive artistic creations, they have played an important role in expressing its democratic soul. The strength of democracy, according to West, is dependent upon the extent to which those on the margins are actual participants in the conversation that shapes the social life of the community. The democratic citizen is not only to find a voice but also to make it heard. He argues that African American music is not just a form of entertainment, but a serious countercultural voice in America's efforts at democratic conversation:

> The blues professes to the deep psychic and material pains inflicted on black people within the sphere of a mythological American land of opportunity. The central role of the human voice in this heritage reflects the

---

[97] Willie James Jennings, *The Christian Imagination*, New Haven: Yale University Press, 2010, 8.
[98] West, *The Cornel West*, 25.   [99] West, *The Cornel West*, 31.
[100] West, *The Cornel West*, 70.
[101] Cornel West, *Race Matters*, first published 1993, 25th anniversary edition, Boston: Beacon Press, 2017, 37–8.

commitment to the value of the individual and of speaking up about ugly truths: it asserts the necessity of robust dialogue – of people needing to listen up – in the face of entrenched dogma . . . The stress the blues placed on dialogue, resistance, and hope is the very lifeblood for a vital democratic citizenry.[102]

Jazz and blues paved the way for the civil rights struggles because these were uplifting voices, sounds of hope, not nihilism in the face of serious misery. West wrote, 'I have always marveled at how such an unfree people as blacks in America . . . invented such odes to democratic individuality and commu-nity as in the blues'. He writes of the ethical value of the blues in that this music 'expresses righteous indignation with a smile and deep inner pain without bitterness or revenge'.[103] It is a tool for America to confront its own darkness with hope rather than bitterness. Hope is a profound ethical stance, and for West, one that is best exemplified in the life of Jesus and the work of great artists such as Shakespeare, Beethoven and Chekhov. West struggles to maintain hope in his own life and the blues for him is 'the most profound interpretation of tragicomic hope' that America has so far created.[104] For West, the place of music is central to the soul and suffering of Black people. In one of his interviews, when responding to questions about Louis Farrakhan and the Nation of Islam, West makes an intriguing observation:

I used to tell him that the Nation of Islam could never become a mass movement among Black people because there is no music in their ritual. And music has really been the fundamental means by which Black people have been able to preserve sanity and dignity and, at our best, integrity.[105]

Based on a series of interviews and selections of his writings, West explains in multivalent ways the significance and struggle of the 'black experience' in America. He writes, 'My own work and life have always unfolded under the dark shadows of death, dread and despair in search of love, dialogue and democracy'. He writes of 'black strivings' which he sees as the 'terrifying African encounter with the absurd in America – and the absurd as America'. Like others, Black people had to construct their own structures of meaning and feeling in the face of all of life's despairs and disappointments but Black people had to 'sustain their mental sanity and spiritual health, social life and

[102] Cornel West, *Democracy Matters*, New York: Penguin Press, 2004, 93.
[103] West, *Democracy*, 216 and 219.   [104] West, *Democracy*, 216. See Conlon, *Pragmatic*, 36–8.
[105] Cornel West, *Black Prophetic Fire*, Boston, MA: Beacon Press, 2014, 116. It is interesting to note that later in the conversation, West describes Malcolm X: 'Malcom was music in motion; he was Black music in motion; he was jazz in motion, and of course, jazz has improvisation, swing and the blues . . . Malcom could be improvisational', 118.

political struggle in the midst of a slaveholding, white supremacist civilization that viewed itself as the most enlightened, free, tolerant and democratic
experiment in human history'.[106]

What sits at the centre of this thought is 'the existential quest for meaning
and the political struggle for freedom'. West describes himself as
a 'Chekhovian Christian with deep democratic commitments'. This means
that he is 'obsessed with confronting the pervasive evil of unjustified suffering and unnecessary social misery in our world'.[107] Expressing his interest in
jazz and blue singers as well as the Russian novelists, he writes, 'Like both
Russian novelists and blues singers, I also stress the concrete lived experience
of despair and tragedy and the cultural equipment requisite for coping with
the absurdities, anxieties and frustrations as well as the joys, laughter and
gaiety of life'.

It is in this deep sense that, for West, Marxism is not a religion as it fails to
speak of the ultimate facts of human existence. As Ulf Schulenberg writes,
'West in the 1980s wants to rework and rewrite Marxism as a critical social
theory that opposes the forces of exploitation, oppression, com-
modification, and reification in late-capitalist America, and by doing so he
can embed this theoretical approach within the broader framework of his
black liberationist Christian perspective'.[108] West critiques the excesses of
capitalism, and while he does not wish to discredit Marxism, he still feels that
Marxism's way works as social theory of societies and histories but 'social
theory is not the same as existential wisdom'.[109] Unlike the Christian faith
which has sustained West, Marxism fails to speak on existential and visceral
levels. But West is keen to point out that he is not a theologian and has little
interest in systematising the dogmas and doctrines of the Christian tradition.
This may be worthy endeavour for the life of the church but West sees his
role as that of a cultural critic 'with philosophic training who works out of the
Christian tradition than a theologian who focuses on the coherency or
epistemic validity of Christian claims'.[110]

West mentions 'struggle' frequently as he speaks of the many ways in
which the Black community has suffered, survived and also been a creative
force in America. Throughout American history, Blackness has been dehu-
manised or the communities rendered invisible. The response to these
various kinds of humiliation and subjugation on which the collective Black

[106] West, *The Cornel West*, 101.   [107] West, *The Cornel West*, xv.
[108] Ulf Schulenberg, 'Where the People Can Sing, the Poet Can Live: James Baldwin, Pragmatism
     and Cosmopolitan Humanism' in Susan J. McWilliams, *A Political Companion to James
     Baldwin*, Kentucky Scholarship online, 270–300, 273.
[109] West, *The Cornel West*, 13.   [110] West, *The Cornel West*, 14.

response is predicated is, according to West, that of prophetic love. This is the love that suffers but bears witness to the truth of this suffering and keeps a 'vision of a black redemption'. For West, the legacy of writers, musicians and comedians such as Martin Luther King, Nat King Cole, Richard Pryor, Toni Morrison and James Baldwin is that they all sustained a 'hope against hope for black freedom'.[111]

On 11 October 2014, West delivered the keynote address to nearly 600 students at the regional Leadership & Social Justice Conference, hosted at Saint Mary's College of California. The conference took place two days before West was arrested in Ferguson, Missouri, during a demonstration to protest the killing of young Black men by White police officers, as in the case of eighteen-year-old Michael Brown in Ferguson. Speaking of the students, West said,

> I would like to see these precious young people commit themselves to lives of integrity, honesty and decency, where they are vigilant against all forms of evil – White supremacists, male supremacists, anti-Jewish, anti-Arab, anti-Muslim and homophobia. Live lives never losing sight of the humanity of other people. Be true to the Lasallian ideal that says each one of us is made in the image and likeness of God. We need to love that image in each and every one of us human beings, wherever and whoever we are.

In his speech he encourages the crowd to hold onto decency and virtue in the face of insult, the imperative to hold onto integrity even as people fight back:

> We're going to fight back the hand of revenge, but we want the world to know, and we want the young folks to know, you're not in it by yourself. They may send you to decrepit schools and try to murder your soul, but you're not in it by yourself. They may have you deal with massive unemployment and act as if you are disposable and superfluous but you're not in it by yourself. They may convince you that you have less beauty and less morality and less character, but you come from a tradition that says you can look that vicious legacy of White supremacy in the face and still learn how to love, learn how to love yourself. Justice is what love looks like in public. Connect that love to bearing witness and put pressure on the powerful elites.

He continues later:

> Life, death, joy, justice, trust, fidelity, these are things that matter, the things they will talk about when you are in your coffin. It won't be a story about how much money you made. It won't be a story about how big your

---

[111] West, *The Cornel West*, 106.

mansion was. It won't be a story about how many material toys you accumulated. They will want to say something about the things that matter, with your body in that coffin before the worms get you.

He tells the students that the most important thing they have to think about is what kind of human are they going to be:

> That's the most terrifying question we will ever raise as mortals made in the image and the likeness of God, not a question about what kind of job you have, not a question about your career. It's not a question about how much money you have, or the question even of about your educational attainment. The essential terrifying question: What kind of human being are you going to be?[112]

West situates his reflections of the Black American struggle in the long history of their suffering and their resistance. His works contain many references to the names which precede him including the foremost sociologist, Black leader and civil rights activist W. E. B. Du Bois (1868–1963), the abolitionist and statesman Frederick Douglass (1818–95), a leading female civil rights activist Ella Baker (1903–86) and the novelist and activist James Baldwin (1924–87). But like many African American writers, he pays a particular tribute to Malcolm X (1925–65). His references to Malcolm X show admiration and sympathy but also critique of this most controversial and powerful figure who continues to be a reference point for human rights activists and scholars alike. Malcolm X, whose original name was Malcolm Little and later Muslim name el-Hajj Malik el-Shabazz, was one of the most prominent African American leaders promoting Black nationalism and a pivotal figure in the Nation of Islam.[113] For a while, he was a leading figure in the NOI and his keen intellect and charisma made him formidable public speaker and critic of American society. But as tensions arose with NOI, he left the organisation in 1964, and founded the Muslim Mosque Inc. Later that year he went on the Hajj pilgrimage to Mecca and embraced Sunni Islam as the true orthodox faith. In 1965, he founded the Organization for Afro-American Unity, which he saw as a secular vehicle to internationalise the plight of Black Americans as well as reaching out to the people of the developing world in his move from civil rights to human rights. After his assassination in February 1965, the widespread distribution of his life story,

---

[112] Cornel West, 'Prophetic Imagination: Confronting The New Jim Crow & Income Inequality in America', in *Engaging Pedagogies in Catholic Higher Education (EPiCHE)*, 1:1, 2015, 1–5.

[113] The Nation of Islam or NOI is an African-American movement and organization, founded in 1930 and known for its teachings combining elements of traditional Islam with Black nationalist ideas.

The Autobiography of Malcolm X, made him an ideological hero, especially among Black youth. All introductions to his life and work reflect his presence and power. Robert Terrill introduces Malcom X:

> Mention Malcolm X, and you are almost certain to receive a reaction. Many admire him, many loathe him, but even now, more than four decades after his death, few lack an opinion about him. A polarizing figure, in death as in life, Malcolm X continues to haunt American national consciousness like few other figures. His name is known around the world, his autobiography is on American high school and college reading lists around the country, his life was the subject of a blockbuster Hollywood film, hundreds of websites are dedicated to his legacy, and he has even appeared on a United States postage stamp. And yet he resists now, as he did then, being fully accepted – or coopted, depending on your point of view – by the culture that he spent his life critiquing.[114]

Terrill sees Malcolm X as one who will always speak from the margins as he points out the 'collective failure to live according to the ideals we proclaim, taking us to task for the inconsistencies and hypocrisies that riddle our politics, revealing our complicity and reviling our complacency'. Malcolm X's voice cannot be 'placated or patronized, a voice both self-righteous and self-educated, passionate and cerebral, angry and eloquent'.[115] A few months after Martin Luther King Jr's 'I have a Dream' speech, Malcolm X delivered his famous 'Ballot or the Bullet' speech at the Cory Methodist Church in Cleveland, Ohio. In this speech he argued, 'I see America through the eyes of the victim. I don't see any American dream; I see an American nightmare'. Malcolm X explained that he was not an American. Rather, he considered himself to be 'one of the 22 million black people who are victims of Americanism. One of the 22 million black people who are victims of democracy, nothing but disguised hypocrisy'. He saw himself neither as an American or a patriot but 'as a victim of [the] American system'.[116] In response to the critique that Malcom X did not articulate any form of political action, Terrill writes that Malcolm's speeches do not encourage his listeners to engage in specific political actions or to explicitly take up violence as a mode of resistance. Rather, his rhetoric showed his audiences the tactics of 'judgment and critique that do not lead toward liberation so

[114] Robert E, Terrill, 'Introduction' in Robert E. Terrill (ed.), *The Cambridge Companion to Malcolm X*, Cambridge: Cambridge University Press, 1–9, 1.

[115] Terrill, 'Introduction', 1.

[116] James Tyner, 'Nightmarish Landscapes: Geography and the Dystopian Words of Malcolm X', in Terrill, *Cambridge Companion*, 137–49, 137. The 'Ballot or the Bullet' speech is considered a masterpiece of rhetoric.

much as they are a liberation from the constraints and norms of the dominant culture'.[117] Black liberation would only occur when African Americans were seen as equals.

In this speech, Malcolm X repeats the force of the African American vote, the need to expand the civil rights struggle to a higher level by making international alliances. For Malcolm X, the Nation of Islam offered little opportunity for political engagement. It was 'a sort of a religious political hybrid, all to ourselves. Not involved in anything but just standing on the sidelines condemning everything'. The organisation had become politically mute, 'actually alienated, cut off from all type of activity with even the world that we were fighting against'.[118]

> Yet, activists still wanted to do something about the problems confronting all Black people. Malcolm X saw the racism in America as similar to the racism which confronts all dark-skinned people everywhere; the problem had to connect the domestic to the international. As he writes, the key technique of the practice of racism everywhere is that it is 'a science that's called image making' designed to make it 'look like the victim is the criminal, and the criminal is the victim. He insists: 'Any kind of movement for freedom of Black people based solely within the confines of America is absolutely doomed to fail'.[119] Cornel West speaks of this distinct move in Malcolm X's vision: 'We can't stop at civil rights; we have to move onto human rights, and then the struggle becomes international, and that's another kind of we-identity. It is no longer limiting because it turns into a freedom to unite and identity with ideals that could be shared by all'.[120]

In a speech delivered in 1964, Malcolm X asked what type of country the United States was. His response was a series of questions and answers:

> Why should we do the dirtiest jobs for the lowest pay? Why should we do the hardest work for the lowest pay? Why should we pay the most money for the worst kind of food and the most money for the worst kind of place to live in? I'm telling you we do it because we live in one of the rottenest countries that has ever existed on this earth. It's the system that is rotten; we have a rotten system. It's a system of exploitation, a political and economic

[117] Terrill, 'Judgement and Critique in the Rhetoric of Malcolm X' in Terrill, *Cambridge Companion*, 125–36, 125.
[118] Terrill, 'Judgement', 132.
[119] Steve Clark, *Malcolm X, February 1965: The Final Speeches*, New York: Pathfinder, 1992, 150 and 167–8.
[120] West, *Black Prophetic*, 132.

system of exploitation, of outright humiliation, degradation, discrimination.[121]

America was a place of broken dreams for the African Americans and for Malcolm X, the goal was not to convince white people with evidence but to give a Black point of view to a world struggling and fighting for human dignity. Malcolm X implored his listeners to make the connection between institutional racism and the suppression of African American individuality and humanity. He explained:

> 'Negro' doesn't give you a language, because there is no such thing as a Negro language. It doesn't give you a country, because there is no such thing as a Negro country. It doesn't give you a culture – there is no such thing as a Negro culture, it doesn't exist. The land doesn't exist, the culture doesn't exist, the language doesn't exist, and the man [sic] doesn't exist. They take you out of existence by calling you a Negro'.[122]

Tyner sees Malcolm X's writings as exemplars of justice and warning. Tyner draws on the conceptual framework of Robin Kelly, for whom certain conditions enabled people to 'imagine something different, to realize that things need not always be this way'. Kelly called this seeing the future in the present, poetic knowledge. His language of maps and spatial analogies refers to the physical geography and landscape which affects the cultural context in which lives are lived. Tyner explains that for Kelly the 'poetics of struggle and lived experience, in the utterances of ordinary folk, in the cultural products of social movements, in the reflections of activists, we discover the many different cognitive maps of the future, of the world not yet born'. The most radical art is 'not protest art but works that take us to another place, that envision a different way of seeing, perhaps a different way of feeling'. For Tyner, Malcolm X imagined a different society but his realism meant that he grounded his political and ethical thought in what he saw around him and the experiences of his audience. Unlike many dystopian writers who imagined a different society from totalitarian regimes, Malcolm X directs his attention 'to the racial underscoring of dystopian landscapes and the interconnections of self and place'. He wanted his African American audiences to 'resist the dehumanizing tendencies of a racist and undemocratic capitalist society'. Tyner distinguishes Malcolm X's writings and speeches in which Malcolm X 'did not follow the lead of dystopian writers through the creation

---

[121] George Breitman (ed.), *Malcolm X, By Any Means Necessary: Speeches, Interviews and a Letter by Malcolm X*, New York: Pathfinder Books, 1970, 46.

[122] Stere Clark (ed.), Malcolm X, *Malcolm X on Afro-American History*, New York: Pathfinder Press, 1967, 25.

of a fictionalized and distant society'. Malcolm X had 'constructed composite landscapes, scenes of oppression and exploitation which his African American audiences would readily see and thus could relate to'. Tyner situates Malcolm X, a radical orator, within the literary tradition of dystopian writings. He states 'I do so from the standpoint that both Malcolm X and many dystopian writers sought to discursively produce alternative geographies in the minds of their audiences'.[123]

For West, Malcolm X articulated Black rage in a manner unprecedented in American history:

> Malcolm X was the prophet of black rage primarily because of his great love for black people. His love was neither abstract nor ephemeral. Rather, it was a concrete connection with a degraded and devalued people in need of psychic conversion. This is why Malcolm X's articulation of black rage was not directed first and foremost at white America.[124]

West explains that this hope for psychic conversion was so that Black people would no longer see themselves through white lenses and constantly feel devalued. Although Malcolm X was demonised by the mainstream as his photos show sinister facial expressions, no one can do justice to his legacy. Malcolm X's prophetic witness is his critique of idolatory in America. Having turned to Sunni Islam, he was going to open his own mosque and reach out to the poor. West remains fascinated by the development which could have taken place if Malcolm X had not been assassinated and he imagines that Malcolm X could have created 'a paradigmatic model of what it means to be a revolutionary Muslim in the way in which King at the end of his life becomes a revolutionary Christian'. West's beautiful homage to Malcolm X is that this kind of prophetic witness 'can never fully and thoroughly be crushed. Even when you kill the body, the words still linger in the air, and it touches people ... its impossible to even think about the Black prophetic tradition without making Malcolm X a central figure in it'.[125]

It is said that Malcolm X never abandoned his commitment to Islam. While he softened his views on many issues, he continued to be hugely fearless in his condemnation of the structures of white oppression. Terrill writes:

> He never wavered on his insistence that violence was justified in self-defense; he never endorsed simple assimilation; he never described the

---

[123] Tyner, 'Nightmarish Landscapes', 138, 141 and 146.   [124] West, *Race*, 95–6.
[125] West, *Black*, 132, 124, 126 and 137.

political system in the United States as anything other than thoroughly and institutionally corrupt; and he never publically imagined that America could one day throw back the cloak of racism and emerge as a society characterised by justice, equity, and brotherhood.[126]

Even as he explores the complex and often tragic history of Black struggle through the lives of so many who preceded him, Cornel West sees American life as 'suffering from social amnesia'. He writes that American religious people have little memory or sense of collective struggle. But West, writing from the prophetic stream of the Christian tradition, is all too aware of the tragic character of life and history. His sense of hope is present in his writing even as he remains critical of American culture in relation to the history and plight of African Americans. He recognises and affirms the struggles of those Black writers, thinkers and activists who precede him, and their legacy which is present in his own works. As an intellectual and a Christian he is always caught in different tensions but the questions with which he wrestles are, in his own words, 'How does a present day Christian think about and act on enhancing the plight of the poor, the predicament of the powerless and the quality of life for all in a prophetic manner?'[127]

Towards the conclusion of this chapter, the news making global headlines was the murder of George Floyd in America.[128] As an unarmed man, who died after the police officer kneeled on his neck for more than eight minutes while he kept pleading, saying, "I can't breathe," his death was particularly brutal. This killing has sparked protests and riots around the world with hundreds of thousands of people demanding justice for Floyd's death. The public conversation around race and, especially, the systemic violence and racism against African Americans, has mobilised people of all backgrounds to demand accountability. Racial justice isn't just America's struggle: it's the moral challenge in every society which values others mainly by the colour of their skin. The public conversations now speak of real change beyond the immediate show of solidarity to create a legacy where everyone can breathe real freedom. While West wrote the Epilogue to his book, *Race Matters* in 1994, his concluding remarks still carry weight, reflecting both the struggle and the hope African Americans carry within them:

> In these downbeat times, we need as much hope and courage as we do vision and analysis; we must accent the best of each other even as we point

---

[126] Terrill, 'Introduction', 9.   [127] West, *The Cornel West*, 359.
[128] https://news.sky.com/story/who-was-george-floyd-the-gentle-giant-who-loved-his-hugs-11997206

out the vicious effects of our racial divide and the pernicious consequences of our maldistribution of wealth and power. We simply cannot enter the twenty-first century at each other's throats, even as we acknowledge the weighty forces of racism, patriarchy, economic inequality, homophobia and ecological abuse on our necks.[129]

---

[129] West, *Race*, 109.

Epilogue

$\mathcal{I}$ N THIS BOOK, THE TOPIC OF HUMAN STRUGGLE HAS BEEN EXPLORED through the writings of Christian, Western and Muslim theologians, philosophers and thinkers. The purpose of the comparative approach is to show that the language and experience of struggle and suffering is universal and can lead to a similar search for meaning across the religious experience. Furthermore, while Christians and Muslims anchor this search in their faith in God, very often faith itself can become our greatest struggle.

The great theologians, philosophers and thinkers mentioned in this book have assumed almost legendary status. Their arguments and reflections live on in a diverse array of scholarship. Their own lives are often testament to various kinds of personal struggle yet they continue to live with hope even in the face of sickness, torture and death. For some, such as Bonhoeffer and Qutb, the quest for greater societal justice comes at a huge personal cost but their religious faith compels them to take action. Others like Ghazali commit to pious devotion despite the desperate quest for certainty. The contemporary sociologists and cultural theorists regard the onset of modernity as both liberating the human self and accentuating human impermanence; thus meaning itself is contested. Beyond the personal lives of the great religious thinkers, a poet such as Rilke imagines God and transcendence in his intellectual restlessness; but if solitude brings solace, solitude also costs.

Faith itself needs new understanding and for Muslim scholars like El Fadl and Arkoun, Islamic thought and life must be revived with an appeal to the moral and the aesthetic. For Cornel West, the long history of the Black struggle in America continues. For all the progress made in winning civil rights, African Americans can still face injustice and discrimination at almost every level of society. In May 2020 this particular struggle assumed a new moral urgency with the death of George Floyd at the hands of a White police officer in Minneapolis. This gruesome death became the tipping point in the long history of police violence against members of the African American community. The subsequent protests and vigils around the world, greatly mobilized through the Black Lives Matter campaign, demand accountability and justice. The struggle for racial equality continues to be one of the longest and most brutal struggles in human history.

This incident and the subsequent protests happened against the background of the COVID-19 pandemic. Beginning in December 2019, the world watched as this highly infectious disease emerged as a cluster of cases in Wuhan, China. As it spread to Thailand and then other parts of the world over the next few weeks, it gradually took its toll on lives and societies everywhere. The alarming spread of the virus meant that in March 2020, the UK, like many other countries, had to take drastic measures to try and curb the potentially devastating effect of the virus and went into lockdown. Overnight, a free and liberal society came to a virtual standstill. While around 80 per cent of people who become infected suffer relatively mild symptoms, the disease has created a global health crisis leaving a deep impact on the way we perceive our world and our everyday lives. The rate of contagion and patterns of transmission meant that for weeks, people were told to stay indoors and the phenomenon of social distancing was born when coming into contact with others. Almost all businesses either shut down or worked online, including educational establishments such as schools and universities. The travel and hospitality industry have suffered enormous losses and many businesses may never recover. People were unable to travel to meet family or attend weddings and funerals and many could not be with their loved ones at the most vulnerable stage of their lives. But most importantly, it is the number of deaths which have been recorded as a result of COVID-19 which is the most poignant statistic; December 2020, deaths in the UK involving Covid-19 total 78000.

The COVID-19 pandemic has created a new urgency around public health and there is a concerted international effort among scientists to create an effective vaccine. But the loss of so many lives in such a short period of time has also heightened our sense of our own mortality. That we cannot control and plan our lives as before has become a startling reality; that we had grown to thinking long term about our hopes and ambitions, but must now take life a day at a time, unsettles and frustrates us. Many, especially those living on their own, express their pain and loneliness as well as fear of greater uncertainty on social media., Vague information and at times, improper communications through media creates greater fear and panic. And while the UK along with several other countries, has now begun the gradual easing of lockdown, no one knows for certain what we can return to from our former lives.

The economic and psychological impact of both the quarantine and the post-quarantine period will be unknown for years to come. Trust in governments and the scientific communities fluctuates but most people have remained compliant and obeyed government rules and regulations. Life as we know it has changed in many ways and although many of us are struggling in minor ways, we all know someone who feels overwhelmed by all this. Yet despite these challenging times, people searched for hope in ordinary acts of generosity and kindness. Community and togetherness in separation has become the narrative of the day. For now, most of us are less indifferent to the destiny of others, we are more empathetic towards those taking risks every day and we remain grateful. Big companies and corporations are rethinking how to do business which demands less travel and fewer face-to-face meetings, and is fairer as well as ecologically just. Crisis management is everywhere. We are also witnessing the beauty of clearer skies, cleaner air and observing the wonders of nature and wildlife a little more closely. Life has become quieter and against this relative stillness, people are being urged to be kinder to themselves as well as to others. Once this struggle has passed, maybe a gentler and kinder future for all could be based on nurturing compassion and gratitude as a way of life. Both 9/11 and the 2008 financial crisis were socially divisive turning points in our lives. Today, however, we share common struggles because of this virus and it may be years before we will be able to measure its true impact on the world. But if the virus has made us aware of our vulnerabilities, it is this shared vulnerability which continues to help us recognise our common humanity.

Bibliography

Elisa Aaltola, 'Philosophical Narratives of Suffering: Nietzsche, Levinas, Weil and Their Cultural Roots', in *Suomen Antropologi*, 43:3, 2019, 22–40

Binyamin Abrahamov, 'A Re-examination of Al-Ash'ari's Theory of "Kasb" According to *Kitab al-Luma*', in *Journal of the Royal Asiatic Society of Great Britain and Ireland*, 2, 1989, 210–21

Melitta W. Adamson, *Food in Medieval Times*, Westport, CT: Greenwood Press, 2004

Theodor W. Adorno, *Minima Moralia: Reflections on a Damaged Life*, trans. and ed. by E. F. N. Jephcott, London: Verso, 2005

Shahrough Akhavi, 'Syed Qutb' in John L. Esposito and Emad El-Din Shahin (eds.), *The Oxford Handbook Of Islam and Politics*, New York: Oxford University Press, 2013

Al-Ash'ari, *The Theology of al-Ash'ari: The Arabic Texts of al-Ash'ari's Kitab al-Luma' and Risalat Istihsan al-khawd fi 'ilm al-kalam* trans. by R. J. McCarthy, Beyrouth: Impr. Catholique, 1953.

Al-Ghazali, *Deliverance from Error: Al-Munqidh min al-Dalal*, trans. by Richard Joseph McCarthy (originally Twayne Publishers), Louisville, KY: Fons vitae, 1980

Al-Ghazali, *The Remembrance of Death and the Afterlife, Kitab dhikr al-mawt wa-ma ba'dahu*, Book XL of *The Revival of Religious Sciences, Ihya' 'ulum al-din*, trans. by T. J. Winter, Cambridge: The Islamic Texts Society, 1989

Al-Ghazali, *On Disciplining the Soul, Kitab Riyadat al-nafs* and *On Breaking the Two Desires (Kitab kasr al-shahwatayn)*, Books XXII and XXIII of *The Revival of the Religious Sciences, Ihya' 'ulum al-din*, trans. by T. J. Winter, Cambridge: The Islamic Texts Society, 1995

Al-Ghazali, *The Incoherence of the Philosophers: A Parallel English–Arabic Text Translated, Introduced, Annotated by Michael E. Marmura*, Provo, UT: Brigham Young University Press, 2000

Al-Ghazali, *On Love, Longing and Contentment*, trans. by Muhammad Nur Abdus Salam, Chicago, IL: Great Books of the Islamic World, 2002

Al-Ghazali, *The Alchemy of Happiness*, trans. by Claude Field, Chicago: SIME Journal (http://majalla.org), [1910] 2004, http://data.nur.nu/Kutub/English/Ghazali_Alchemy-of-Happiness.pdf

Al-Ghazali, *Letter to a Disciple, Ayyuha'l-Walad*, trans. by Tobias Mayer, Cambridge: The Islamic Texts Society, 2005

Al-Ghazali, *Love, Longing, Intimacy and Contentment, Kitab al-mahabba wa'l-shawq wa'l-uns wa'l-rida.* Book XXXVI of *The Revival of the Religious Sciences, Ihya' 'Ulum al-din,* trans. by Eric Ormsby, Cambridge: The Islamic Texts Society, 2011

Muhammad M. Al-Hudaibi, *The Principles of Politics in Islam* (2nd ed.), Cairo: Islamic Inc. Publishing and Distribution, 2000

Al-Qushayri, *Epistle on Sufism,* trans. by Alexander D. Knysh, Reading, UK: Garnet Publishing, 2007

Mohammed Arkoun, 'Rethinking Islam Today', in *Annals of the American Academy of Political and Social Science,* 588, Islam: Enduring Myths and Changing Realities, 2003, 18–39

Brooks Atkinson (ed.), *The Essential Writings of Ralph Waldo Emerson,* New York: New York Modern Library, 2000

Mahmoud M. Ayoub, *Redemptive Suffering in Islam: A Study of the Devotional Aspects of Ashura in Twelver Shi'ism,* The Hague: Mouton Publishers, 1978

Ulrich Baer, *The Poet's Guide to Life: The Wisdom of Rilke,* New York: The Modern Library, 2005

James Baldwin, *Collected Essays,* New York: Literary Classics of the United States, 1998

Zygmunt Bauman, *Liquid Love,* Cambridge: Polity Press, 2003

Zygmunt Bauman, *Identity: Conversations with Benedetto Vecchi,* Cambridge: Polity Press, 2004

Zygmunt Bauman, *Liquid Times; Living in an Age of Uncertainty,* Cambridge: Polity Press, 2007

Zygmunt Bauman and Leonidas Donskis, *Moral Blindness,* Cambridge: Polity Press, 2013

George K. A. Bell, Bishop of Chichester, 'The Church and the Resistance Movement' in W. D. Zimmermann and R. G. Smith (eds.), *I Knew Dietrich Bonhoeffer,* trans. by K. G. Smith, London: Collins, 1966

John C. Bennett, 'The Problem of Evil', in *The Journal of Religion,* 18:4 1938, 401–21

Albert J. Bergesen, 'Qutb's core ideas' in Albert J. Bergesen (ed.), *The Sayyid Qutb Reader,* London: Routledge, 2008

Albert J. Bergesen, 'The Earth's Suffocating Expanse' in Albert J. Bergeson (ed.), *The Sayyid Qutb Reader,* London: Routledge, 2008

Paul Berman, 'The Philosopher of Islamic Terror', *New York Times Magazine,* 23 March 2003

Eberhard Bethge, *Bonhoeffer: Exile and Martyr,* Collins: London, 1975

Eberhard Bethge, *Dietrich Bonhoeffer: A Biography – Theologian, Christian, Man for His Times,* Minneapolis: Fortress Press, 2000

Albert L. Blackwell, 'Schleiermacher's "Sermon at Nathanael's Grave,"' in *Pastoral Theology,* 26:1, 1977, 23–36

Dietrich Bonhoeffer, *Ethics,* New York: Macmillan, 1965

Dietrich Bonhoeffer, *Discipleship, Dietrich Bonhoeffer Works,* English edition, Volume 4, (henceforth *DBWE*), John W. De Gruchy (ed.), Minneapolis: Fortress Press, 2003, 43–4. This volume is part of the series of translations of the German, *Dietrich Bonhoeffer Werke* (1986–1999). Each of these definitive English translations in *DBWE* contains a very useful introduction and background. But for a helpful overview of the history of the Fortress Press project of translating and publishing Bonhoeffer's works in English, see John W. Matthews, 'The Dietrich Bonhoeffer Works English Edition,' *Word and World,* 34:4, 2014, 412–420.

Dietrich Bonhoeffer, *Creation and Fall: A Theological Exposition of Genesis 1–3*, John W.
    De Gruchy (ed.), trans. by Douglas Bax, Minneapolis, MN: Fortress Press, 2004
Jonathan Burnside, 'The Spirit of Biblical Law', in *Oxford Journal of Law and Religion*,
    1:1, 2012, 127–150
John Calvert, 'The World Is an Undutiful Boy: Sayyid Qutb's American Experience', in
    Islam and Christian–Muslim Relations, 11:1, 2000, 87–103
John Calvert, *Sayyid Qutb and the Origins of Radical Islamism*, London: Hurst &
    Company, 2010
John Calvert, https://foreignpolicy.com/2010/12/15/the-afterlife-of-sayyid-qutb/
Karen J. Campbell, 'Rilke's Duino Angels and the Angels of Islam', in *Alif: Journal of
    Comparative Poetics*, 23, 2003, 191–211.
Antonella Castelveder, 'Neither Religion nor Philosophy', in *German Life and Letters*,
    63: 2, 2010, 133–45
Dan Chiasson, 'Ecstasy of Influence', in *The New Yorker*, 91:26, 7 Sept. 2015
Keith Clements 'Ecumenical Witness for Peace' in John W. De Gruchy (ed.), *The
    Cambridge Companion to Dietrich Bonhoeffer*, Cambridge: Cambridge University
    Press, 1999, online 2006
James Conlon, 'Cornel West's Pragmatic Understanding of America', in *Journal of
    Black Studies*, 28:1, 2017, 26–42
Amena Coronado, *Suffering & The Value of Life*, a PhD dissertation submitted to the
    University of California, Santa Cruz, 2016
Harvey Cox, *The Future of Faith*, New York: HarperCollins Publishers, 2009
Don Cupitt, *The Meaning of the West*, London: SCM Press, 2008
Mike Davies, 'Planet of Slums', *New Left Review*, 26 March–April 2004
John W. De Gruchy, 'Bonhoeffer' in Gareth Jones (ed.), *The Blackwell Companion to
    Modern Theology*, Oxford: Blackwell Publishing, 2004
John W. De Gruchy (ed.), *The Cambridge Companion to Dietrich Bonhoeffer*, Cambridge:
    Cambridge University Press, 1999, online 2006
John W. De Gruchy (ed.), *Dietrich Bonhoeffer: Letters and Papers from Prison*, DBWE 8,
    Minneapolis, MN: Fortress Press, 2010
Jan de Vos, 'Christopher Lasch's *The Culture of Narcissism*', in *Theory and Psychology*,
    20:4, 2010, 528–48
Peter Dews, '"Radical Finitude" and the Problem of Evil' in María Pía Lara (ed.),
    Rethinking Evil, London: University of California Press Ltd, 2001
Kelly Brown Douglas, *Stand Your Ground: Black Bodies and the Justice of God*,
    Maryknoll, NY: Orbis Books, 2015
Terry Eagleton, *Ideology: An Introduction*, London: Verso, 1991
Terry Eagleton, *Culture and the Death of God*, New Haven: Yale University Press, 2015
Matthew T. Eggemeier, 'Levinas and Ricoeur on the Possibility of God after the End of
    Theodicy', in *Philosophy and Theology*, 24:1, 2012, 23–48
Khaled Abou El Fadl, *Rebellion and Violence in Islamic Law*, Cambridge: Cambridge
    University Press, 2001
Khaled Abou El Fadl, *The Place of Tolerance in Islam*, Boston: Beacon Press, 2002
Khaled Abou El Fadl, *The Search for Beauty in Islam: A Conference of the Books*,
    Lanham, MD: Rowman and Littlefield Publishers, 2005
Khaled Abou El Fadl, 'When Happiness Fails: An Islamic Perspective', in *The Journal of
    Law and Religion*, 29:1, 2014, 109–23

Roxanne L. Euben, 'Comparative Political Theory: An Islamic Fundamentalist Critique of Rationalism', in *The Journal of Politics*, 59:1, 1997, 28–55

Roxanne L. Euben and Muhammad Qasim Zaman (eds.), *Princeton Readings in Islamist Thought*, Princeton, NJ: Princeton University Press, 2009

David Fergusson, *Church, State and Civil Society*, Cambridge: Cambridge University Press, 2004

Ludwig Feuerbach, *The Essence of Christianity*, trans. by George Eliot, United Kingdom: Create Space Independent Publishing Platform, 2018

Michel Foucault, 'Technologies of the Self' in Luther H. Martin, Huck Gutman, Patrick H. Hutton (eds.), *Technologies of the Self: A Seminar with Michel Foucault*, Amherst: University of Massachusetts Press, 1988

Michel Foucault, *The Hermeneutics of the Subject: Lectures at the Collège de France 1981–82*, ed. by Frédéric Glos and trans. by Graham Burchell, New York: Picador, 2001

Richard M. Frank, 'The Structure of Created Causality According to Al-Ash'ari: An Analysis of the *Kitab al-Luma'*, pars 82–164', in *Studia Islamica* 25, 1966, 13–75

Viktor E. Frankl, *Man's Search for Meaning*, London: Ebury Publishing, 2004

Sigmund Freud, *Civilisation and Its Discontents*, 1941, trans. by David McLintock, London: Imago Publishing, 2002

Erich Fromm, *Man for Himself*, London: Routledge & Kegan Paul, Ltd, 1949

Francis Fukuyama, *The End of History and the Last Man*, London: Hamish Hamilton, 1992

Louise Glück, 'Disruption, Hesitation, Silence', in *Proofs & Theories: Essays on Poetry*, New York: Ecco, 1994

Johanes Goebel, 'When He Sat Down at the Piano' in Wolf-Dieter Zimmermann and Ronald Gregor Smith (eds.), *I Knew Dietrich Bonhoeffer*, trans. by Kathe Gregor Smith, London: Collins, 1966

Graham Good, *Rilke's Late Poetry*, Vancouver: Ronsdale Press, 2015

Philip Goodchild, 'Capitalism and Global Economics' in Craig Hovey and Elizabeth Phillips (eds.), *The Cambridge Companion to Political Theology*, New York: Cambridge University Press, 2015

Rudiger Görner, 'Rilke: A Biographical Exploration' in Karen Leeder and Robert Vilain (eds.), *The Cambridge Companion to Rilke*, Cambridge: Cambridge University Press, 2010

Clifford J. Green, 'Pacifism and Tyrannicide: Bonhoeffer's Christian Peace Ethic', in *Studies in Christian Ethics*, 18:3, 2005, 31–47

Clifford Green, 'Human Sociality and Christian Community' in John W. De Gruchy (ed.), *The Cambridge Companion to Dietrich Bonhoeffer*, Cambridge: Cambridge University Press, 1999, online 2006

Christian Gremmels and Hans Pfeiffer, *Theologie und Biographie: Zum Beispiel Dietrich Bonhoeffers*, Munich: Chr. Kaiser Verlag: 1983

Frank Griffel, *Al-Ghazali's Philosophical Theology*, New York: Oxford University Press, 2009

Wilhelm Guggenberger, 'Muslim Brotherhood, Social Justice and Resentment' in M. Kirwan and A. Achtar (eds.), *Mimetic Theory and Islam*, Palgrave Macmillan: Cham, 2019

Adrian Gully, *The Culture of Letter Writing in Pre-Modern Islamic Society*, Edinburgh: Edinburgh University Press, 2008

Nadine Hamilton, 'Dietrich Bonhoeffer and the Necessity of Kenosis for Scriptural Hermeneutics', in *Scottish Journal of Theology*, 71:4, 2018, 441–59

Andy Hargreaves, *Teaching in the Knowledge Society: Education in the Age of Insecurity*, Open University Press, 2003

Patrick Hart (ed.), *The Literary Essays of Thomas Merton*, New York: New Directions Book, 1981

Rupert Hart-Davis (ed.), *Selected Letters of Oscar Wilde*, New York: Oxford University Press, 1989

Franz Hildebrandt, 'An Oasis of Freedom' in W. D. Zimmermann and R. G. Smith (eds.), *I Knew Dietrich Bonhoeffer*, trans. by K. G. Smith, London: Collins, 1966

Willem A. Visser't Hooft, 'An Act of Penitence' in W. D. Zimmermann and R. G. Smith (eds.), *I Knew Dietrich Bonhoeffer*, trans. by K. G. Smith, London: Collins, 1966

Jon Hoover, *Ibn Taymiyya's Theodicy of Perpetual Optimism*, Leiden: Brill, 2007

Craig Hovey, 'Liberalism and Democracy' in Craig Hovey and Elizabeth Phillips (eds.), *The Cambridge Companion to Political Theology*, New York: Cambridge University Press, 2015

Ben Hutchinson (ed.), *Rainer Maria Rilke's* The Book of Hours: *A New Translation with Commentary*, trans. by Susan Ranson, Woodbridge: Boydell and Brewer, 2008

Andreas Huyssen, 'The Notebooks of Malte Laurids Brigge' in K. Leeder and R. Vilain (eds.), *The Cambridge Companion to Rilke*, Cambridge Companions to Literature, Cambridge: Cambridge University Press, 2010

Muhammad ibn 'Abd Allah al - Kisa'i, Tales of the Prophets, Qisas al-anbiya', trans. by Wheler M. Thackston Jr, Chicago: Great Books of the Islamic World, 1997

Ibn Qayyim al-Jawziyya, *On Divine Wisdom and the Problem of Evil*, trans. by Tallal M. Zeni, Cambridge: The Islamic Texts Society, 2017

Ezzeddin Ibrahim and Denys Johnson Davies, *Forty Hadith Qudsi*, Cambridge: Islamic Texts Society, 1997

Imam al-Juwayni, *A Guide to Conclusive Proofs for the Principles of Belief*, trans. by Paul E. Walker, Doha: Garnet Publishing, 2000

Muhammad Iqbal, *Tulip in the Desert: A Selection of Poetry*, trans. and ed. by Mustansir Mir, London: Hurst & Company Publishers, 2000

William Irvine, *On Desire: Why We Want What We Want*, New York, Oxford University Press, 2006

Christopher Janaway, *Schopenhauer: A Very Short Introduction*, Oxford: Oxford University Press, 2002

Willie James Jennings, *The Christian Imagination*, New Haven: Yale University Press, 2010

Immanuel Kant, 'Conjectural Beginnings of Human History,' trans. by Emil Fackenheim, from in Lewis White Beck (ed.), *Kant on History*, Indianapolis: Bobbs-Merrill, 1963

Geffrey. B. Kelly and F. Burton Nelson (eds.), *A Testament to Freedom: The Essential Writings of Dietrich Bonhoeffer*, New York: Harper Collins, 1990

Philip Kennedy, Review of John W. De Gruchy (ed.), The Cambridge Companion to Dietrich Bonhoeffer, Cambridge: Cambridge University Press, 1999, in *Journal of Ecclesiastical History*, 52:1, 2001, 169–70

Giles Kepel, *Muslim Extremism in Egypt: The Prophet and the Pharaoh*, Berkeley: University of California Press, 1993

Giles Kepel, *Muslim Extremism in Egypt: The Prophet and the Pharaoh* (2nd ed.), Berkeley: University of California Press, 2003

Atif Khalil, 'Tawba in the Sufi Psychology of AbuTalib al-Makki', in *Journal of Islamic Studies*, 23:3 2012, 294–324

Sayyed Khatab, *The Political Thought of Sayyid Qutb: The Theory of Jahiliyya*, London: Routledge, 2005

Richard Kilminster, 'Narcissism or Informalization? Christopher Lasch, Norbert Elias and Social Diagnosis', in *Theory, Culture & Society*, 25:3, 2008, 131–51

Martin Luther King Jr and Coretta Scott King, *Words of Martin Luther King Jr.*, New York: Newmarket Press, 2001

Galway Kinnell and Hannah Liebmann, *The Essential Rilke*, New York: HarperCollins Publishers, 2000

Michael Kirwan, 'Vox victima, vox moderna? Modernity and Its Discontents' in M. Kirwan and A. Achtar (eds.), *Mimetic Theory and Islam*, Cham: Palgrave Macmillan, 2019

Kathleen L. Komar, 'The Duino Elegies' in K. Leeder and R. Vilain (eds.), *The Cambridge Companion to Rilke*, Cambridge Companions to Literature, Cambridge: Cambridge University Press, 2010

Christopher Lasch, *The Culture of Narcissism*, New York: W.W. Norton & Company, 1979

Christopher Lasch, *The Minimal Self: Psychic Survival in Troubled Times*, London and New York: W.W. Norton, 1984

Jon K. Lauck, 'Christopher Lasch and Prairie Populism', in *Great Plains Quarterly*, 32:3, 183–205

Jackson Lears, 'The Grim Optimism of Christopher Lasch', *New Republic*, 2 October 1995.

Karen Leeder and Robert Vilain, 'Introduction' in K. Leeder and R. Vilain (eds.), *The Cambridge Companion to Rilke*, Cambridge Companions to Literature, Cambridge: Cambridge University Press, 2010

Sabine Leibholz, 'Childhood and Home' in W. D. Zimmermann and R. G. Smith (eds.), *I Knew Dietrich Bonhoeffer*, trans. by K. G. Smith, London: Collins, 1966

Gottfried Wilhelm Leibniz, *Theodicy: Essays on the Goodness of God, the Freedom of Man and the Origin of Evil*, trans. by E. M. Huggard, Whithorn: Anodos Books, 2017

Emmanuel Levinas, *Figuring the Sacred: Religion, Narrative, Imagination*, trans. by David Pellauer, ed. Mark I. Wallace, Minneapolis: Fortress Press, 1995

Emmanuel Levinas, *Entre Nous: Thinking-of-the-Other*, trans. Michael Smith and Barbara Harshav, New York: Columbia University Press, 1998

D. Stephen Long, Nancy Ruth Fox, with York Tripp, *Calculated Futures*, Waco, TX: Baylor University Press, 2007

Joanna Macy and Anita Barrows (eds.), *A Year with Rilke*, London: Harper Colllins, 1996

Sabu George Maddathikunnel, 'Secularism and the Crisis of Secularization in India: A Taylorian Response', in *A Journal of Religion, Education and the Arts*, 7, 2001

Jeff Malpas, 'Suffering, Compassion, and the Possibility of a Humane Politics' in Jeff Malpas and Norelle Lickiss (eds.), *Perspectives on Human Suffering*, Springer: Dordrecht, 2012

Andrew March, 'Taking People as They Are: Islam as a "Realistic Utopia" in the Political Theory of Sayyid Qutb', in *The American Political Science Review*, 104:1, 2010, 189–207

Michael E. Marmura, 'Ghazali and Ash`arism Revisited', in *Arabic Sciences and Philosophy*, 12, 2002, 91–110

Charles Marsh, *A Life of Dietrich Bonhoeffer: Strange Glory*, New York: A.A. Knopf, 2014

Thomas Martinec, 'Sonnets to Orpheus' in K. Leeder and R. Vilain (eds.), *The Cambridge Companion to Rilke*, Cambridge Companions to Literature, Cambridge: Cambridge University Press, 2010

Martin E. Marty, *Dietrich Bonhoeffer's Letters and Papers from Prison*, Princeton: Princeton University Press, 2011

Tobias Mayer, *Al-Ghazali: Letter to a Disciple, Ayyuha'l-Walad*, Cambridge: The Islamic Texts Society, 2005

William McKane, *Al-Ghazali's Book of Fear and Hope*, Leiden: Brill, 1962

Simon Sebag Montefiore, *Written in History: Letters That Changed the World*, Weidenfeld and Nicolson: London, 2019

Thomas Moore, *Care of the Soul*, London: Piatkus, 1992

Ebrahim Moosa 'Introduction' in Fazlur Rahman (ed.), *Revival and Reform in Islam*, Oxford: OneWorld Publications, 2000

Toni Morrison, *The Source of Self-Regard*, New York: Alfred A. Knopf, 2019

Richard Mullender, 'Review of "Zygmunt Bauman, Identity: Conversations with Benedetto Vecchi"', in *History of Political Thought*, 28:2, 2007, 368–71

Adnan A. Musallam, 'Sayyid Qutb and Social Injustice, 1945–1948', in *Journal of Islamic Studies*, 4:1, 1993, 52–70

Adnan A. Musallam, *From Secularism to Jihad: Sayyid Qutb and the Origins of Radical Islamism*, Connecticut: Westport, 2005

F. Burton Nelson, 'Report on a Period of Study at the Union Theological Seminary in New York, 1930–31' in Edwin H. Robinson (ed.), *D. Bonhoeffer, No Rusty Swords: Letters, Lectures and Notes, 1928–1936, Collected Works of Dietrich Bonhoeffer*, trans. by Edwin H. Robinson and John Bowden, New York: Harper & Row, 1965

F. Burton Nelson, 'The Life of Dietrich Bonhoeffer' in John W. De Gruchy (ed.), *The Cambridge Companion to Dietrich Bonhoeffer*, Cambridge: Cambridge University Press, 1999, online 2006

Reinhold Niebuhr, 'To America and Back' in W. D. Zimmermann and R. G. Smith (eds.), *I Knew Dietrich Bonhoeffer*, trans. by K. G. Smith, London: Collins, 1966

Friedrich Nietzsche, *The Will to Power*, London: Penguin, 2017

Paul T. Nimmo, *Barth: A Guide for the Perplexed*, London: Bloomsbury T&T Clark, 2017

James L. Nolan Jr, 'From Musha to New York: Qutb Encounters American *jahiliyya*' in *What They Saw in America: Alexis de Tocqueville, Max Weber, G. K. Chesterton and Sayyid Qutb*, Cambridge: Cambridge University Press, 2016

Martha C. Nussbaum, 'Political Animals: Luck, Love, and Dignity', in *Metaphilosophy*, 29:4, 1998, 273–88

Simon O' Meara, 'The Space between Here and There: The Prophet's Night Journey as an Allegory of Islamic Ritual Prayer', in *Middle-Eastern Literatures: Incorporating Edebiyat*, 15:3, 2012, 232–9

Mary Oliver 'Introduction' in Brooks Atkinson (ed.), *The Essential Writings of Ralph Waldo Emerson*, New York: The Modern Library, 2000

Eric Ormsby, *Theodicy in Islamic Thought: The dispute over al-Ghazali's 'Best of All Possible Worlds'*, Princeton: Princeton University Press, 1984

Jean-Michel Oughourlian, *The Genesis of Desire*, East Lansing: Michigan State University Press, 2010

John Passmore, *The Perfectibility of Man*, London: Gerald Duckworth and Company Limited, 1970

Stephen Plant, *Bonhoeffer*, London: Continuum, 2004

Pope John Paul 11, *Salvifici Doloris*, http://w2.vatican.va/content/john-paul-ii/en/apos t_letters/1984/documents/hf_jp-ii_apl_11021984_salvifici-doloris.html

Donald Prater, *A Ringing Glass: The Life of Rainer Maria Rilke*, Oxford: Clarendon Press, 1986

Princess Marie Von Thurn Und Taxis, *The Poet and the Princess: Memories of Rainer Maria Rilke*, Amazon printed, UK, 2017

Sayyid Qutb, *Islam: The Religion of the Future*, Beirut: The Holy Koran Publishing House, 1978

Sayyid Qutb, *The Islamic Concept and Its Characteristics*, Plainfield, IN: American Trust Publication, 1991

Sayyid Qutb, *Al-'Adala al-Ijtima'iyya fi'l-Islam*, Cairo: Dar al Shuruq, 1993

Sayyid Qutb, *Milestones Ma'alim fi'l-tariq*, New Delhi: Islamic Book Services Ltd, 2002

Sayyid Qutb, *In the Shade of the Qur'an*, trans. by Adil Salahi and Ashur Shamis, Leicester, UK: The Islamic Foundation, 2003

Sayyid Qutb, *A Child from the Village*, trans. and ed. by John Calvert and William Shepard, Syracuse, NY: Syracuse University Press, 2004

Sayyid Qutb, *Fi Zilal al-Qur'an*, 6 vols, Cairo: Dar al-Shuruq, 2004

Fazlur Rahman, *Islam and Modernity*, Chicago: The University of Chicago Press, 1982

Vanessa Rampton, 'Dostoevskii and the Book of Job: The Struggle to Find Faith', in *Studies in Religion*, 39:2, 2010, 203–17

John Rawls, 'Justice as Fairness: Political not Metaphysical', in *Philosophy and Public Affairs*, 14:3, 1985, 22–51

Paul Ricoeur, *Evil: A Challenge to Philosophy and Theology*, trans. by John Bowden, London: Continuum, 2007

Rainer Maria Rilke, *Das Florenzer Tagebuch*, 1942, Ruth Sieber-Rilke and Carl Sieber (eds.), Insel: Frankfurt and Leipzig, 1994

Rainer Maria Rilke, *Letters to a Young Poet*, trans. by Charlie Louth, London: Penguin Books, 2011

Richard H. Rouse and Mary A. Rouse, *Bound Fast with Letters*, Notre Dame, IN: University of Notre Dame Press, 2013

Martin Rumscheidt, 'The Formation of Bonhoeffer's Theology' in John W. De Gruchy (ed.), *The Cambridge Companion to Dietrich Bonhoeffer*, Cambridge: Cambridge University Press, 1999, online 2006

Jalaluddin Rumi, 'The Progress of Man' in R. A. Nicholson, *Persian Poems*, ed. by A. J. Arberry, Everyman, 1972

Bertrand Russell, *The Autobiography of Bertrand Russell, vol. 1, 1872–1914*, London: Allen & Unwin, 1967

Nerina Rustomji, *The Garden and the Fire*, New York: Columbia University Press, 2009

Malise Ruthven, *A Fury for God: The Islamist Attack on America*, London & New York, Granta Books, 2006

Walid A. Saleh, 'The Etymological Fallacy and Qur'anic Studies: Muhammad, Paradise, and Late Antiquity' in Angelika Neuwirth, Michael Marx and Nicolai Sinai (eds.), *The Qur'an in Context: Historical and Literary Investigations into the Qur'anic Milieu*, Leiden: Brill, 2010

Robert Saler, 'The Transformation of Reason in Genesis 2–3: Two Options for Theological Interpretation', in *Currents in Theology and Mission*, 36:4, 2009, 275–86

Michael Sandel, *Liberalism and Its Critics*, Oxford: Blackwell, 1984

Michael Sandel, *What Money Can't Buy: The Moral Limits of Markets*, London: Allen Lane, Penguin Books, 2012

Deborah Ann Niederer Saxon, *Representations of the Care of the Soul in Early Christian Texts*, PhD Thesis, Faculty of the University of Denver, Iliff School of Theology, 2013

Annemarie Schimmel, 'Some Aspects of Mystical Prayer in Islam', in *Die Welt des Islams*, 2:5, 1952, 112–25

Annemarie Schimmel, *Rumi's World: The Life and Work of the Great Sufi Poet*, Boston and London: Shambala Publications, 2001

Arthur Schopenhauer, *The World as Will and Representation*, vols. 1&2 (1819, 1844), trans. by E. F. J. Payne, New York: Dover Publications, 1969

Arthur Schopenhauer, *On the Suffering of the World*, trans. by R. J. Hollingdale, London: Penguin Books, 2004

Ulf Schulenberg, '"Where the People Can Sing, the Poet Can Live": James Baldwin, Pragmatism and Cosmopolitan Humanism' in Susan J. McWilliams (ed.), *A Political Companion to James Baldwin*, Kentucky Scholarship online, 2017

Frithjof Schuon, *Islam and the Perennial Philosophy*, United Kingdom: World of Islam Publishing Company, 1976

Peter Selby, 'Christianity in a World Come of Age' in John W. De Gruchy (ed.), *The Cambridge Companion to Dietrich Bonhoeffer*, Cambridge: Cambridge University Press, 1999, online 2006

Richard Sennett, *The Uses of Disorder: Personal Identity and City Life*, London: Faber, 1996

Richard Sennett, *Together: The Rituals, Pleasures and Politics of Cooperation*, London: Allen Lane, 2012

Reza Shah-Kazemi, 'Review of *Conference of the Books* by Khaled Abou El Fadl', in *Journal of Islamic Studies*, 15:2, 2004, 220–1

William E. Shepard, 'Sayyid Qutb's Doctrine of "Jahiliyya"', in *International Journal of Middle East Studies*, 35:4, 2003, 521–45

Ayman Shihadeh, 'Theories of Ethical Value in Kalam: A New Interpretation' in Sabine Schmidtke (ed.), *The Oxford Handbook of Islamic Theology*, Oxford: Oxford University Press, 2016

Russell Shorto, 'The Anti-Secularist: Can Pope Benedict XVI Re-Christianize Europe?' *The New York Times Magazine*, 8 April 2007

Mona Siddiqui, *The Good Muslim*, Cambridge: Cambridge University Press, 2012

Angus Slater, 'Khaled Abou el Fadl's Methodology of Reform, Law, Tradition and Resisting the State', in *Journal of Law, Religion and State*, 4, 2016, 293–321

Stewart Smith, *Nietzsche and Modernism*, London: Palgrave Macmillan, 2018

Wilfred Cantwell Smith, *Islam in Modern History*, New York: New American Library, 1957

Ana Belén Soage, 'Islamism and Modernity: The Political Thought of Sayyid Qutb', *Totalitarian Movements and Political Religions*, 10:2, 2009, 189–203

Stephen Spender, 'Rilke and the Angels; Eliot and the Shrines', *The Sewanee Review*, 61:4, 1953, 557–81

Charles Taylor, *A Secular Age*, Cambridge, MA: Beelknap Press of Harvard University Press, 2007

Charles Taylor, *The Ethics of Authenticity*, Cambridge, MA: Harvard University Press, 2018.

Robert E, Terrill, 'Introduction' in Robert E. Terrill (ed.), *The Cambridge Companion to Malcolm X*, Cambridge: Cambridge University Press, 2010

Robert E. Terrill, 'Judgement and Critique in the Rhetoric of Malcolm X' in Robert E. Terrill (ed.), *The Cambridge Companion to Malcolm X*, Cambridge: Cambridge University Press, 2010

William Thompson, 'Review of Al-Ghazali, O Disciple!', trans. by George H. Scherer. (Collections des Grande Oeuvres l'UNESCO, Arabic Series), Beirut: Catholic Press, 1951, ppxxvi, 75', in *Speculum*, 29:3, 1954, 561–4

Colm Tóibín in www.theguardian.com/books/2016/aug/26/oscar-wilde-de-profundis-greatest-love-letter

Leo Tolstoy, *A Confession and Other Religious Writings*, London: Penguin, 1987

Andrew Turnbull (ed.), *The Letters of F. Scott Fitzgerald*, New York: Penguin Books, 1963

James Tyner, 'Nightmarish Landscapes: Geography and the Dystopian Words of Malcolm X' in Robert E. Terrill (ed.), *The Cambridge Companion to Malcolm X*, Cambridge: Cambridge University Press, 2010

Roberto Mangabeira Unger and Cornel West, *The Future of American Progressivism: An Initiative for Political and Economic Reform*, Boston: Beacon Press, 1998

Frederic Vanson, 'Rilke's "Stories of God"' in *Renascence*, 1962; 14:2, 90–2

Adolf von Harnack, *What Is Christianity?*, London: Williams and Norgate, 1912

W. Montgomery Watt, 'The Authenticity of the Works Attributed to al-Ghazali', in *The Journal of the Royal Asiatic Society of Great Britain and Ireland*, 1:2, April, 1952, 24–45

Itzchack Weismann, 'A Perverted Balance: Modern Salafism between Reform and Jihad', in *Die Welt Des Islams*, 57, 2017, 33–66

Cornel West, *The American Evasion of Philosophy*, Madison: University of Wisconsin Press, 1989

Cornel West, *Race Matters*, New York: Vintage Books, 1993

Cornel West, 'Preface' to *The Cornel West Reader*, New York: Basic Civitas Books, 1999

Cornel West, *Democracy Matters*, New York: Penguin Press, 2004

Cornel West, *Black Prophetic Fire*, Boston: Beacon Press, 2014

Cornel West, 'Prophetic Imagination: Confronting the New Jim Crow & Income Inequality in America', in *Engaging Pedagogies in Catholic Higher Education (EPiCHE)*, 1:1, 2015

Cornel West, *Race Matters*, 25th anniversary ed., Boston: Beacon Press, 2017

Richard White, 'Levinas, The Philosophy of Suffering, and the Ethics of Compassion', in *The Heythrop Journal*, 53, 2012, 111–23

Rowan Williams, *Being Human: Bodies, Minds, Persons*, London: SPCK, 2018

Haddon Willmer, 'Bonhoeffer's Sanctity as a Problem for Bonhoeffer Studies' in *Celebrating Critical Awareness: Bonhoeffer and Bradford 60 Years On*, London: International Bonhoeffer Society, 1993

Haddon Willmer, 'Costly Discipleship' in John W. De Gruchy (ed.), *The Cambridge Companion to Dietrich Bonhoeffer*, Cambridge: Cambridge University Press, 1999, online 2006

Malcolm X, *Malcolm X on Afro-American History*, Steve Clark (ed.), New York:
   Pathfinder Press, 1967
Malcolm X, *By Any Means Necessary: Speeches, Interviews and a Letter by Malcolm X*,
   George Breitman (ed.), New York: Pathfinder Books, 1970
Malcolm X, *Malcolm X, February 1965: The Final Speeches*, Steve Clark (ed.), New York:
   Pathfinder, 1992
Muhammad Qasim Zaman, *Modern Islamic Thought in a Radical Age*, Cambridge:
   Cambridge University Press, 2012
Ruth Zerner, 'Church, State and the Jewish Question' in John W. De Gruchy (ed.), *The
   Cambridge Companion to Dietrich Bonhoeffer*, Cambridge: Cambridge University
   Press, 1999, online 2006

Online Sources

www.bl.uk/collection-items/manuscript-of-de-profundis-by-oscar-wilde
www.esquire.com/news-politics/a14443780/james-baldwin-mlk-funeral/
www.gutenberg.org/files/921/921-h/921-h.htm
https://news.sky.com/story/who-was-george-floyd-the-gentle-giant-who-loved-his-
   hugs-11997206
https://referenceworks-brillonline-om.ezproxy.is.ed.ac.uk/entries/encyclopaedia-of-
   islam-2/*-COM_0233
https://viewing.nyc/dr-martin-luther-king-jr-1962-civil-rights-speech-in-new-york-
   city/
www.who.int/emergencies/diseases/novel-coronavirus-2019/coronavirus-disease-answers

Index

`Azif, `Abd al-Salam, 95
'Abbasids, 51
Abwehr (German military intelligence), 127
Acedia/tristitia (apathy/melancholy), 131
Adam, 24, 25, 30
   In Islamic thought, 29, 30, 41
   In the Qur'an, 26, 28
'*Adl* (justice), 36
Adorno, Theodor W., 157
African-Americans, 6, 16, 118, 180, 181, 182, 183, 184, 189, 190, 191, 193
   African-American Christianity, 118
   Civil rights movement, 10, 180, 185, 188, 190, 195
Afterlives/Afterworlds (comparison of Christian and Islamic concepts), 58
Al-Juwayni, 51
Al-Qaeda, 87
Al-Qushayri, 42
Al-`Aqqad, Mahmud, 90
Al-aghbiya' (ignorance), 52
Al-Ash`ari, 37
   Kitab al-Luma', 36, 37
Al-Azhar University, 90
Al-Banna, Hassan, 85, 92, 97
Al-Baqillani, 51
Al-bari' (The Creator), 37
Al-Basri, Hasan, 64
Al-Farabi, 51
Al-fasam al-nakd ('hideous schizophrenia' – secularism), 89
Al-Ghazali, Abu Hamid, 5, 47, 48, 50, 51, 60, 61, 62, 63, 64, 79, 81, 195
   Aristotelian logic, 51, 53
   Deliverance/The Deliverer from Error/Al-Munqidh min al-Dalal, 49, 53, 54, 63
   Hajj, 54
   Hujjat-al-Islam (Proof of Islam, title given by contemporary scholars), 48

Ibn Rushd/Averroes critique/
   The Incoherence of the Incoherence, 53
Letter to a *Disciple/ 'O boy/disciple'/
   'Ayyuha'l-Walad*, 57, 58, 59, 60, 80
Letters, 5, 49, 79
Nizamiyya Madrasah, 48, 51, 55
On Breaking the Two Desires/ Kitab kasr al-shahwatayn, 61
On Disciplining the Soul/ Kitab Riyadat al-nafs, 61
The Alchemy of Happiness/Kimiya Sa`dat, 55
The Incoherence of the Philosophers, Tahafut al-Falasifa, 52
The Revival of the Religious Sciences/Ihya `Ulum al-Din, 55, 56, 57, 59
Theodicy, 38
Travels, 54
Views on *Jihad*, 3, 62
Views on *Sawm*, 61
Views on *shari'a*, 55, 56, 60
Al-Junayd, 60
Al-Makki, Abu Hazim, 60
Al-Makki, Abu Talib, 28
Al-Qaeda, 86, 137
Al-salaf al-salih (first generations of Islam), 84
Al-Wahhab, Muhammad ibn 'Abd, 91
American civil rights movement, 180, 185, 188, 190, 195
   Dr Martin Luther King Jr, 10
Anfechtung (temptation), 130, 131
Anglo-Saxonism, 183
Antisemitism, 120, 121, 122, 126, 187
Anwar al-ma`arifa (Gnosis), 62
Aqbah (morally wrong), 36
Aqida, 50
Arab Spring, 85
Arkoun, Mohammed, 6, 150, 153, 154, 195
   'Rethinking Islam Today', 150, 151, 152, 153
Aryan Clause (boycott of Jewish Businesses), 121

Ash'arite School, 36, 48, 51, 64
Auden, W.H., 69
Aufheben (stage in the Hegelian dialectic view of history), 32
Auschwitz, 9, 33
Ayoub, Mahmoud, 38, 39
Ayyub (Job in the Qur'an), 44

Baker, Ella, 188
Baldwin, James, 188
    Reflections on Martin Luther King Jr and Malcolm X, 11
Barmen Declaration, 121
Barth, Karl, 113, 114, 120, 121
Bauman, Zygmunt, 168, 171, 172, 173, 174
    Liquid modernity, 168, 169, 171, 174
Bell, George Bishop of Cirencester, 120, 124, 128
Bennet, John, 31
Bethel Confession, 120
Bethge, Eberhard, 128, 129, 132
    Dietrich Bonhoeffer
    Theologian, Man for His Times, 109, 110, 118
Bible, 25, 42, 112, 114, 119, 120, 123, 134, 161
Billige gnade/teure gnade (cheap grace/costly grace), 124, 125
Black Abyssinian Baptist Church, 118
Black Lives Matter, 196
Bonhoeffer, Dietrich, 5, 83, 107, 195
    'Paradox of discipleship', 119
    Antisemitic or ambivalent attitude towards Jews, 123
    Christus als Gemeinde existierend, 116
    Correspondence with brother Karl Friedrich, 118
    Creation and Fall, 119
    Discipleship, 108, 118, 123, 124, 125
    Early years, 107, 109, 110, 111
    Ecumenicism, 112, 121, 122
    Encounters with Islam, 112
    Ethics, 127
    Finkenwalde Preachers' Seminary, 110
    Forerunner to socially engaged Theology/ Christian activism, 108
    Habilitation/Act and Being, 116
    Help with smuggling Jews out of Germany, 122, 127
    Imprisonment and execution, 6, 108, 127, 128, 129, 130, 131, 132, 133, 134, 137
    Involvement with plot to overthrow Hitler, 108, 127, 138
    Lectureship at Berlin, 119
    Letters and Papers from Prison, 108, 128, 129, 130, 131, 132, 137
    Life Together, 123
    On Original Sin/The Fall, 25

Opposition to Nazism, 108, 118, 120, 121, 122, 123, 126, 127, 128, 135, 137
Posts Barcelona, New York, London, 112, 117, 118, 119, 120, 121
Relationship with Maria von Wedemeyer, 123, 129, 131
Studies, 111, 112, 113, 115, 117
The Communion of Saints, Sanctorum Communio, 115
Theology, 115, 116, 118, 119, 123, 124, 125, 126, 130, 132, 133, 134, 136, 137, 138
Travels, 112, 120
Boulainvillier The Life of Mohamed/La Vie Mohamed, 66
Brown, Michael, 187
Buchenwald, 127

Capitalism, 92, 93, 97, 160, 170, 186
Catholic Social Teaching, 100
Catholicism/Catholic Church/Catholics, 100, 112, 163
Christology, 116, 119, 132
Christusgemeinschaft (Christ community), 116
Cold War, 97, 175
Colonialism, 4, 91, 92, 99, 102, 149, 183
Communism, 92, 97, 106, 179
Communist Party, 168
Confessing Church, 107, 116, 121, 123, 126
    Pastorial Oath to Hitler, 126
COVID-19,6, 7, 193, 196

Da'arah (immorality), 91
Dawla (the state), 101
Descartes, Rene, 166
Dhawq (direct experience of God), 56
Dhiliz (threshold), 156
Din al-fitra (natural religion), 102
Diwan School
    'Abbas Mahmud al-'Aqqad, 90
Dostoevskii, Fyodor
    Interpretation of Job, 43
Douglass, Frederick, 188
Du Bois, W.E.B., 181, 188
Du'a' (prayer), 60
Durkheim, Emile, 162

Ecclesia (church), 112
Ecclesiology, 116
El Fadl, Khaled Abou, 6, 139, 140, 143, 144, 145, 146, 148, 149, 150, 153, 154, 155, 195
    The Place of Tolerance in Islam, 147
    The Search for Beauty in Islam
        A Conference of the Books, 139, 145, 147
    Views on shari'a , 145
El-Hudaibi, Mohammad Ma'mun, 91
Emerson, Ralph Waldo, 12, 13, 181
    Compensation, 12

Experience, 12, 13
Entzweiung (breaking apart), 25
Eve, 24
Evikgeit (eternity), 107

Falah (success, also refers to salvation), 30, 39, 41, 44
Falasifa (philosophers), 52, 53
Farrakhan, Louis, 185
Fascism, 97
Fasting in Christianity, 61 (*see Sawm* for fasting in Islam)
Fatimid caliphs, 51
Fatwa (legal opinion), 146
Felix culpa (happy fault), 28
Ferguson, Missouri, 187
Fergusson, David, 159, 163
Feuerbach, Ludwig
    The Essence of Christianity/Das Wesens des Christentums, 35
Fisher, Albert E., 118
Fitra (human nature), 92, 102
Fitzgerald, F. Scott, 11
Flossenbürg concentration camp, 108, 127
Floyd, George, 193, 195
Foucault, Michel
    Technologies of the Self, 166
Frankl, Viktor, 9, 10
    Imprisonment in Auschwitz, 9
Freud, Sigmund, 178
    Connections to Lou Andreas Salome, 66
    Libido theory, 176
    'Paradox of Civilisation', 8
Fukuyama, Francis, 159

Gabriel
    In Islam, 29
Gadamer, Hans, 172
Gandhi, M.K. (Mahatma), 126
Gemeinde (community/congregation), 115
Gestapo, 123, 127
Girard, René, 22
Globalisation, 160, 162, 168, 171, 172, 174
Gospels, 24, 79, 104, 108, 113, 114, 124, 125, 133, 138, 163

Hadith
    Al-Ghazali's commentaries on *Hadith*, 55, 56, 60
    Hadith on jihad, 3
Hakimiyya (sovereignty), 99
Hanbali School, 27
Haqa'iq al-umur (the true meaning of things), 50
Hegel, Georg Wilhelm Friedrich, 32, 114, 115, 159
Hildebrant, Franz, 117
Hitler, Adolf, 84, 108, 120, 121, 126, 128, 137

Assassination attempt, 127, 134
Holl, Karl, 115
Human rights, 6, 140, 164, 169, 172

Ibada (service), 142
Iblis (Satan), 26, 27, 29
Ibn Qayyim al-Jawziyya, 27, 40
Ibn Rushd/Averroes, 53
    The Incoherence of the Incoherence/critique of Al-Ghazali, 53
Ibn Sa'ud, 'Abd al-'Aziz, 91
Ibn Sina/Avicenna, 51
Ibtala (suffering), 27
Ihsan/Hasan (good, proper, beautiful), 139, 144
Ijtihad (effort), 151
'ilm (knowledge), 154
Imam Husayn, 39
Imam Shafi'i, 152
Iman (faith), 40
Inequality, 4, 193, 194
    Racial, 6, 182, 183, 184, 185, 187, 188, 189, 190, 192, 193, 195
Iqbal, Muhammad, 29
Irada (desire), 42
Irvine, William, 18
Islamic Studies, 140, 143
Islamism, 84, 85, 86, 87, 102
Ismailis, 51
    Views of Al-Ghazali, 51
Isodore of Seville, 46
Itlaq (release), 57

Jahiliyya (ignorance and unbelief), 83, 98, 99, 100, 102, 103, 104, 106
Jalal (majesty), 143
Jama'at al-Ikhwan al-Muslimin. See Muslim Brotherhood
Jamal (beauty), 143
Janna (paradise), 39
Jefferson, Thomas, 183
Jesus Christ, 22, 23, 24, 25, 78, 84, 113, 114, 115, 116, 117, 120, 121, 122, 123, 124, 125, 130, 133, 134, 136, 137, 138, 163, 164, 183, 185
Jews, 121, 122, 126, 127, 168
    'Jewish question', 118, 121
Jihad, 3, 106
    Al-Ghazali on jihad, 3, 62
    Greater and lesser, 2, 3
    Reduction to militancy, 3, 83, 86, 147
    Sufi thought on *jihad*, 3
    Views of Sayyid Qutb, 103, 104, 136
Job, 43
    Dostoevskii's interpretation, 43, 44
    Job (Ayyub) in the Qur'an, 44
    Rilke's reading of *Job*, 68
Judaism, 102, 151, 161
Jung, Carl, 165

Kalam (Islamic Theology), 37, 48, 49,
    50, 53
Kant, Immanuel, 18, 30, 31, 142
Kasb (theory of acquisition), 36
Khânqâh (Sufi convent), 55, 57
Khutba (sermon), 146
Kierkegaard, Soren, 157
    Der Einzelne und die Kirche
    Uber Luther Protestantismus, 124
King Jr, Dr Martin Luther, 10, 192
    'I have a dream' speech, 189
    Speech at Sheraton Hotel New York City,
    1962, 10
Kirchenkampf (Church struggle), 116
Kreuzweg (crossroad, Also Way of the Cross/
    Via Crucis), 78
Kristallnacht (crystal night), 126

Lasch, Christopher, 175, 178
    The Culture of Narcissism, 175, 176, 177,
    179, 180
Lasserre, Jean, 118
Leibniz, Gottfried Wilhelm von, 31
    Resemblance to Al-Ghazali, 38
    Théodicée, 32
Leise (delicacy), 71
Letter writing, historical/cultural significance,
    45, 46
Lévinas, Emmanuel, 33, 34
Liberalism, 105, 148, 158, 159, 160, 175, 176, 196
Liquid modernity, 168, 169, 171, 174
Luther, Martin, 115, 124
    De Servo Arbitrio, 118

Mahfouz, Naguib, 91
Maqamat (Sufi spiritual journey), 30
Marx, Karl, 107, 174
Marxism, 186
Mawdudi, Sayyid Abu Ala, 85, 98, 103
Merton, Thomas, 16
Minhaj Islami (the Islamic way), 101
Mixophobia, 171
Moore, Thomas, 165, 166, 167, 168
Moosa, Ebrahim, 142
Morrison, Toni
    Reflections on Martin Luther King Jr, 11
Mu'tazilite School, 53, 149
Mujahada (struggle), 30
Murid (desire for God)/*Murad* (to be desired
    by God), 42
Muslim Brotherhood, 94, 100
    Banning by Nasser, 95
    Hassan al-Banna, 85, 92, 97
    Massacre of, 1957, 95
    Mohammad Ma'mun El-Hudaibi, 91
Mutakamil (complete system), 97
Mu'tazilite School, 36

Nasser, Gamal Abdel, 104
    Assassination attempt/banning of Muslim
    Brotherhood, 95
    Overthrow of Monarchy, 94
Nation of Islam
    Louis Farakhan, 185
    Malcolm X, 188, 190
National Party (Egypt), 90
Nationalism, 90, 94, 95, 97, 135
Native Americans, 183
Nazi regime, 5, 84, 108, 116, 117, 120, 121, 122, 123,
    126, 127, 128, 135, 137, 168
    Concentration camps, 9
Negro spirituals, 16
Niebuhr, Reinhold, 117, 126
Nietzsche, Friedrich, 21, 23
    'The death of God', 21, 23
    The Gay Science, 21
    Thus Spake Zarathustra, 66
Nizam al-Mulk, 48
Nizamiyya Madrasa, 48, 51, 55
Non posse non peccare (inability to avoid
    sinning), 24
Nussbaum, Martha, 17

Old Testament, 104
Origen
    Comparisons with Al-Ghazali, 48
Ovid
    Metamorphoses, 72

Pan-Arabism, 94, 105
Pan-Islamism, 105
Pastor's Oath of Loyalty to Hitler, 126
Patripassianism (suffering of God), 23
Plato, 18, 78, 168
Political Islam, 84, 85, 105, 106
Pope Benedict XV, 1, 105
Pope John Paul II, 16
    On the Christian Meaning of Human
    Suffering, 16
Pope Leo XIII
    Catholic Social Teaching, 100
Pope Paul V, 1, 8
Posse non peccare (unable to sin), 24
Prophet Muhammad, 27, 59, 66, 70, 84, 100, 102,
    107, 142, 144, 152

Qaddara laka (what has been predestined), 63
Qibla (Direction of prayer), 154
Qur'an, 25, 26, 27, 28, 39, 40, 41, 42, 44, 48, 54, 55,
    56, 57, 58, 60, 70, 79, 84, 85, 87, 89, 96,
    104, 107, 135, 136, 137, 141, 142, 143, 144,
    147, 148, 154, 155
Qutb, Sayyid, 5, 83, 86, 106, 135, 195
    'The Philosopher of Islamic Terror', 86
    A Child from the Village/Tifl min al-Qarya, 89

Critique of Egypt/the Muslim world, 83, 90, 91, 92, 102, 105, 136
Critique of the west, 83, 87, 89, 92, 93, 94, 97, 99, 102, 105
Early life, 89, 90
Editorship of *The New Thought/al-Fikr al-Jadid*, 92
Imprisonment, torture and execution, 5, 95, 106, 107, 137
In the Shade of the Qur'an/Fi Zilal al-Qur'an, 87, 95, 107
On the polyethnicity/universality of Islam, 98
Poetry, 90
Signposts along the Road or Milestones/ Ma'alim fi'l-tariq, 95, 96, 97, 98, 100, 103, 104, 105, 136
Social Justice in Islam/`Adalal-ijtima'iyya fi'l-Islam, 92
Speculation on Qutb's views on September 11th, 86
Teaching career, 90, 91, 94
The Future of This Religion, 89
Theology/Ideology, 96, 97, 98, 99, 101, 102, 103, 104, 106, 107, 135, 136, 137, 138
Travels in the USA, 93
Views on *jihad*, 103, 104, 136
Views on *shari'a*, 88, 92

Racism, 4, 10, 11, 93, 117, 118, 180, 182, 183, 184, 186, 187, 188, 189, 190, 191, 192, 193, 195
Rahma (Divine mercy), 64
Rahman, Fazlur, 141, 142, 154
Rawls, John, 88, 158
Reformation, 115
Regensberg, 127
Ricoeur, Paul, 9, 33, 34
Rilke, Rainer Maria, 5, 47, 64, 71, 79, 80, 81, 82
    Acclaim of W.H. Auden, 69
    Comparison to Dylan Thomas, 47
    Correspondence with Franz Xaver Kappus/ *Letters to a Young Poet/Briefe an einen jungen Dichter*, 74, 74, 75, 76, 78
    Daughter – Ruth, 66
    Duino Elegies/Duineser Elegien, 68, 69, 70
    Early years, 65, 66, 67
    Florentine Diary, 66
    Frustrations with/critique of contemporary Christianity, 66, 77, 78, 81
    Influence of Nietzsche, 66
    Interest in Islam, 66
    Islamic angels and Gabriel in Rilke's work, 70
    Later years and death, 68, 73, 73
    Letters, 5, 72, 79
    Marriage to Clara Westhoff, 66
    Patronage of Princess Marie von Thurn and Taxis Hohenlohe, 68, 73
    Popularity in French literary circles, 73
    Reading of *The Book of Job*, 68
    Relationship with and influence of Lou Andreas Salome, 66
    The Book of Hours/Das Stunden-Buch, 67
    The Notebooks of Malte Laurids/Die ufzeichmungen des Malte Laurids Brigge, 67
    The Sonnets to Orpheus/Die Sonnette an Orpheus, 69, 71
    Translations of Paul Valéry work into German, 73
    Travels in Russia/Meetings with Tolstoy, Pasternak and Drozhzhin, 65, 66
    Travels in Tunisia and Egypt, 66
    Work with Auguste Rodin, 67
Rodin, Auguste
    Employment of Rilke, 67
Rorty, Richard, 181
Rumi, Jalaluddin, 60
Russell, Bertrand, 17

Sa'dist Party (Egypt), 92
Sabr (patience or endurance), 40
Salaf (predecessors), 56
Salafis/Salafism, 84, 147
    Muhammad ibn 'Abd al-Wahhab, 91
Salome, Lou Andreas
    Female Figures in Ibsen's Plays (1892), 66
    Friedrich Nietzsche (1894), 66
    Marriage to Friedrich Carl Andreas, 66
    Relationship with Rilke, 66
    Training under Freud/first female Psychoanalyst, 66
Sawm (fasting), 61
Schlatter, Adolf, 111
Schleiermacher, Friedrich, 13, 14, 113
    'Sermon at Nathanael's Grave', 14
Schonberg, 127
Schopenhauer, Arthur, 18, 19, 21
    The World of Will and Representation/Die Welt als Wille und Vorstellung, 18, 19
Secularism/Anti-Secularism, 6, 93, 99, 118, 133, 152, 161, 162, 163
    In the Muslim world, 88, 89, 95, 100, 105, 147
    Laicite, 152
Seeberg, Reinhold, 115, 117
Seljuks, 48
September the 11th, 86, 140, 147, 149, 153, 197
Shafi'I school, 28, 48
Shahadah (Islamic 'creed'), 97
shari'a, 85, 101
    Islamist attitudes to *shari'a*, 84, 85
    Role in Islamism, 84, 85
    Views of Al-Ghazali, 54, 56, 60

shari'a (cont.)
Views of Khaled Abou El-Fadl, 144
Views of Sayyid Qutb, 88, 92
Shi'a Islam, 38, 39, 48, 51
Six Days War, 95
Slavery, 4, 16, 180, 182, 183
Socialism, 105, 106, 182
St Augustine, 24, 28
St Jerome, 61
St Paul, 23, 24, 28
Struggle, comparison with suffering, 9
Suffering, etymology of, 8
Sufis/Sufism, 28, 42, 60, 143
Al-Ghazali's Sufism, 48, 49, 53, 55, 56, 57, 60
khânqâh (Sufi convent), 55, 57
Maqamat (stages on Sufi Spiritual
journey), 30
Mujahada (struggle, part of ascetic self-
discipline), 30
Prayer (Du'a) in Sufism, 60
Sufi thought on jihad, 3
Sunna (words and deeds of the Prophet), 152
Sunni Islam, 38, 41, 48, 51, 56, 79, 147,
188, 192

Takfir (excommunication), 104, 105
Taqlid al-haqq (imitation of what is true)/taqlid-
al-batil (imitation of the false), 52
Taqwa (righteousness), 41
Tawakkul (trust and reliance on God), 38, 41
Tawba (repentance), 28
Tawhid (divine unity), 96, 136
Taylor, Charles, 158, 160, 164, 165
Tegel prison, 110, 127, 128, 133
Tertullian, 61
Thomas, Dylan
Comparison to Rilke, 47
Tolstoy, Leo, 20
Torah, 103, 126, 161, 162
Troeltsch, Ernst, 113
Tuhfa (gift), 57

Ulama (Islamic scholars), 140, 150
Umma (The global Muslim Community),
101
Union Theological Seminary, New York, 117,
118, 119
USSR, 175

Via Crucis (Way of the Cross), 78
von Harnack, Adolf, 113, 115
Vorstellung (representation), 18

Wafd Party (Egypt), 90, 92
Wahhabism. See Salafis/Salafism
Wahy (revelation), 142
Weber, Max, 25, 162
Weimar Republic, 117, 120
West, Cornel, 6, 180, 181, 182, 184, 187, 188,
193, 195
'Chekhovian Christian', 186
Music, 184, 185
Race Matters, 184, 193
The American Evasion of Philosophy,
180
Views on Malcolm X, 188, 192
Wilde, Oscar, 78
De Profundis, 14, 15, 16, 46, 75
Imprisonment and death, 14, 15
Relationship with Alfred Lord Douglas,
14
Wille (will), 18
Williams, Rowan, 172
Wirklichkeit (statement about reality), 120

X, Malcolm, 188, 189, 190, 191, 192
'Ballot or the bullet' speech, 189
Conversion from NOI to Sunni Islam,
188, 192
Hajj, 188
The Autobiography of Malcolm X, 189

Zaghlul, Sa'd, 92